# Lecture Notes in Computer Science

*Commenced Publication in 1973*
Founding and Former Series Editors:
Gerhard Goos, Juris Hartmanis, and Jan van Leeuwen

## Editorial Board

George Pavlou   Toufik Ahmed
Tasos Dagiuklas (Eds.)

# Management of Converged Multimedia Networks and Services

11th IFIP/IEEE International Conference on Management
of Multimedia and Mobile Networks and Services, MMNS 2008
Samos Island, Greece, September 22-26, 2008
Proceedings

 Springer

Volume Editors

George Pavlou
University College London
Department of Electonic and Electrical Engineering
Torrington Place, London, WE1E 7JE, UK
E-mail: G.Pavlou@ee.ucl.ac.uk

Toufik Ahmed
University Bordeaux 1
CNRS LaBRI Lab
351 Cours de la Libération, 33405 Talence Cedex, France
E-mail: tad@labri.fr

Tasos Dagiuklas
TEI of Mesolonghi
Dept. of Telecommunications and Networks
30300 Nafpaktos, Greece
E-mail: ntan@teimes.gr

Library of Congress Control Number: 2008934861

CR Subject Classification (1998): C.2, H.4, H.5, H.2.4, H.4.3

LNCS Sublibrary: SL 5 – Computer Communication Networks
and Telecommunications

ISSN      0302-9743
ISBN 978-3-540-87358-7 Springer Berlin Heidelberg New York

Springer is a part of Springer Science+Business Media

springer.com

© IFIP International Federation for Information Processing, Hofstrasse 3, A-2361 Laxenburg, Austria 2008

Typesetting: Camera-ready by author, data conversion by Scientific Publishing Services, Chennai, India
Printed on acid-free paper      SPIN: 12523825      06/3180      5 4 3 2 1 0

# Preface

This volume presents the proceedings of the *11th IFIP/IEEE International Conference on Management of Multimedia and Mobile Networks and Services (MMNS 2008)*, which was held on Samos, Greece during September 22–26 as part of the 4th International Week on Management of Networks and Services (Manweek 2008). As in the previous three years, the Manweek umbrella allowed an international audience of researchers and scientists from industry and academia – who are researching and developing management systems – to share views and ideas and present their state-of-the-art results.

The other events co-located with Manweek 2008 were the 19th IFIP/IEEE International Workshop on Distributed Systems: Operations and Management (DSOM 2008), the 8th IEEE Workshop on IP Operations and Management (IPOM2008), the Third IEEE International Workshop on Modeling Autonomic Communications Environments (MACE 2008), the 4th IEEE/IFIP International Workshop on End-to-End Virtualization and Grid Management (EVGM 2008) and the 5th International Workshop on Next-Generation Networking Middleware (NGNM 2008).

Under this umbrella, MMNS again proved itself as a top public venue for dissemination of results and intellectual collaboration with specific emphasis on the management of emerging mobile and wireless networks. The objective of the conference is to bring together researchers and scientists from academia and industry interested in state-of-the-art management of converged multimedia networks and services across heterogeneous networking infrastructures.

Contributions from the research community met this challenge with a total of 46 paper submissions from four continents. A comprehensive review process was carried out by the Technical Program Committee and additional subject area experts, with all papers receiving three reviews. Subsequently, all submissions were ranked based on review scores as well as the wider Technical Program Committee's view of their contribution and relevance to the conference scope. After a relevant discussion, it was decided to accept 15 full papers and 1 short paper, presenting work in progress. The overall acceptance rate was 32.6%, which is in line with previous events and guarantees a high-quality technical program. The diverse topics in this year's program included services and user experience, management aspects of wireless and cellular networks, monitoring and control and resource management, IMS platforms for the management of applications, P2P overlays for multimedia applications and services  all contributing to the management of real-time mobile multimedia services, as expressed in this year's motto.

The high-quality MMNS 2008 program is a delicate concoction based on the accepted papers of the original and novel contributions of all the authors who submitted their work to the conference, purified by the hard work of the

MMNS 2008 Technical Program Committee members and the rigorous review process accomplished by this set of worldwide experts, supported by the 2008 Manweek Organizing Committee, and enabled by the generous contribution of IFIP, IEEE and the sponsor companies, all of whom are gratefully thanked by the conference Technical Program Committee Chairs. In addition, we thank the Publication Chair Tom Pfeifer and the Springer LNCS team for their support of these proceedings.

We have no doubt that the MMNS 2008 conference was another significant step towards the ability to develop, manage and control truly scalable end-to-end multimedia-based services over next-generation wired and wireless networks.

September 2008                                                    George Pavlou
                                                                 Toufik Ahmed
                                                                 Tasos Dagiuklas

# MMNS 2008 Organization

## Workshop and Program Co-chairs

George Pavlou      University College London, UK
Toufik Ahmed      University Bordeaux 1, France
Tasos Dagiuklas      TEI of Mesolonghi, Greece

## Publication Chair

Tom Pfeifer      Waterford Institute of Technology, Ireland

## Publicity Co-chair

Luciano Paschoal Gaspary      Universidade Federal do Rio Grande do Sul,
Brazil

## Treasurers

Sofoklis Kyriazakos      Converge, Greece
Brendan Jennings      Waterford Institute of Technology, Ireland

## Website and Registration Chair

Sven van der Meer      Waterford Institute of Technology, Ireland

## Submission Chair

Lisandro Granville      Universidade Federal do Rio Grande do Sul,
Brazil

## Sponsoring Co-chairs

E. Pallis      Centre for Technological Research of Crete,
Greece
I. Venieris      National Technical University of Athens,
Greece

## Manweek 2008 Chair

George Kormentzas      University of the Aegean, Greece

## Manweek 2008 Vice Chair

Francisco Guirao                    European Commission

## Manweek 2008 Advisors

| | |
|---|---|
| Raouf Boutaba | University of Waterloo, Canada |
| Brendan Jennings | Waterford Institute of Technology, Ireland |
| Sven van der Meer | Waterford Institute of Technology, Ireland |

## MMNS 2008 Technical Program Committee

| | |
|---|---|
| Ahmed Mehaoua | University of Paris, Descartes - CRIP5, France |
| Aiko Pras | University of Twente, The Netherlands |
| Alan Marshall | The Queen's University of Belfast, UK |
| Alexander Clemm | Cisco Systems, USA |
| Bert-Jan van Beijnum | University of Twente, The Netherlands |
| Brendan Jennings | TSSG, Waterford Institute of Technology, Ireland |
| Burkhard Stiller | University of Zurich and ETH Zurich, Switzerland |
| Chadi Assi | CIISE Concordia University, Canada |
| Christian Timmerer | Klagenfurt University, Austria |
| Danny Raz | Technion University, Israel |
| Dilip Krishnaswamy | Qualcomm, Inc., USA |
| Dorgham Sisalem | Tekelec, Germany |
| Francine Krief | LaBRI Laboratory, Bordeaux 1 University, France |
| Gabriel-Miro Muntean | Dublin City University, Ireland |
| Gang Ding | Olympus Communication Technology of America, USA |
| Gerard Parr | University of Ulster, UK |
| Go Hasegawa | Osaka University, Japan |
| Guy Pujolle | Université de Paris 6, France |
| Hanan Lutfiyya | University of Western Ontario, Canada |
| John Vicente | Intel Corporation, USA |
| Jun Li | University of Oregon, USA |
| Karim Seada | Nokia Research Center, Finland |
| Liam Murphy | UCD, Ireland |
| Lukas Kencl | Czech Technical University (CTU), Czech Republic |
| Maja Matijasevic | University of Zagreb, Croatia |
| Masum Hasan | Cisco Systems, USA |
| Mihaela van der Schaar | UCLA, USA |
| Nazim Agoulmine | University of Evry, France |

| | |
|---|---|
| Ralf Steinmetz | Darmstadt University, Germany |
| Roger Zimmermann | National University of Singapore, Singapore |
| Sasitharan Balasubramaniam | Waterford Institute of Technology, Ireland |
| Sven van der Meer | Waterford Institute of Technology, Ireland |
| Theodore Willke | Intel Corporation, USA |
| Theodore Zahariadis | TEI of Chalkida, Greece |
| Thomas Magedanz | FhG FOKUS, Germany |
| Tom Pfeifer | Waterford Institute of Technology, Ireland |
| Viji Raveendran | QUALCOMM Incorporated, USA |
| Yacine Ghamri-Doudane | LRSM - ENSIIE, France |
| Yangcheng Huang | Ericsson, USA |

# Table of Contents

## Wireless Ad Hoc and Sensor Networks

## Multimedia Distribution

## Quality of Experience

## QoS Mechanisms and Tools for Multimedia

# A Knowledge Plane for Autonomic Context-Aware Wireless Mobile Ad Hoc Networks

Daniel F. Macedo[1], Aldri L. dos Santos[2],
José Marcos S. Nogueira[3], and Guy Pujolle[1]

[1] Université Pierre et Marie Curie-Paris6, France
[2] Federal University of Paraná, Curitiba-PR, Brazil
[3] Federal University of Minas Gerais, Belo Horizonte-MG, Brazil
{Daniel.Macedo,Guy.Pujolle}@lip6.fr, aldri@inf.ufpr.br, jmarcos@dcc.ufmg.br

**Abstract.** Due to the emergence of multimedia context-rich applications and services over wireless networks, networking protocols and services are becoming more and more integrated, thus relying on context and application information to operate. Further, wireless protocols and services have employed information from several network layers and the environment, breaking the layering paradigm. In order to cope with this increasing reliance on knowledge, we propose MANKOP, a middleware for MANETs that instantiates a new networking plane. The *Knowledge Plane* (KP) is a distributed entity that stores and disseminates information concerning the network, its services and the environment, orchestrating the collaboration among cross-layer protocols, autonomic management solutions and context-aware services. We use MANKOP to support the autonomic reconfiguration of a P2P network over MANETs. Simulation results show that the MANKOP-enabled solution is applicable to more scenarios than the classic approaches, as the network adapts its query dissemination strategy to match the current conditions of the peers.

## 1 Introduction

With the evolution of networking and electronics, communication capabilities are nowadays implemented in a huge set of devices, such as notebooks, PDAs, cell phones or even household appliances. Those devices can provide multimedia and interactive content, such as pictures, audio, video or online gaming, requiring strict QoS guarantees from the underlying networking infrastructure. Further, although some of those devices face several connection challenges due to mobility, users expect a responsive and efficient experience at all times.

Those severe performance requirements have led to the creation of cross-layer protocols, which aim at optimizing the operation of the network by breaking the encapsulation and isolation principles, sharing information with several layers at the same time [1]. Further, ubiquitous mobile devices and networks should seamlessly blend with their surroundings, thus requiring that networking solutions and services adapt automatically to changes in their environment and in

G. Pavlou, T. Ahmed, and T. Dagiuklas (Eds.): MMNS 2008, LNCS 5274, pp. 1–13, 2008.

user needs (their *context*) [2]. Finally, the complexity and dynamics of wireless networks has spurred the research on autonomic network management solutions, which also require a view of the network as a whole [3].

The urgent need of information driven by *cross-layer protocols, context-aware services* and *autonomic networking* was hence the driving force for the conception of middlewares and mechanisms that promote information sharing. However, existing solutions tend to be specific to one of the three problems above, thus requiring multiple independent information services. Due to the use of disparate systems, information is not entirely shared, requiring replicated effort to maintain the same data on several systems.

In order to solve this problem, we advocate the use of a single distributed information service that stores any knowledge required to the operation of the network. This service can be seen as a new networking plane, called *Knowledge Plane* (KP), that deals with knowledge sharing. The KP lies between networking protocols and services[1], serving the information needs of both. Thus, all information concerning a service or protocol would be stored on this plane, spurring the free flow of information among services. The KP would replace the information repositories of autonomic management solutions and context-aware systems, storing context, knowledge, policies and past network behavior. It would also work as a cross-layer framework, exposing the interdependency among protocols and allowing the sharing of information using rich information models.

The use of a KP is natural in MANETs, since the resource restrictions of such networks impose the development of integrated, multi-layer context-aware solutions. For example, it is impossible to think of a routing or transport protocol that does not take link quality and battery life into account [4,5]. Further, node movement and node and link failures demand that each protocol autonomically reconfigures some of its parameters. Since such networks are highly dynamic, due to the unpredictability of the hardware and of wireless links, existing information services for wired networks are not applicable because of their high overhead. The low bandwidth and high latency of the links make data synchronization too costly, thus services deployed over MANETs should rely on a partial knowledge of the state of the network [6,7].

This paper proposes a middleware that instantiates a KP over MANETs. This KP, called MANKOP (MANet KnOwledge Plane), is adapted to the characteristics of the wireless medium and the resource restrictions of mobile nodes. It provides secure access to context and knowledge, as well as mechanisms for automatic information dissemination among MANET nodes. Due to the availability of more knowledge for the optimization of network protocols, services and autonomic management solutions, MANKOP allows a smoother operation of demanding applications such as multimedia and cooperative services. In order to show the benefits of MANKOP, we evaluated a MANKOP-aware Peer-to-Peer (P2P) network that automatically reconfigures the way queries are disseminated based on information stored on the KP. Simulation results show that the

---

[1] In this text we also consider management protocols and overlay networks such as P2P networks as services.

MANKOP-enabled solution is applicable to more scenarios than the classic approaches, as it presents a performance comparable to that of the classic query strategy more suitable for each scenario.

This paper is organized as follows. Section 2 describes the related work. Section 3 details the MANKOP architecture. Section 4 shows the case study and simulation results. Finally, Section 5 shows our conclusions and future work.

## 2 Related Work

In order to adapt the autonomic concepts to the networking world, Clark et al. added a plane to the OSI model, called knowledge plane [8]. Clark's knowledge plane manages the networking protocols (the *data plane*) using artificial intelligence algorithms that automatically react to changes in the network, in user requirements and in the environment[2]. Clark's as well as other autonomic management architectures [8, 9, 10] use context and application awareness to base their decisions upon rich models of the services and the environment. Those works usually assume that there is an information base from where knowledge can be stored and fetched in a scalable way. However, such information systems are still an open research issue [10, 11]. MANKOP is an instance of such a knowledge base, and thus could be support the operation of those architectures on MANETs.

Due to the scarce resources and the harshness of the wireless medium, *cross-layer design* is frequent in MANETs [12]. Cross-layering might induce a high layer interdependency, producing less modular code. To reduce those effects, several works proposed middlewares for MANETs providing standardized mechanisms for information sharing [13, 14, 15]. Usually, however, those middlewares are restricted to the information stored in each node, and employ simple information models or no model at all. Our work allows the representation of information using elaborate models and provides means to fetch information from any node in the network, thus improving the state of the art.

Conti et al. proposed event-based cross-layer interfaces [13]. Razzaque et al. created a middleware that is dynamically fed by the protocol stack, using *contextors* [14]. Each protocol has its contextor, which inserts and queries information from the middleware. In both approaches the stored information is limited to the current node. Further, there is still replication of information, since protocols cannot see each other's data unless they are explicitly exported. Winter et al. created a cross-layering middleware that divides information into local and global views [15]. The local view concerns the host node, while the global view represents the aggregated state of the network. The lack of information pertaining individual nodes precludes the use of those solutions for tasks such as management.

Other middlewares for information dissemination on MANETs support multi-agent systems. They limit the amount of information available to each agent

---

[2] Throughout this paper we refer to a knowledge plane as the plane responsible only for the dissemination and management of knowledge.

to reduce their resource usage. In the spatial programming paradigm, the data available to each node varies according to its location [16]. This model is handy for applications where nodes in a region tend to perform similar computations (e.g. for target tracking, detection of natural events), being simple to implement and highly scalable. The problem is that certain applications, such as Peer-to-Peer overlays, require information from nodes that are far away. TOTA (Tuples Over The Air) is an information dissemination middleware for multi-agent systems [17]. It employs the concept of stigmergy, that is, individual agents communicate by changing their local environment. Although simple and scalable, protocols and services must be modeled using stigmergic patterns, which may be hard for tasks such as distributed management. Also, this middleware may not scale well with complex dissemination and maintenance rules.

Haggle is an autonomic middleware designed for opportunistic MANETs [18], which are networks where nodes face frequent disconnections for extended periods of time. Nodes access remote information as if it were local, in a secure and simple way. This approach also has its drawbacks, such as the lack of trap-based access, which is extensively used in network management.

## 3   The MANKOP Middleware

The MANKOP middleware constructs a distributed information base, called Knowledge Plane (KP). The KP stores information and knowledge pertaining all the protocols and services of the network. Further, the KP acts as a collaboration layer, encouraging the adoption of context-aware, cross-layer protocols and services by providing interfaces for information dissemination and sharing. This plane lies between the service plane, composed by the services and management solutions, and the data plane, composed of devices and networking protocols, as shown in Figure 1. This organization allows services and autonomic managers to incorporate context-awareness or use the KP as a database for services and capabilities of the network, in order to compose more complex services. Further, protocols could use MANKOP to optimize their operation through cross-layering and context awareness.

In order to improve scalability, each node stores information concerning itself and also replicates data from local neighbors or other nodes with which it communicates. Information from distant nodes can be either queried directly from the nodes that produced it, or cached locally. However, the middleware does not guarantee that the cached copies are synchronized with the original data. The middleware also supports event notification services.

Data stored in MANKOP can be accessed using push/pull commands like GETS and TRAPS. Even though MANKOP does not specify a standalone data model, it is advisable to use one that supports rich information models. For instance, XML-RPC has been shown to be feasible in MANETs composed of modest PDAs [19]. Further, the content stored in MANKOP is updated in one of two ways. Either the services that produced the information specify an information dissemination policy, or they disseminate the information themselves. In

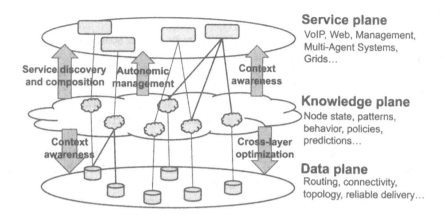

**Fig. 1.** The three planes in autonomic networks

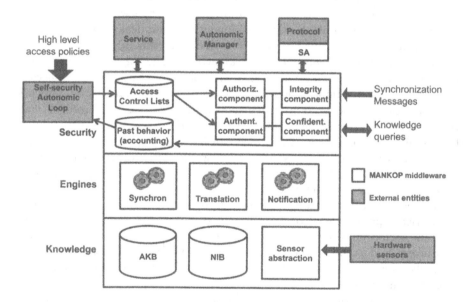

**Fig. 2.** The MANKOP module and its interaction with protocols and services

both cases, MANKOP provides interfaces that encapsulate the sending of messages, allowing piggybacking several pieces of information in a single packet. This reduces the control overhead of the network, which reduces energy consumption.

The organization of the MANKOP middleware is depicted in Figure 2. It is composed of three tiers: the *knowledge tier*, which stores the knowledge produced by the network, the *engine tier*, which performs several tasks over the stored knowledge, and a *security tier*, which secures the access to information.

## 3.1 The Knowledge Tier

MANKOP's knowledge tier has three components, which store knowledge produced by the application and provide abstractions for physical sensors. MANKOP should model information following a standardized information model, such as DEN-ng [20], DMTF's CIM [21] or RDF schemas.

The *Sensor Abstraction Component* deals with access to hardware sensors. In this paper we differentiate among hardware sensors and virtual sensors, as it is usual in the literature of context-aware and multi-agent systems [2]. Hardware sensors monitor physical devices, e.g. a GPS, a battery indicator, an accelerator. Virtual sensors, on the other hand, monitor software, providing readings such as the occupation of a packet queue, the number of TCP flows or the version of a program. The sensor abstraction layer provides a standardized interface for the access to hardware sensors, hiding device-specific interfaces and commands from other MANKOP components. For example, location data from diverse devices, such as a GPS or infrared-based systems, would be translated into a standardized representation for location, e.g. coordinates in degrees with their associated imprecision. The sensor abstraction component does not deal with virtual sensor data, which would be stored either at the AKB or at the NIB.

The *AKB* and *NIB Components* store knowledge. The Application Knowledge Base (AKB) stores knowledge coming from applications and high-level services, whereas the Network Information Base (NIB) stores information from networking protocols. This separation is due to performance reasons. Protocols have stronger real-time requirements and must respond very fast to events. Further, they usually require simple data, which can be easily represented using simple data structures (e.g. a floating-point number would suffice to represent queue occupation, signal-to-noise ratio and link reliability). Autonomic services, on the other hand, rely on complex information describing services, policies and products (a book, a VoIP connection). Hence, such services demand object-oriented, feature-rich representations of information. However, this capacity comes with a certain performance penalty. In order to allow fast access to information to lower layers, and at the same time provide support to rich information models to the applications and services, the knowledge tier stores the information in two different components.

The difference between AKB and NIB lies on the data models. While AKB should use object-oriented data models (e.g. a OO-DBMS), the NIB should use simple data models (e.g. ASN.1 or SMI). Lower level services would still access data on the AKB, providing that they accept a higher response time. The two data models are bridged using the translation engine described later. We chose not to define standard data models to allow each developer to pick one that fits the restrictions of the network.

In order to allow a higher degree of interoperability, the information stored in MANKOP should follow clearly defined information models. Using a standard representation, applications and/or protocols implemented by different vendors would be able to communicate (e.g. a free source FTP client could use information stored by a commercial client). Furthermore, a standardized representation reduces the effort to develop MANKOP compatible solutions, since developers are already familiar with such a representation.

## 3.2 The Engine Tier

The Engine tier of MANKOP offers engines for event notification, data synchronization and translation among different data representations.

The *Translation Engine* converts data among the different data models used in AKB and NIB to the format used for queries coming from protocols and services. Suppose, for example, that queries to information stored on MANKOP could be performed using XML-RPC. The translation engine would interpret the queries, identify where the information is stored (AKB or NIB), fetch it and marshal the data following a defined XML schema. Also, when receiving a SET command, MANKOP would employ the translation engine to translate the incoming information into its AKB and NIB representations. The translation engine should support two or more representations to data queries. For example, it could use XML-RPC for applications and services and ASN.1 for protocols. This would allow a faster response time for protocols that require a timely response (e.g. MAC and PHY level algorithms).

The *Notification Engine* watches the state of the local copy of data stored in the MANKOP middleware to create alarms whenever a certain condition happens. Applications can subscribe to events happening at the local node, or at other nodes. As an example, events could indicate low link reliability or an alarm for insufficient battery.

The *Synchronization Engine* automatically disseminates information based on simple rules. Those rules are defined by the application in terms of a distance in hops, a timeout and a periodicity of updates. Automatic synchronization is useful for services and protocols where the information required by each node is clearly divided in regions, for example as in routing and clustering [7]. The synchronization rules also allow nodes joining the network to easily populate their local AKB and NIB bases by issuing a synchronization request to its neighbors. Those nodes, in turn, will check the stored dissemination rules to determine which data will be sent to the arriving node. The engine uses broadcast messages, profiting from the broadcast nature of the wireless medium.

The synchronization of each piece of information is determined by a tuple $(D, R, T, S)$. $D$ defines the dissemination policy, that is, when the information should be disseminated. The possible values are *on every change*, *periodical* and *do not disseminate*. Next, the reach of the dissemination is defined by $R$, which defines the range in hops. Thus, if node $X$ has data marked with a range of 5, its direct neighbors will cache it with a value of 4, and the neighbors of the neighbors will be marked with a value of 3. Each tuple also defines an Access Control List (ACL), stored in S, and a time to live, the value $T$. The time to live is reset on every update. In order to minimize the amount of packets sent, and thus reduce energy consumption, the synchronization engine should aggregate information updates as much as possible. For instance, defining a minimum interval among updates rather than disseminating changes as soon as they happen.

As mentioned before, some applications do not adopt a range-based neighborhood. In P2P applications, for example, neighbor peers may be several hops away, or even at the other side of the network. Thus, such applications would define themselves their propagation policy. Also, for applications where the propagated data is highly dynamic, each application would define what and when to send. For this scenario, MANKOP allows applications to either piggy-back their own data on MANKOP synchronization messages or to send their own MANKOP messages. In order to do so, the developer would implement a *Synchronization Agent* (SA) to select which and how information must be updated. This agent would autonomously manage the synchronization of all data concerning the service.

### 3.3 The Security Tier

Security is essential to MANKOP knowledge exchanges, once attacks to MANKOP could disrupt the operation of the entire network. The security tier assumes that a running PKI system exists on the network.

The *Confidentiality* and *Integrity* components perform encryption, decryption and signing of MANKOP messages. The *Authentication* component deals with the identification of services and protocols. Whenever a request arrives, the source must authenticate within MANKOP. Since in MANETs we should not rely on a central authority, authentication should be performed either by tickets created by a group of nodes [22] or by a PGP-like trust model. Finally, the *Authorization* component uses access control lists (ACLs) to define in a per-object granularity the access privileges of nodes, users and services. The definition of ACLs is not in the scope of MANKOP, which only enforces them. All the components produce traces (or past behavior), which are used for accounting as well as the automatic adaptation of the security tier by means of an external self-security component.

### 3.4 Interoperability with Regular Nodes

Due to the number of mobile devices already deployed, MANKOP-based nodes will have to interact with nodes that do not employ a KP, called *regular nodes*. Thus, MANKOP-aware protocols will provide both KP-based and traditional information dissemination methods. If no regular node is in the neighborhood of a MANKOP-aware node, it will employ the MANKOP approach. If a MANKOP-aware node receives traditional update messages (e.g. a routing message), it should respond using regular messages, based on the information stored on MANKOP. Only MANKOP-aware nodes in contact with regular nodes would operate on compatibility mode, as the others may communicate using MANKOP messages. Regular nodes, on the other hand, will discard MANKOP messages.

## 4    Case Study: Self-configuration of P2P Networks

In this case study we implemented a self-configuration management module for unstructured peer-to-peer (P2P) networks, since our previous work [23] showed that such networks perform better than structured ones on MANETs. Unstructured networks can be divided into *flooding-based* and *random walk-based*. In flooding-based networks, nodes forward queries to all their neighbors, bringing fault tolerance to protocols, however at a high energy and load cost. Random walk-based networks disseminate a fixed amount of queries, called *walkers*, which wander randomly around the network [24]. Usually flooding-based techniques have a higher hit rate (the amount of successful queries) due to the high number of messages sent. However, random walks perform better than flooding on high load networks.

In this case study we use MANKOP to support an autonomic manager that automatically selects the best query technique according to the conditions of the MANET. As in TCP, where the data rate is determined by the congestion of the network, the autonomic manager uses flooding when the network allows, switching to random walk (a more economic strategy) when the charge reaches a critical level. This adaptation indirectly optimizes the number of successful P2P file queries (the hit rate), the response time perceived by the user and the energy consumption by reducing the amount of collisions in the MAC layer. The manager requires information from different layers (the application and the MAC layers) and from several nodes, which justify the use of a middleware such as MANKOP.

A *MANKOP-aware Autonomic Manager* (MAM) is installed in all nodes. It divides the network in clusters, where the cluster-heads (CH) coordinate the monitoring of the network condition and also decide if the nodes on the cluster should change the employed query strategy. In order to create clusters, the MAM sets a periodic timer on all nodes. Upon its timeout, nodes choose if they will become CHs with a probability of 10%. Those nodes will then advertise themselves, so non-CH nodes can choose which cluster they will join. Next, the CH watches two events on all member nodes, as described below.

The decision to change the query strategy is based on the queue occupation (the amount of the packet queue that is being used) of a k-hop neighborhood, which is calculated using the information stored in MANKOP. Each node inserts in the KP its queue occupation as well as the aggregated queue occupation of its one-hop neighborhood (*ohocc*), using the formula $ohocc = max(max(N.occ), occ)$, where $N$ is the set of all the one-hop neighbors of a node, and $occ$ is the node's occupation. Next, each node calculates the two-hop occupation $thocc = max(N.ohocc)$ in order to obtain the maximum occupation in two hops. We used two hops since empirical results showed that this configuration performed better than zero (local) and one-hop knowledge. If $thocc$ is below a threshold, the network does not seem to be congested, hence flooding should be employed. In this case, nodes produce a FLOOD_THRESHOLD_EVT MANKOP event. However, if the two-hop estimate is above a second pre-defined threshold, the network is saturated, and thus random walk should be used. To signal this to the CH, nodes produce a RW_THRESHOLD_EVT event. An operator defines the values of those thresholds.

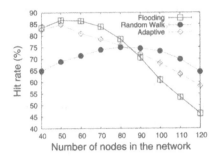
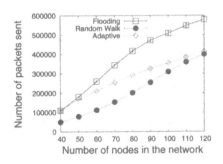

**Fig. 3.** Average hit rate

**Fig. 4.** Average number of query packets sent

The evaluation was performed on NS-2 over an IEEE 802.11b network with nodes having a Cisco Aironet radio [25]. The radio model supports adaptive modulation and coding, thus the transmission range varies from 355 to 1061 meters. We use a proactive routing protocol (DSDV). For flooding-based queries, we employ the Gnutella protocol, while for random walk we employ the model presented in [24]. Random walks use four walkers with a TTL equal to 25% of the number of nodes. For Flooding, the TTL was set to four, following the results in [23]. The FLOOD_THRESHOLD_EVT and RW_THRESHOLD_EVT events are triggered when the occupation is below 10% and over 50%, respectively. Likewise, the MAM changes from flooding to random walk if 40% of the nodes signal a FLOOD_THRESHOLD_EVT event within a clustering interval (set as 30s), and changes from random walk to flooding if 90% of the nodes signal the corresponding event. Those values were defined using empirical experiments. Results are averaged over 35 independent simulations and are plotted with a confidence interval of 99%.

Figure 3 presents the hit rate. The figure shows that flooding performs better on smaller networks, however on networks with more than 90 nodes, random walk performs better, as expected. This is due to the number of packets required for queries, shown in Figure 4. Flooding sends more than the double of packets than Random Walk, thus the network becomes congested faster. Hence, it would be recommended to use flooding for networks up to 80 nodes, and random walk for bigger networks. This is the idea of the Adaptive protocol, which employs the MAM described previously. The adaptive method had a performance between flooding and random walk techniques, performing up to 5% worse than Flooding on networks of up to 80 nodes, and performing from 1% to 6% worse than Random Walk on bigger networks. This behavior is due to the addition of the MAM, which reduces the amount of query packets in order to reduce collisions (Figure 5).

Figure 6 shows the percentage of nodes using each query strategy. When the load increases, the autonomic manager gradually reconfigures the nodes. Thus, for lighter networks most nodes use flooding, while nodes on busy networks usually resort to random walk. The adaptive solution has an intermediary energy

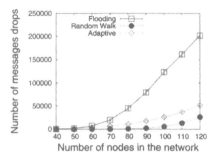

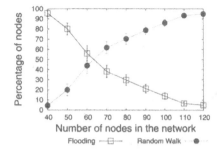

**Fig. 5.** Average number of packet drops

**Fig. 6.** Average percentage of nodes using each query strategy

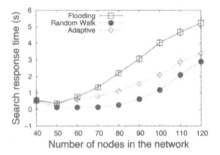

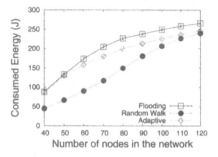

**Fig. 7.** Average query response time

**Fig. 8.** Average energy consumption

consumption and response time, as shown in Figures 7 and 8. The response time and energy consumption of the Adaptive solution are not as low as that of Random Walk for two reasons. First, the operation of the MAM requires additional control traffic. Second, large networks still have a small amount of nodes running Gnutella, which increase the energy consumption and the response time. This mix of query strategies reduces the hit rate of the adaptive method when compared to pure methods. However, this degradation is acceptable once the autonomic solution has a more predictable response time and energy consumption.

## 5  Conclusions

This work presented a knowledge plane for ad hoc networks called MANKOP in order to face the challenges raised by multimedia, context-aware and autonomic services. Each node having a MANKOP module stores information from all layers and from other nodes of the network in one single abstraction, accessible to protocols and applications. Thus, protocols and services may use algorithms that take into account context, service and network information to improve their operation.

We showcased the benefits of MANKOP with a self-configuration manager that automatically adapts the query strategy on unstructured P2P networks. The insertion of a MANKOP manager has produced a protocol that is more adapted to a higher range of scenarios. The autonomic solution presents a hit rate, response time and energy consumption comparable to the best P2P protocol on each scenario. However, since the manager imposes a small control overhead, there is a small but acceptable performance degradation.

As future work, we will define the network-level information stored at the control plane and investigate the correlation of this information to improve the treatment of events such as node and link failures, security attacks, among others.

## Acknowledgements

We would like to thank CNPq, an organization from the Science and Technology Ministry of Brazil, for partially funding this research.

## References

1. Srivastava, V., Motani, M.: Cross-layer design: A survey and the road ahead. IEEE Comm. Mag. 43(12), 112–119 (2005)
2. Baldauf, M., Dustdar, S., Rosenberg, F.: A survey on context-aware systems. International Journal of Ad Hoc and Ubiquitous Computing 2(4), 263–277 (2007)
3. Dobson, S., Denazis, S., Fernández, A., Gaïti, D., Gelenbe, E., Massacci, F., Nixon, P., Saffre, F., Schmidt, N., Zambonelli, F.: A survey of autonomic communications. ACM Trans. on Autonomic and Adaptive Systems 1(2), 223–259 (2006)
4. Akkaya, K., Younis, M.: A survey of routing protocols in wireless sensor networks. Elsevier Ad Hoc Network Journal 3(3), 325–349 (2005)
5. Katabi, D., Handley, M., Rohrs, C.: Congestion control for high bandwidth-delay product networks. In: ACM SIGCOMM, pp. 89–102 (2002)
6. Hollos, D., Karl, H., Wolisz, A.: Regionalizing global optimization algorithms to improve the operation of large ad hoc networks. In: IEEE Wireless Communications and Networking Conference, pp. 819–824 (2004)
7. Biskupski, B., Dowling, J., Sacha, J.: Properties and mechanisms of self-organizing MANET and P2P systems. ACM Trans. on Autonomic and Adaptive Systems 2(1-34), 1 (2007)
8. Clark, D., Partridge, C., Ramming, J.C., Wroclawski, J.T.: A knowledge plane for the internet. In: ACM SIGCOMM, pp. 3–10 (2003)
9. Niebert, N., Abramowicz, H., Malmgren, G., Sachs, J., Horn, U., Prehofer, C., Karl, H.: Ambient networks: an architecture for communication networks beyond 3G. IEEE Wireless Communications 11(2), 14–22 (2004)
10. Malatras, A., Hadjiantonis, A.M., Pavlou, G.: Exploiting context-awareness for the autonomic management of mobile ad hoc networks. Journal of Network and System Management 15(1) (March 2007)
11. Giaffreda, R., Pentikousis, K., Hepworth, E., Agüero, R., Galis, A.: An information service infrastructure for ambient networks. In: IASTED Multi-Conference on Parallel and Distributed Computing and Networks, pp. 21–27 (2007)
12. Kawadia, V., Kumar, P.R.: A cautionary perspective on cross layer design. IEEE Wireless Communications 12(1), 3–11 (2005)

13. Conti, M., Gregori, E., Turi, G.: A cross-layer optimization of gnutella for mobile ad hoc networks. In: ACM MobiHoc, pp. 343–354 (2005)
14. Razzaque, M., Dobson, S., Nixon, P.: A cross-layer architecture for autonomic communications. In: Autonomic Networking, pp. 25–35 (November 2006)
15. Winter, R., Schiller, J.H., Nikaein, N., Bonnet, C.: Crosstalk: Cross-layer decision support based on global knowledge. IEEE Comm. Mag. 44(1), 93–99 (2006)
16. Borcea, C., Intanagonwiwat, C., Kang, P., Kremer, U., Iftode, L.: Spatial programming using smart messages: Design and implementation. In: International Conference on Distributed Computing Systems, pp. 690–699 (2004)
17. Mamei, M., Zambonelli, F.: Programming stigmergic coordination with the TOTA middleware. In: International Joint Conference on Autonomous Agents and Multiagent Systems, pp. 415–422 (2005)
18. Scott, J., Hui, P., Crowcroft, J., Diot, C.: Haggle: A networking architecture designed around mobile users. In: IFIP Conference on Wireless On-demand Network Systems and Services (January 2006)
19. Pavlou, G., Flegkas, P., Gouveris, S., Liotta, A.: On management technologies and the potential of web services. IEEE Comm. Mag. 42(7), 58–66 (2004)
20. Strassner, J.: DEN-ng: achieving business-driven network management. In: IEEE/IFIP Network Operations and Management Symposium, pp. 753–766 (2002)
21. DMTF, Inc.: DMTF Common Information Model (CIM) (March 2008),
    http://www.dmtf.org/standards/cim/
22. Luo, H., Kong, J., Zerfos, P., Lu, S., Zhang, L.: Ursa: ubiquitous and robust access control for mobile ad hoc networks. IEEE/ACM Trans. on Networking 12(6), 1049–1063 (2004)
23. Oliveira, L.B., Siqueira, I., Macedo, D.F., Loureiro, A.A., Nogueira, J.M.: Evaluation of peer-to-peer network content discovery techniques over mobile ad hoc networks. In: IEEE WoWMoM, pp. 51–56 (June 2005)
24. Gkantsidis, C., Mihail, M., Saberi, A.: Random walks in peer-to-peer networks: Algorithms and evaluation. Performance Evaluation 63(3), 241–263 (2006)
25. Cisco Systems: Cisco aironet 350 series client adapters (March 2008),
    http://www.cisco.com/en/US/products/hw/wireless/ps4555/products_data_sheet09186a0080088828.html

# Policy Distribution Using the Publish/Subscribe Paradigm for Managing MANETs

Vasilis Sourlas, Paris Flegkas, and Leandros Tassiulas

Dept. of Computer and Communication Engineering,
University of Thessaly, Volos, Greece
{vsourlas,pflegkas,leandros}@inf.uth.gr

**Abstract.** Policy management has been an emerging management paradigm that has been extensively studied for the case of fixed networks and limited work has already been done for migrating it to mobile environments. Publish/subscribe has become an important architectural style for designing distributed systems and especially for mobile environments due to the loose coupling of the components involved. In this paper, we present a policy-based management system for Mobile Ad hoc Networks (MANETs) using the publish/subscribe paradigm for distributing policies to the managed nodes. Moreover, we enhance the publish/subscribe system with a novel request/response mechanism for tackling the problem of how newly joined nodes will retrieve previously introduced policies.

## 1 Introduction

Management of Mobile Ad hoc Networks (MANETs) has recently attracted a lot of attention due to the proliferation of mobile/pervasive devices and their ability and need to communicate. The nature and their inherent characteristics such as topology changes, mobility of nodes and limited terminal capabilities of such networks pose new challenges and requirements for their management. Traditional management approaches in fixed networks based on centralized approaches (SNMP) cannot be applied in ad hoc networks. MANETSs are self-creating in the sense that mobile hosts need to dynamically discover other nodes and form spontaneously a network from a collection of mobile hosts that have the ability to route information. It is evident that the highly dynamic environment of MANETs can benefit from the self-management capabilities provided by Policy-based Management (PBM). PBM has been applied to fixed networks using also a centralized architecture where a Policy Decision Point (PDP) resides in a management server and is responsible for retrieving policy rules, defined by the operator in the Policy Management Tool (PMT), stored in the Policy Repository (PR) and translating them to management operations on the network elements i.e. Policy Enforcement Points (PEPs), realizing this way the business objectives of the operator [1]. In order to apply PBM in ad hoc networks, a hierarchically distributed management approach has to be followed, based on their characteristics and behavior as described by related work in the literature [2].

The publish/subscribe paradigm has become an important architectural style for designing distributed systems. Applications that exploit a publish/subscribe

G. Pavlou, T. Ahmed, and T. Dagiuklas (Eds.): MMNS 2008, LNCS 5274, pp. 14–19, 2008.

communication paradigm are organized as a collection of autonomous components (clients), which interact by publishing event notifications and by subscribing to the classes of events they are interested in. The event dispatcher (broker), is responsible for collecting subscriptions and forwarding events to subscribers. The anonymity and dynamism of publish/subscribe allow the systems to adapt quickly to frequent connections and disconnections of mobile nodes.

Network management has always been one of the most popular applications using an event-based paradigm where managers subscribe to events published by the managed elements. In this paper, we present a policy-based management architecture for mobile ad hoc networks based on the publish/subscribe communication paradigm for distributing policy rules from the points they are introduced to all the responsible components for their enforcement. We believe that the dynamic environment of MANETs can benefit from such a communication paradigm. Policy distribution is a critical task in managing MANETs since there is a need to assure that all nodes comply with policies introduced by the operator leading the system to stability. Moreover, we enhance the publish/subscribe paradigm with a request/response mechanism so that nodes that join the network can retrieve previously introduced policies. This is important since nodes might not have joined the network when the operator defines a policy and current publish/subscribe systems do not support retrieval of previous or missing events.

The rest of the paper is organized as followed. Section 2 describes related work in the area of management of MANETs and publish/subscribe systems. Section 3 presents our proposed policy management architecture based on the publish/subscribe paradigm for distributing policies. Section 4 describes the enhanced request/response mechanism while section 5 presents our initial design and implementation. Finally, section 6 concludes this paper and gives pointers to our future work.

## 2  Related Work

Limited work has been done in the area of management of ad hoc networks where most approaches follow a hierarchical oragnisation model. The first attempt was made by [3], proposing an Ad hoc Network Management Protocol (ANMP) based on hierarchical clustering of nodes in a three level architecture. The "Guerilla" architecture [4] adopts an agent-based two-tier distributed approach where at the higher level "nomadic managers" make decisions and mobile agents exploit a utility function to decide their migration and probe deployment to fulfill management objectives Finally in [2], a hybrid hierarchical and distributed approach is adopted, presenting a system architecture that uses the policy-based management paradigm together with context awareness for managing MANETs. While all the above approaches were designed for solving relevant problems in the area of ad hoc network management, none of them has dealt with the critical issue of policy distribution in MANETs. The use of a publish/subscribe architecture for distributing policies in MANETs has not been considered in the past and comprises one of the most innovative aspects of our approach.

There are several research efforts concerned with the development of an event notification service such as Siena [5] and REDs [6] which implement the publish/subscribe architecture. REDs defines a protocol to organize the nodes of a mobile ad hoc network in a single, self-repairing tree that efficient supports content-based routing. In achieving this goal REDs implement COMAN (Content-based routing for Mobile Ad hoc Networks) [7], which was designed to tolerate the dynamics of the underlying physical network, characteristic of MANETs.

## 3  System Architecture

We adopt a 2-tier hierarchical and distributed approach for our management organization model where nodes of the network are categorized based on their management functionality. The simplest nodes are the ones only with the PEP functionality, offering only a management interface to nodes with enhanced management intelligence denoted as cluster managers in [4]. Depending on the degree of distribution policy repositories (PR) can be hosted in several nodes in the network avoiding this way the retrieval of all policies from the PDPs from a single point in the network. Finally, in the highest level of our hierarchy are the nodes with the PMT functionality, enabling the administrator of the network to introduce policies that should be stored in the repositories and enforced by all the nodes with the PDP functionality.

In order to incorporate a robust and efficient policy distribution mechanism all the policy management components described above communicate using the publish/subscribe paradigm. In order to achieve that, several nodes of the network take the role of the event broker i.e. a publish/subscribe (pub/sub) router as it is shown in Figure 1 forming an overlay publish/subscribe network handling the distribution of policies from the point they are introduced to the repositories and the PDPs responsible to enforce them. All the policy components are the clients of the pub/sub network namely the publishers and the subscribers. Our system architecture is depicted in Figure 1 where all nodes with PDP functionality subscribe to the pub/sub router they are connected to waiting for a relevant policy to be introduced/published by the administrator (PMT).

In our work, we assume the following well adopted representation of a policy as defined by IETF [8] and used in our previous work on policy management [9]:

*{Roles} [TimePeriod] if {conditions} then {actions}*

The concept of roles is critical in our architecture since it defines the scope of the policy i.e. to which nodes it applies and comprises the subscription filter in the pub/sub network. Nodes with only the PEP functionality first supply their role to their cluster manager node that creates an aggregated subscription with all the roles of the managed nodes in order to receive all the relevant policies. Nodes with the PDP functionality present and not in a Cluster manager role subscribe only to policies related to their own operation.

The operator of the network defines the policies in a node with the PMT functionality which publishes the policy to the pub/sub router it is attached to (or physically co-located) and the pub/sub network is responsible for delivering this policy to all the relevant components based on the Roles attribute and the subscription tables of the pub/sub routers that were created by the client subscriptions. With the recent advances in the pub/sub systems and their enhancements for mobile environments the pub/sub overlay network takes all the reconfigurations actions needed to assure a minimum

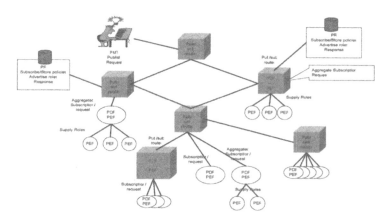

**Fig. 1.** System Architecture

amount of lost messages. Finally, nodes with the Policy Repository component also subscribe to receive policies and are responsible to store them for later retrieval by new subscribers or for validation and conflict detection checking before a new policy is introduced.

## 4 Enhancing Publish/Subscribe with Request/Response

In our pub/sub system, we use the subscription forwarding routing strategy [5] where the routing paths for policies are set by subscriptions, which are propagated throughout the network so as to form a tree that connects the subscribers to all the brokers in the network. This scheme is optimized to avoid forwarding the same subscriptions in the same direction by exploiting "coverage" relations among filters. This means that a subscription is forwarded to a neighboring broker only if it is not being covered by a subscription already forwarded to the same neighbor. Particularly we say that a sub-scription $S_1$ covers another subscription $S_2$, denoted by $S_1 \geq S_2$, iff any event matching $S_2$ also matches $S_1$ [10]. When a client (PMT) publishes a message (policy) that matches a subscription, the message is routed towards the subscriber following the reverse path put in place by the subscription.

The subscription forwarding routing algorithm and all its known implementations ([5] and [6]) does not provide the capability of retrieving a published message (pol-icy) at a time later than the time of its publication. In order to achieve this, we en-hance the pub/sub system with advertisement messages. Each broker maintains a set ST "Subscription Table" containing the identifiers of the brokers to which the broker is connected and the subscriptions that those neighbors had sent to the broker. In our case, we add to each broker another set AT "Advertisement Table" which contains the identifiers of the brokers to which the broker is connected and the advertisements that those neighbors had sent to the broker.

Advertisements are messages sent by the PR nodes containing the Roles to which the stored policies are referred to and are treated similarly to subscription messages so as to form a tree that connects the PRs to all the brokers in the network. Coverage also

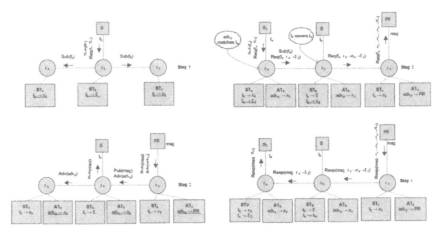

**Fig. 2.** Enhanced publish/subscribe paradigm. Step 3 and step 4 illustrates the novel introduced Request() and Response() messages.

occurs with advertisements and as in subscriptions is used to avoid forwarding the same advertisements to the same direction.

We also add to the system two additional types of messages. We call them Request() and Response(). As shown in figure 2, when a client node $s_2$ (PDP) subscribes to a broker node $n_a$ (step 3), sending a Subscribe($f_a$) message also sends a Request($f_a$, $s_2$) message. The Request() message is similar to the Subscribe() message but apart from the filter it also carries the sequence of the nodes that passes from. Node $n_a$ upon receiving the Request() message checks in $ATn_a$ for advertisements matching filter $f_a$. If such an advertisement occurs ($adv_a$), the broker forwards the Request() message to the identifier for which the $adv_a$ was in the table otherwise the Request() message is dropped.

When a broker $n_b$ receives a Request() checks in $ATn_b$ for matching advertisements and according to the findings, it forwards the Request() appending its identifier. In this case, there will be an entrance in a brokers' AT ($ATn_c$) which points in a PR node. Upon receiving the Request() the PR client checks for the matching messages and sends back a Response() message (step 4) for each matching message. The Response() message is similar to the Publish() one but apart from the message it also carries the sequence of nodes carried by the Request(). When a broker receives a Response() message pops off its identifier from the sequence and forwards it to the first broker of the remaining sequence. In the end, client $s_2$ will receive the message. With the above procedure every new subscriber and only that one will receive every old message (policy) matching its role.

## 5 Design and Implementation

Two of the most popular publish/subscribe systems, where the subscription forwarding routing algorithm is implemented, are Siena [5] and REDS [6]. We used REDS since it was designed to tolerate dynamic reconfigurations of the dispatching infrastructure. We mainly modified the Routing layer of the REDS systems in order to implement the newly introduced messages and support the storage of the advertisements (Advertisement Table). We have also altered the Overlay layer in such a way that can transfer the new type of messages. Of course, minor changes had been made to other modules in order to make the system compatible.

# 6 Conclusion and Future Work

In this paper, we described an architecture for policy-based management of mobile ad hoc networks focusing on the critical problem of policy distribution. We showed how we can incorporate a publish/subscribe communication paradigm, providing a robust and efficient policy distribution mechanism in such a volatile network environment.

Initial tests showed very promising results and our future work focuses on performing experiments in different mobility scenarios, evaluating our system both in terms of message (policy) delivery as well as in terms of overhead.

# Acknowledgement

This paper is part of the 04EP106 research project implemented within the framework of ENTER-2004 and co-financed by National and Community funds (25% from the Greek Ministry of Development – General Secretariat of Research and Technology and 75% from E.U.- European Social Fund).

# References

1. Strassner, J.: Policy-Based Network Management, Solutions for the next generation. Morgan Kaufmann, San Francisco (2003)
2. Hadjiantonis, M., Malatras, A., Pavlou, G.: A Context-aware Policy-based Framework for the Management of MANETs. In: 7th IEEE International Workshop on Policies for Distributed Systems and Networks, Canada, pp. 23–32 (2006)
3. Chen, W., Jain, N., Singh, S.: ANMP Ad hoc network management protocol. IEEE Journal on Selected Areas in Communications 17 (1999)
4. Shen, C., Srisathapornphat, C., Jaikaeo, C.: An adaptive management architecture for ad hoc networks. IEEE Communication Magazine 41 (2003)
5. Carzaniga, A., Rosenblum, D., Wolf, A.: Design and evaluation of a wide-area event notification service. ACM Transaction On Computer Systems 19, 332–383 (2001)
6. Cugola, G., Picco, G.: REDS, A Reconfigurable Dispatching System. In: 6th International workshop on Software Engineering and Middleware, Oregon, pp. 9–16 (2006)
7. Mottola, L., Cugola, G., Picco, G.: A Self-repairing Tree Topology Enabling Content-Based Routing in Mobile Ad Hoc Networks. IEEE Transaction on Mobile Computing 7, 946–960 (2008)
8. Moore, B., Ellesson, E., Strassner, J., Westerinen, A.: Policy Core Information Model. RFC 3060, IETF (2001)
9. Flegkas, P., Trimintzios, P., Pavlou, G., Liotta, A.: Design and Implementation of a Policy-based Resource Management Architecture. In: IEEE/IFIP Integrated Management Symposium, Colorado, pp. 215–229 (2003)
10. Chand, R., Felber, A.: A scalable protocol for content-based routing in overlay networks. In: 2nd IEEE International Symposium on Network Computing and Applications, pp. 123–130 (2003)

# D-Sense: An Integrated Environment for Algorithm Design and Protocol Implementation in Wireless Sensor Networks

Kazushi Ikeda[1], Shunsuke Mori[1], Yuya Ota[1,*], Takaaki Umedu[1,2], Akihito Hiromori[1,2], Hirozumi Yamaguchi[1,2], and Teruo Higashino[1,2]

[1] Graduate School of Information Science and Technology, Osaka University
[2] Japan Science Technology and Agency, CREST
{k-ikeda,s-mori,umedu,hiromori,h-yamagu,higashino}@ist.osaka-u.ac.jp,
*ohta@am.sanken.osaka-u.ac.jp

**Abstract.** Since Wireless Sensor Networks (WSNs) are regarded as large-scale distributed systems in nature, it is (i) difficult to implement their distributed low-level codes, (ii) hard to analyze their performance and (iii) almost impossible to operate a number of nodes manually. In this paper, we propose an integrated environment called *D-sense* to solve these problems in WSN development. By providing algorithm-level APIs, D-sense tries to hide distributed, low-level operations in the NesC programming language. The algorithm-level APIs and other NesC codes can automatically be converted into simulator codes to avoid code-writing for simulation purpose. In addition, D-sense provides useful functions like monitoring, logging and debugging of distributed programs. We have implemented several known protocols and evaluated the performance by simulation and real environmental experiments to demonstrate the functions of D-sense.

## 1 Introduction

In Wireless Sensor Networks (WSNs), due to heterogeneity of architecture, network scale and applications, new protocols are often developed or existing protocols are tuned accordingly. Thus many protocols have been designed with different design goals [1,2,3,4,5,6,7,8]. However, protocol designers and developers face with typical problems which have been experienced in designing distributed systems. Even though the developers wish to concentrate on abstract behavior of protocols, they at last need to write target-dependent low-level codes. Then they carry out performance analysis and validation in simulated networks or real environment. However, additional effort may be required to prepare another implementation of the protocol for network simulators, since in most cases it is not compatible with real codes. Also experiments in real environment require to set up many sensor nodes, to log their behavior, and to manipulate them to validate (debug) the implementation. Obviously all of these tasks are really hard and complex.

G. Pavlou, T. Ahmed, and T. Dagiuklas (Eds.): MMNS 2008, LNCS 5274, pp. 20–32, 2008.

In this paper, we design and develop *D-sense*, an integrated development environment to support protocol development in WSNs efficiently. D-sense mainly assumes NesC on TinyOS as the target language and architecture, and experiments have been carried out on Mica Motes accordingly. However, for other languages such as C or Java, D-sense's design concept can also be applied. The advantages of D-sense are three-fold. First, D-sense offers algorithm-level APIs which are derived by classifying and studying existing protocols. Thus developers can design distributed algorithms in NesC language directly with these APIs. Secondly, it enables seamless integration of simulated and real sensor networks. To accomplish this, we provide a translator from NesC codes into QualNet simulator application codes. Also the physically sensed events and sensor node status observed in real environment are made available in the simulator. These capabilities increase repeatability and fidelity of experiments. Thirdly, monitoring and run-time manipulation of sensor node behavior is possible. We will later show how this functionality can powerfully support developers in test and maintenance of WSN protocols.

Using the D-sense APIs, we have implemented GPSR [1], SPEED [2], BIP [3] and Rumor Routing [4]. In particular, we have evaluated the performance of SPEED in both real and simulated networks and compared the results with [2] to validate the D-sense implementation. It was also confirmed how D-sense contributed to alleviate the development cost.

This paper is organized as follows. In Section 2, we address the related work and show the features of D-sense. In Section 3, we describe the functions of D-sense that support design, experiments and protocol debugging of WSN. In Section 4, we show example implementation of the existing WSN protocols by using the D-sense design APIs, and Section 5 shows the experimental results. Section 6 concludes the paper.

## 2   Related Work

Large-scale testbeds such as MoteLab [9] and CitySense [10] usually provide management functions like online distribution of execution codes to mitigate maintenance costs. D-sense differs from them since it is aimed at comprehensive support of design, development and performance analysis.

TinyDB [11] and COUGAR [12] support designing query processing in sensor networks. They provide SQL-like APIs to implement event acquisition and search processes. MATE [13] also provides APIs for more generic purposes, but only low-level APIs like sensing events, pushing data to stack or sending data are designed. EnviroSuite [14] is an object-based programming model framework for tracking and environmental monitoring. Meanwhile, we attempt to help high-level design of more generic protocols including geographic/random-based routing and data fusion/diffusion by extracting their typical behavior. This appropriately hides both distributed and low-level behavior so that developers concentrate on algorithm description. For example, geographic routing protocols like GPSR which employ greedy forwarding strategy need a series of the following atomic actions at each node; (i) obtaining positions of neighbors, (ii) computing distances between the node and the neighbors and between the neighbors and the destination, (iii) finding the neighbor which is closer to the destination than the node and is the closest to the destination among the other neighbors, and (iv) sending a packet. D-sense defines an API for each atomic action, and also provides a single API for a series of these actions by using those atomic APIs.

In summary, as far as we know, no environment has been provided that comprehensively supports algorithm design, low-level implementation, seamless use of simulator and real terminals, and online debugging/monitoring in real environment.

## 3   Functions of D-Sense

### 3.1   High-Level Design Support

One of the most important features of D-sense is high-level design support. Using the *D-sense design APIs*, developers can give algorithm-level NesC descriptions. Then the *D-sense design API translator* takes them as inputs, and expands the embedded APIs that are implemented as macros into pure NesC implementation automatically. In order to support as many types of protocols as possible, the D-sense design APIs are developed based on property analysis of existing typical protocols. These protocols are classified by the criteria which are inspired from [15]. A classification example by these criteria is given in Figure 1. For example, GPSR ("g" in Figure 1) is a position-based routing method and is used in GHT [16] or some other methods that employ position-based event accumulation and search mechanisms. In implementing this protocol, we may use the APIs for "position-based routing" and "store and search application". Similarly, some other known protocols are classified in the figure.

For each type in the classification, we provide type dependent APIs, and also provide generic APIs which are commonly used in all the types. Furthermore, we design more functional APIs that are realized by using these APIs. Part of

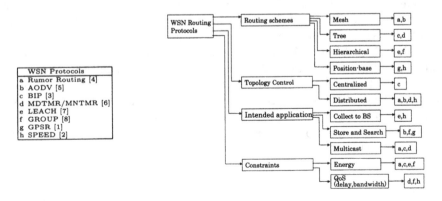

**Fig. 1.** Criteria in Classification of WSN Protocols

**Table 1.** Part of D-sense Design API

| Generic APIs | Energy Constraint Protocol APIs |
|---|---|
| Get the IDs of the one hop neighbor nodes<br>   -> get_neighbors(IDs[],len_IDs)<br>Send a packet to the designated node<br>   -> send_unicast_packet(ID,pkt) | Get the residual battery of the designated node<br>   -> get_residual_energy(ID)<br>Get the energy consumption to send a packet<br>   -> get_transmission_energy() |
| **Position base protocol APIs** | **QoS Constraint Protocol APIs** |
| Get the position of the designated node<br>   -> get_position(ID)<br>Compute the distance between the designated<br>two nodes<br>   -> get_distance(ID,ID) | Get the delay between the designated two nodes<br>   -> get_delay(ID,ID)<br>Get the packet loss ratio at the designated node<br>   -> get_packet_loss_rate(ID) |
| | **Functional (Combined) API** |
| **Hierarchical protocol APIs** | Get the ID of the maximum residual battery node |
| Get the IDs of the cluster members<br>   -> get_cluster_nodes(IDs[],len_IDs)<br>Get the cluster head of the neighbor cluster<br>   -> get_neighbor_clusterhead() | in a cluster<br>Get the minimum delay node which has the spe-<br>cific data<br>Get the packet loss ratio in the tree |

them is shown in Table 1. Using these D-sense design APIs, developers can write codes concentrating on algorithmic behavior, and other low-level descriptions are hidden. The details of the APIs and their implementation are shown in our web site [17].

In Section 4, we will exemplify how typical protocols are implemented using these APIs.

## 3.2 Seamless Integration of Simulated and Real Networks

The NesC codes derived by the D-sense design API translator can be directly executed on Mica Mote, or can further be translated into codes for QualNet simulator [18] written in C++ by the *D-sense NesC translator*. Also environmental events and sensor node status logged automatically by the D-sense debugging component in real environment and can be animated by the QualNet animator (Figure 2) in which we provide special graphics to visualize residual amount of battery and LED status (we assume Mica MOTE here) for more realistic animation.

## 3.3 Protocol Debugging Support

We explain our powerful support facility for online debugging. Debugging sensor node software in distributed environments requires many efforts to implement the complicated communication schemes for confirming the node status. To mitigate these efforts, D-sense offers *debug scenarios* which enable developers to get information about the nodes and to make debugging easy. At each node, we run a "debug_agent", and at the base station we run a "debug controller". Each debug agent can monitor specified variables on that node, and communicate with the debug controller. The debug controller operates those agents to realize the scenario in distributed environment.

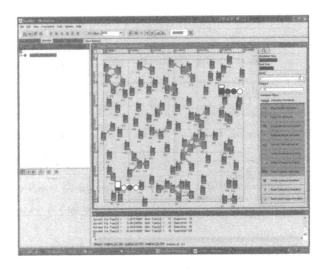

**Fig. 2.** A Snapshot from QualNet Simulator (Sensor Node Status is Visualized)

A debug scenario is composed of a *condition* followed by an *action*. As the condition, we may refer to function names which become true when the corresponding function of the NesC code is called. We may also specify boolean expressions over the variables of the NesC code. The action can be specified as a set of statements which are executed when the condition is satisfied.

An important feature is that we may specify the "owners" of the variables and functions that appear in the scenario. These owners may be a specific node or a set of nodes, which are determined statically or dynamically. For the static case, we may directly specify node ID as the prefix of each variable or function. If we wish dynamic assignment to the node ID, we may use symbol $ in the condition, which implies the first node that satisfies the condition. Also we may define a set of nodes that satisfy specified conditions. This node set can be determined statically by debug APIs, or can be defined dynamically in the action part.

In the following part, we give two examples of debug scenarios. The first one is given below.

```
$.on_loop_detected ->|
  nodeIDs = $.receive_packet->recent_visit_nodes;
  foreach u in nodeIDs {
      u.refresh_table();
  }
```

The prefix of a variable or a function indicates its owner node. Those without prefix are variables defined and held by the debug controller (at the base station). Thus, this scenario means that if a sensor node (symbolized by $) calls *on_loop_detected* function, then *recent_visit_nodes* (this is a list of nodes) included in structure *receive_packet* of node $ is set on the list variable *nodeIDs* of the base station. Then each node specified in *nodeIDs* executes function *refresh_table()*.

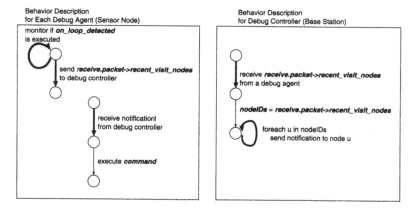

**Fig. 3.** Distributed Execution of Debug Scenario

This code can be used as an assertion and a post-condition in routing protocols. Once a loop is detected by a sensor node in forwarding a packet, the routing tables on the nodes that the packet recently traversed are refreshed.

The second example is a scenario for system monitoring and maintenance.

```
ave_energy(S = region(a,b)) < 0.2 ->|
  foreach u in S {
    u.beacon_interval = u.beacon_interval * 2
  }
```

This scenario means that if the average residual energy of the nodes in the square region defined by two corner points $a$ and $b$ (the set of the nodes in the region is obtained by the debug API "$region(a, b)$") is less than 20%, these nodes double their beacon intervals to extend network lifetime of the region. $ave\_energy(S)$ is also a debug API that returns the average residual energy of the nodes in set $S$.

To realize these scenarios by the debug controller and the debug agents, we need to derive protocols to exchange necessary data or notification, and to execute statements. For example, the first example can be distributed over the agents and controller as shown in Figure 3. Formally, each debug agent (or controller) collects arguments to execute a statement that updates its own variable. For example, the first statement of the action part,

```
nodeIDs = $.receive_packet->recent_visit_nodes;
```

is executed by the controller because $nodeIDs$ is the variable of the controller. However, the right-hand value is the variable held by the node symbolized by $. Since we do not know which node becomes $, the agent on each node sends this value to the controller whenever $on\_loop\_detected$ function is executed, and the controller updates the value of $nodeIDs$.

As seen in this very simple example, we need to define the language specification to describe various scenarios design the architecture of controller, agents, and network to execute the given scenario in distributed environment. More interesting challenge is to execute the scenario in fully-distributed sensor networks where no base station is present. In such a case, sensor nodes need to collaborate to check the condition and execute the action, with less traffic and computation costs. To determine policies of distributed execution, which optimize message exchanges or some other objective functions, is part of our ongoing work.

## 4   Protocol Implementation Examples

In this section, we show example implementation of four existing WSN protocols; GPSR, SPEED, BIP and Rumor Routing by using the D-sense design APIs.

GPSR[1] is a position-based protocol, where each sensor node forwards a packet to the neighbor node nearest to the destination by using a planar graph. Figure 4(a) denotes an example implementation of the algorithm to make a Relative Neighborhood Graph (RNG), which is a kind of well-known planar graph. We can see that the algorithm is implemented simply by using APIs, such as listing neighbor nodes ("get_neighbor" in line 02) and getting the distance between nodes ("get_distance" in line 07). Figure 4(b) shows an example implementation of routing process of GPSR. In this code, each node lists its neighbor nodes (line 01) and forwards a packet to the node nearest to the destination in the listed nodes (lines 05–09).

SPEED[2] is also a position-based routing protocol. In SPEED protocol, Stateless Non-deterministic Geographic Forwarding (SNGF) algorithm is used to select a node which is nearer to the destination and handles lighter traffic to forward packets. Figure 5 shows an example implementation of SNGF. A node

```
01: get_planar_graph(graph g){
02:     len = get_neighbors(neighbor_IDs, sizeof(neighbor_IDs));
03:     for (i = 0; i < len; i++){
04:         nodeID = neighbor_IDs[i];
05:         for (j = 0; j < len; j++){
06:             nodeID' = neighbor_IDs[j];
07:             if (get_distance(myID,nodeID)
                     > max(get_distance(myID,nodeID'),
                         get_distance(nodeID,nodeID')))
08:                 g.remove_edge(myID,nodeID);
09: }
```

(a) RNG Generation

```
01: len = get_neighbors(neighbor_IDs, sizeof(neighbor_IDs));
02: forwardID = get_my_ID();
03: for (i = 0; i < len; i++){
04:     nodeID = neighbor_IDs[i];
05:     if(get_distance(nodeID,targetID)
             < get_distance(forwardID,targetID))
06:         forwardID = nodeID;
07:     if(forwardID != myID) // forward toward a nearer node
08:         send_unicast_packet(forwardID,packet);
09: else peremeter_mode == true; // perimeter mode (omitted)
```

(b) Greedy Forwarding

**Fig. 4.** Example Implementation of GPSR

```
01: SNGF(message){
02:    my_length = get_distance(message->target_ID, myID);
03:    len = get_neighbors(neighborIDs, sizeof(neighborIDs));
04:    num_FS_first = 0; num_FS_Second = 0;
05:    for (i = 0; i < len; i++){
06:       nodeID = neighbor_IDs[i];
07:       diff = my_length
                - get_distance(message->target_ID, nodeID);
08:       if(diff > 0){
09:          if(diff / get_delay(myID,nodeID) > set_point)
10:             FS_first[num_FS_first++] = nodeID;
11:          else
12:                FS_second[num_FS_Second++] = nodeID;
13:       }
14:    }
15:    if(num_FS_first > 0){
16:       forwarding_probability = 0;
17:       forwarding_nodeID = FS_first[0];
18:       for(i = 0;i < num_FS_first; i ++){
19:          nodeID = FS_first[i];
20:          fp = get_probability
                (get_distance(myNodeID,nodeID)
                 get_queue_size(nodeID));
21:          if(fp > forwarding_probability){
22:             forwarding_probability = fp;
23:             forwarding_nodeID = nodeID;
24:          }
25:       send_unicast_packet(nodeID, message);
26:    }
27:    else // forward toward the nodes in FS_second
28: }
```

**Fig. 5.** Example Implementation of SPEED

receiving a packet finds nodes that are nearer to the destination than itself (lines 02–07) and classifies them into two groups. If the transmission efficiency of a node is larger than a threshold *set_point*, it is put into group *FS_first*. The other nodes are put into group *FS_second* (lines 08–13). Then a node is selected from the group *FS_first* of nodes having better transmission efficiency according to the length of the transmission path and the levels of congestion (lines 15–26).

We can see that GPSR and SPEED, both of which are position-based routing protocols, can be implemented by using similar APIs.

BIP [3] is a centralized protocol managing sensor nodes in tree topology, and is designed to minimize the total energy consumption of the network. Due to space limitations, we omit the explanation. The interested readers may refer to our web [17].

Rumor Routing [4] is a routing protocol based on mesh topology, and is designed for accumulation and search of data. Figure 6 shows an example implementation. In Rumor Routing, an agent manages event tables kept in sensor nodes as follows. A node receiving an agent adds information written in the agent to its event table. The information consists of the number of hops to the event *num_hops*, and the direction and the hop count from the node that sends the agent *source_ID* to each event (lines 01–02). At the same time, the node puts information recorded in its event table to the agent and sends it to another node. In this process, a node where agents have not visited long time is selected (lines 03–06). When a node receives a query packet, the node searches the path

```
01:   on_agent_received(source_ID,agent_packet){
02:       event_table = set_event_distance(
                  agent_packet->num_hops,source_ID);
03:       agent_packet = set_event_info(
                  agent_packet, event_table);
04:       if(agent_packet->ttl-- > 0)
05:          send_unicast_packet(
                  get_not_visited_neighbor(agent_packet),
                  agent_packet);
06:   }
07:
08:   on_query_received(source_ID,query_packet){
09:       query_packet->ttl--;
10:       if(get_num_hops(event_table,query_packet->data)==0)
11:          doQuery(query_packet)
12:       else if (get_hops(query_packet->data) > 0)
13:          send_unicast_packet(query_packet,
                  get_forwarding_direction(event_table,query_packet))
14:       else
15:          send_unicast_packet(
                  get_not_visited_neighbor(query_packet),
                  queryPacket)
16:   }
```

**Fig. 6.** Example Implementation of Rumor Routing

to the event queried by the packet using its event table (line 10). If the node has the target event information itself, it processes the query, otherwise the node searches a direction to forward it to (lines 11–13). If the node has no information regarding the query at all, the query is forwarded to a node where the query packet has not visited recently (lines 14–15).

At last, in order to show the effectiveness of the D-sense design APIs, we counted the LOC (lines of code) of SPEED codes implemented (1) by using the design APIs, (2) in C++ for QualNet simulator and (3) in NesC for MOTE terminals.

|     | (1) Design API | (2) C++ | (3) NesC |
|-----|----------------|---------|----------|
| LOC | 221            | 1044    | 1147     |

Without using APIs, the implementation required more than 1000 lines. On the other hand, by using the APIs, the LOC is decreased to about 200 lines. Thus, much effort dedicated to implementation was reduced.

## 5   Performance Evaluation

In order to validate the D-sense implementation and show its usefulness, we evaluated the performance of the SPEED protocol in simulation and real environment by using D-sense, and compared the performance in the simulation to the performance reported in [2].

We used the same scenario as [2]. This scenario is aimed at testing the congestion avoidance capability of the SPEED protocol. A few nodes are randomly selected from the left side of the terrain and send periodic data to the base station at the right side of the terrain. Each sender generates one CBR flow with 1 packet/second. To create congestion, two randomly chosen nodes in the middle of the terrain create a flow between them at half time of the 150 second experiment. In order to evaluate the congestion avoidance capability under different congestion levels, the rate of this flow is increased by 10 from 0 up to 100 packets/second over several simulations. We have evaluated the delay and loss ratio of the packets to the base station.

We show the experimental environment in Table 2. Because of the limitation on the number of MOTEs, we evaluated the SPEED protocol with 25 nodes in real environment. To compare the reported performance with the real environmental performance, simulation experiments were also conducted in the same configurations. We adjusted the wireless ranges of MOTEs and simulator according to the network scale. Figure 7 shows a snapshot from the experiments in real environment where MOTE terminals were uniformly arranged.

**Table 2.** Experimental Environment

| | Reported | Simulation | Real Env. |
|---|---|---|---|
| PHY & MAC | 802.11 | 802.11 | 802.15.4 |
| Bandwidth | 200 Kb/s | 200Kb/s, 250Kb/s | 250Kb/s |
| Payload Size | 32 Bytes | 32 Bytes | 32 Bytes |
| Terrain | (200m, 200m) | (200m, 200m), (20m, 20m) | (20m, 20m) |
| # of Nodes | 100 | 100, 25 | 25 |
| Node Placement | Uniform | Uniform | Uniform |
| Radio Range | 40m | 40m, 8m | 8m |

**Fig. 7.** Arrangement of MOTEs in Real Environment

Figure 8(a) shows the end to end delay. In the experiments with 100 nodes, the performance observed in the simulation well follows the reported performance although small difference is seen around 40 packet/sec congestion. We observed the same level delays in the experiments with 25 nodes as observed in those with 100 nodes. In each congestion level, delays in real environment were smaller than those in simulation.

Figure 8(b) shows packet loss ratio (the ratio of packets that failed to reach the base station). In the experiments with 100 nodes, the simulation performance is nearly equal to the reported performance. In the experiments with 25 nodes, the packet loss ratio is greatly higher than that in the experiments with 100 nodes. This is mainly because each node had too few nodes in its neighbor table to avoid the congestion area at the center of the network in the experiments with 25 nodes. In particular the packet loss ratio is much higher in real environment than that in the simulation.

As shown in Figure 8, compared to the simulation results, we can see small delays and large packet loss ratio in real environmental results. We attribute these differences to large fluctuation of radio ranges in real environment. In

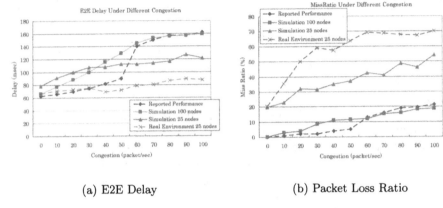

(a) E2E Delay

(b) Packet Loss Ratio

**Fig. 8.** Performance of SPEED Protocol

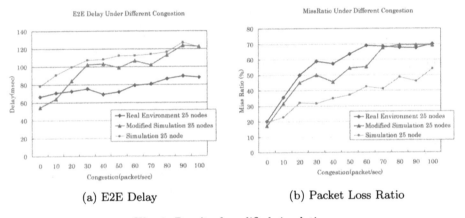

(a) E2E Delay

(b) Packet Loss Ratio

**Fig. 9.** Result of modified simulation

real environment, nodes can receive beacons from further nodes and store the node IDs in its neighbor table. Then, nodes send packets to those further nodes, which have both lower delays and higher probability of packet loss. To solve this problem, we should improve the scheme of neighbor table management. Nodes which receive beacons do not add the IDs of the sender nodes to their neighbor tables until they observe higher success ratio of beacon reception from those nodes than a certain threshold.

On the other hand, as shown in Figure 9, the simulation result gets closer to the real environment one by enlarging the radio range and choosing a proper radio model and height of antenna according to the logs obtained from the experiments in real environment. This shows that we can realize realistic simulation experiments that are closer to the experiments in real environment.

From these performance evaluations, we could validate the D-sense implementation. In addition, we could find some real environmental problems and their causes, discuss their solutions, and improve reality of the simulation by considering them. This shows the importance of implementing and evaluating WSN protocols in real environment, and also shows that D-sense well supports these activities.

## 6  Conclusion

In this paper, we have designed and developed an integrated environment called D-sense for supporting development of WSNs. D-sense supports protocol design by high-level design APIs. Also it provides seamless collaboration of simulated and real networks for performance evaluation, and powerful distributed debugging scheme. We have conducted performance evaluation of the SPEED protocol in simulation and real environment to show the effectiveness of D-sense. For now, we have designed the specification of D-sense and implemented a part of its functions. Our ongoing work includes developing a complete set of design/debug APIs and related tools, and opening them to public domain.

## References

1. Karp, B., Kung, H.T.: GPSR: Greedy Perimeter Stateless Routing for Wireless Networks. In: Proc. of the 6th Annual International Conference on Mobile Computing and Networking (MobiCom 2000), pp. 149–160 (2000)
2. He, T., Stankovic, J.A., Lu, C., Abdelzaher, T.: SPEED: A Stateless Protocol for Real-time Communication in Sensor Networks. In: Proc. of the 23rd International Conference on Distributed Computing Systems(ICDCS 2003), pp. 46–55 (2003)
3. Wieselthier, J.E., Nguyen, G.D., Ephremides, A.: On the Construction of Energy-efficient Broadcast and Multicast Trees in Wireless Networks. In: Proc. of the 19th Annual Conference on Computer and Communications (INFOCOM 2000), pp. 585–594 (2000)
4. Braginsky, D., Estrin, D.: Rumor Routing Algorthim for Sensor Networks. In: Proc. of the 1st ACM international workshop on Wireless Sensor Networks and Applications (WSNA 2002), pp. 22–31 (2002)
5. Perkins, C., Royer, E.: Ad-hoc On-demand Distance Vector Routing. In: Proc. of 2nd IEEE Workshop on Mobile Computing Systems and Applications (WMCSA 1999), pp. 90–100 (1999)
6. Wei, W., Zakhor, A.: Multiple Tree Video Multicast Over Wireless Ad Hoc Networks. IEEE Transactions on Circuits and Systems for Video Technology 17(1), 2–15 (2007)
7. Heinzelman, W.R., Chandrakasan, A., Balakrishnan, H.: Energy-efficient Communication Protocol for Wireless Microsensor Networks. In: Proc. of the 33rd Annual Hawaii International Conference on System Sciences (HICSS-33), pp. 1–10 (2000)
8. Liyang, Y., Neng, W., Wei, Z., Chunlei, Z.: GROUP: A Grid-Clustering Routing Protocol for Wireless Sensor Networks. In: Proc. of the 2nd International Conference on Wireless Communications, Networking and Mobile Computing (WiCOM 2006), pp. 1–5 (2006)
9. Werner-Allen, G., Swieskowski, P., Welsh, M.: MoteLab: a Wireless Sensor Network Testbed. In: Proc. of the 4th International Symposium on Information Processing in Sensor Networks (IPSN 2005), pp. 483–488 (2005)
10. CitySense Project: CitySense - An Open, Urban-Scale Sensor Network Testbed, http://www.citysense.net/

11. Madden, S., Franklin, M., Hellerstein, J., Hong, W.: TinyDB: An Acquisitional Query Processing System for Sensor Networks. ACM Transactions on Database Systems (TODS) 30(1), 122–173 (2005)

12. Bonnet, P., Gehrke, J., Seshadri, P.: Towards Sensor Database Systems. In: Tan, K.-L., Franklin, M.J., Lui, J.C.-S. (eds.) MDM 2001. LNCS, vol. 1987, pp. 3–14. Springer, Heidelberg (2000)

13. Levis, P., Culler, D.: Mate: a Tiny Virtual Machine for Sensor Networks. In: Proc. of the 10th International Conference on Architectural Support for Programming Languages and Operating Systems (ASPLOS-X 2002), pp. 85–95 (2002)

14. Luo, L., Abdelzaher, T.F., He, T., Stankovic, J.A.: Envirosuite: An Environmentally Immersive Programming Famework for Sensor Networks. Trans. on Embedded Computing Sys. 5(3), 543–576 (2006)

15. Al-Karaki, J.N., Kamal, A.E.: Routing Techniques in Wireless Sensor Networks: a Survey. IEEE Transactions on Wireless Communications 11(6), 6–28 (2004)

16. Ratnasamy, S., Karp, B., Yin, L., Yu, F., Estrin, D., Govindan, R., Shenker, S.: GHT: A Geographic Hash Table for Data-centric Storage in Sensornets. In: Proc. of the First ACM International Workshop on Wireless Sensor Networks and Applications (WSNA 2002), pp. 78–87 (2005)

17. D-sense Web, D-sense: An Integrated Environment for Algorithm Design and Protocol Implementation in Wireless Sensor Networks, APIs,
http://www-higashi.ist.osaka-u.ac.jp/software/WSN/D-sense/

18. Scalable Network Technologies, Inc., "Qualnet simulator",
http://www.scalable-networks.com/

# A Case for Multimedia Streaming over the Grid Infrastructure

Lambros Lambrinos[1] and Fotis Georgatos[2]

[1] Dept. of Communication and Internet Studies,
Cyprus University of Technology
Limassol, Cyprus
lambros.lambrinos@cut.ac.cy
[2] National Technical University of Athens,
Athens, Greece
fotis@mail.cern.ch

**Abstract.** The grid infrastructure consists of nodes all over the world which are usually interconnected with high speed network links and provide storage and processing facilities. In this paper, we investigate how this massive infrastructure can be utilized to facilitate efficient and scaleable real-time multimedia streaming. The aim is to avoid the issues usually associated with one-to-many media streaming architectures through the use of a mechanism that initiates reflectors as and when they are needed thereby reducing bandwidth-related bottlenecks and ensuring that the delay between the last media distribution point and the receiving client is as low as possible.

**Keywords:** grid, multimedia, streaming, architecture.

## 1 Introduction

Streaming multimedia data over the packet-switched internet is nowadays a highly popular application. End-user hosts have more than adequate processing power for the decoding of high quality audiovisual streams; mobile devices are also capable of displaying reasonable quality video. The material distributed is usually pre-recorded but an increasing number of live events (ranging from speeches to music festivals and sports events) are streamed in real-time.

The increased user demand for multimedia streaming results in increased network bandwidth requirements. As the data is predominantly carried on a best-effort basis, issues such as jitter and packet loss degrade the user's experience. These problems are not uncommon and are somewhat expected considering that the media data competes with other internet traffic. Researchers have always been examining ways to reduce the load on the infrastructure as this allows more users to be served.

An infrastructure that could be used for multimedia streaming is the grid [1]. So far, the grid is predominantly seen as a massive infrastructure that can be used to perform intensive processing operations and store vast amounts of data. To facilitate these activities, the various nodes (clusters) are in many cases interconnected using

G. Pavlou, T. Ahmed, and T. Dagiuklas (Eds.): MMNS 2008, LNCS 5274, pp. 33–38, 2008.

high speed links. In this paper we propose an architecture that aims to utilize this exact characteristic and use the grid for scalable real-time multimedia streaming.

The paper starts with a brief introduction to the main characteristics of media streaming technologies and the grid. Our rationale for deploying multimedia streaming services over the grid is then presented followed by a description of our proposed architecture and its components and future work plans.

# 2  Background

The use of the internet for distribution of multimedia data to multiple clients has been a highly active research topic for many years. It is expected that it will remain so since commercial applications are already using IP networks for their data delivery [2] and the internet already "hosts" an enormous collection of audiovisual material.

## 2.1  Multimedia Streaming

In our work we concentrate on streaming data from a single source to multiple receivers. Streaming involves the transmission of media data over the packet-switched network. The source of such data may be a stored file or a live feed from audiovisual equipment. A receiving host expects a timely and loss-free delivery of the data packets in order to decode the media streams and present them to the user.

Solutions designed for this purpose are generally categorised as Video-on-Demand (VoD) systems. True Video-on-Demand systems [3] allow users to have total control: they can pause, rewind, fast forward the stream whenever they like. Such activities put additional strain on the provider's resources; to prevent that, near Video-on-Demand [4] systems allow such user actions but at discrete time intervals.

The one-to-many data distribution model prevents such systems from scaling as the media server has a finite bandwidth capacity available. Scaleable multimedia data distribution is a topic that has attracted a lot of research interest in the past years; various solutions [5,6] have been proposed to increase the scalability of systems. The ideal solution for the unnecessary bandwidth consumption (i.e. the multiple unicast streams) is the use of native multicast [7] data distribution; this is not yet supported in the majority of the internet.

## 2.2  The Grid

One definition of the grid is that it is a technology based on a system that collects users and resources in a common infrastructure even if they belong to multiple independent organizations, carriers, companies etc. In practice, this implies that we can view all these resources as a single entity independent of geographical location; the primary reason is that networks such as the internet, make it irrelevant. This method of organization can (and does) have tremendous impact in multiple scientific and/or commercial activities that have to manage systems, data and computations in an intensive way. Furthermore, grids can impact end-users providing benefits both in content search applications as well as content storage and retrieval of any type currently in use: text-audio-video. One particular aspect of the grid is that it combines storage, networking and computational resources in a single infrastructure. This makes it possible to perform all functions necessary for:

- building and running Digital Libraries
- performing on-the-fly signal compression-decompression or de/multiplexing
- doing capacity provisioning/scheduling on both cpu and network resources
- allocating capacity dynamically either based on on-demand requests or on static traffic patterns

## 3  Video Distribution over the Grid

In this section we present the rationale behind the suitability of the grid as a platform for multimedia streaming and describe our proposed architecture. Briefly put, a fixed infrastructure investment is never the optimal solution so the grid is the right environment for applications that exhibit variable resource utilization.

### 3.1  The Grid as a Multimedia Streaming Platform

The concept of utility computing is highly applicable in multimedia content delivery; the consumers of the content are typical human beings following diurnal, weekly or monthly patterns with highs and lows in service utilization levels. This is highly evident in TV broadcasting during popular programs.

If we try to transfer this kind of media broadcasting service on the internet as we know it currently, the end result would be congestion, low latency and bad performance at the very moment of highest demand. The most critical aspect of serving an online user community is service stability. It is a good observation to point out that the Internet, as currently experienced by the vast majority of its users, is a network without guarantees and as such it is unsuitable to provide, for example, a better replacement for existing TV and Radio transmission technologies.

This happens because the dependability aspects of the latter are much more robust and resilient to usage by an excessively large audience population. In order for the internet to be able to reach similar levels of robustness and resilience, a number of items have to be addressed:

- a federation-capable solution is needed, if many content providers are going to coexist in the same infrastructure.
- reflectors have to be placed at or near network branching points and reflector capacity must be tunable on demand at run-time.
- bandwidth reservation must be a standard automatic network service, without a human in the loop, even across network boundaries.
- multiple paths should be provided for media data delivery, so that no single system failure or malfunction can disrupt service.

In fact, grid systems are supposed to be able to manage all these aspects at once:

1) grids are by definition a collection of resources spanning multiple administrative domains. As a result, technology provisioning for many Certification Authorities [8] and entities below them is considered as standard in grids. On top of

that, under the concept of Virtual Organizations [9] one is able to collect entities (resources or users) at arbitrary sets together so an infinite number of policies can be globally applied.

2) grid clusters are typically located near backbone network edges or central junctions, for the very fact that this is the only way to make efficient use of them. Moreover, grid clusters contain multiple CPUs which makes it possible to run as many reflectors as needed on a given moment.

3) bandwidth reservation and network Quality-of-Service are not new topics and they play a major role in many distributed applications today. What is though a whole new topic, is the capability to be able to offer them in a fully automated manner. This will build guaranteed paths across multiple networks (autonomous systems in Internet parlance) querying in the process and following distinct network policies in a federated manner. Recent experience during summer 2007 in European networks attached to GEANT2 [10] showed that this is feasible and the current plan is to integrate this service as a part of the capabilities of grid systems.

4) the internet has provisioning for resilience through the automatic rerouting of traffic through multiple paths. Grids should be able to overcome transient or even permanent failures in a similar manner and in a way which is transparent for the user. The concept applies to all subsystems comprising the grid (CPUs, network links etc.)

It is important to note that although peer-to-peer solutions have been proposed as the underlying mechanisms for multimedia data streaming, the grid offers a far larger and more stable infrastructure that is already being used for data storage and computational purposes. To illustrate our point, a project driven by CERN that involves conducting the largest physics experiment ever, is exploiting grid technology exclusively for the distribution and management of its datasets.

## 3.2  Grid Enhancements

One particular aspect that is related to points 2 and 3 in the previous section, which is worthy of further discussion, is that capacity usage in either the CPU or the network must be a schedulable resource. In the current grid implementation this is not always possible, for the very reason that existing grids are of the batch form, since this is the simplest way to build such a service. For example, in the EGEE grid currently it is not possible to request an allocation of 100 CPUs for the first day of the next month; the basic method of service is based on FIFO queues at Computing Elements (CEs).

In order to schedule CPU and network usage, a slightly revised CE architecture must be developed that includes a scheduler that supports job preemption. Although at first glance someone might comment that such a scheme is not directly supportable by the existing grid, the fact is that the implementation is feasible with only slight modifications. There exist local scheduling systems that are able to do so [11] and have already been tested in the real grid environment. Grid engineers are also currently building the components necessary to provide network performance guarantees for grid-based applications [12]. This is work of very high complexity since the underlying network infrastructure must be able to provide such a service.

### 3.3  System Architecture

The architecture of our proposed solution is shown in Figure 1 below. Essentially our proposed solution falls under the category of application-level multicast data distribution systems.

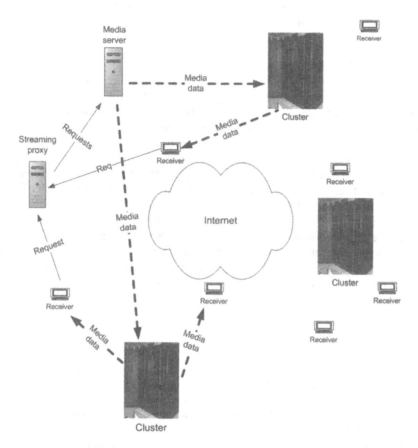

**Fig. 1.** A grid-based multimedia streaming architecture

The *streaming proxy* is the brain of our architecture. It is responsible for handling client requests and associating clients with the most appropriate reflector. The reflectors run on worker nodes in the grid *clusters*; they are responsible for sending the media data to the receivers that the streaming proxy has allocated to them. The media data is sent to the reflectors by the *media server*. For clarity purposes, some receivers in the diagram appear to be idle.

The different stages of the system's operation are as follows:

- the streaming proxy receives a client request
- proxy identifies the best reflector for the client

- media server requested to start sending data to the reflector (if its new)
- reflectors stream data to their clients

The key research issue in the operation outlined here is the identification of the best reflector for the particular client. The definition of "best" here implies that the reflector can accommodate the client (i.e. has not reached its bandwidth capacity) and the round-trip time between client and reflector is reasonable and fairly static.

## 4  Conclusion and Future Work

In this paper we presented our ideas and potential solution for the provision of scalable multimedia streaming services by exploiting the grid infrastructure's wide area and stability characteristics. At the current stage, the proposed architecture does not designate any particular protocol or signaling approach since it is agnostic to them. The benefit of this approach is that it provides a model for diverse implementations.

Our ultimate goal is the development of an algorithm that dynamically optimizes the placement of reflectors as clients join and leave during the "broadcast" of a live event. In the initial parts of our work we will concentrate on analyzing the Grid to ascertain whether it fully meets our requirements as they were defined in this paper; if that is not the case then steps have to be taken towards that direction before a reflector placement algorithm can be defined. In our work we will utilize techniques and solutions that are already developed for VoD systems and modify the Videolan [13] streaming software to add extra messaging functionality as it will form our server and client software.

## References

1. Foster, I., Kesselman, C.: The Grid: Blueprint for a New Computing Infrastructure. Morgan Kaufmann, San Francisco (2004)
2. IPTV Industry, http://www.iptv-industry.com
3. Fonseca, N.L.S., Rubinsztejn, H.K.: Channel allocation in true video-on-demand systems. In: Globecom 2001 (2001)
4. Profeta, E., Shin, K.: Scheduling Video Programs in Near Video-on-Demand Systems. In: ACM Multimedia 1997 (1997)
5. Nguyen, T., Zakhor, A.: Protocols for distributed video streaming. In: ICIP 2002 (2002)
6. Gialama, E., et al.: Distributed Video Server for Streaming. In: CSCC 2001 (2001)
7. Deering, S.: Multicast routing in internetworks and extended lans. In: SIGCOMM 1995 (1995)
8. Astalos, J.: International Grid CA Interworking. In: EGC 2005 (2005)
9. Foster, I., Kesselman, C., Tuecke, S.: The Anatomy of the Grid: Enabling Scalable Virtual Organizations. Journal of High Performance Computing Applications (2001)
10. GEANT, http://www.geant.net
11. Etsion, Y., Tsafrir, D.: A Short Survey of Commercial Cluster Batch Schedulers, Technical Report 2005-13, Hebrew University (2005)
12. Stewart, G.: Grid data management. Reliable file transfer services performance. In: CHEP 2006 (2006)
13. Videolan, http://www.videolan.org

# Resource Management and Signalling Architecture of a Hybrid Multicast Service for Multimedia Distribution

Eugen Borcoci[1], António Pinto[2], Ahmed Mehaoua[3], Li Fang[3], and Ning Wang[4]

[1] University Politehnica Bucharest, Splaiul Independentei 313, Bucharest, Romania
Eugen.Borcoci@elcom.pub.ro
[2] Universidade do Porto, Faculdade de Engenharia, INESC Porto
R. Dr. Roberto Frias, Porto – Portugal
apinto@inescporto.pt
[3] Université Paris Descartes, Faculty of Mathematics & Computer Science 45 rue des
Saints Pères 75006 Paris – France
mea@math-info.univ-paris5.fr
[4] University of Surrey, Guildford, Surrey GU2 7XH UK
n.wang@surrey.ac.uk

**Abstract.** This paper further develops an architecture and design elements for a resource management and a signalling system to support the construction and maintenance of a mid-long term hybrid multicast tree for multimedia distribution services in a QoS guaranteed way, over multiple IP domains. The system called E-cast is composed of an overlay part – in inter-domain and possible IP level multicast in intra-domain. Each E-cast tree is associated with a given QoS class and is composed of unicast pipes established through Service Level Specification negotiations between the domain managers. The paper continues a previous work, by proposing an inter-domain signalling system to support the multicast management and control operations and then defining the resource management for tree construction and adjustment procedures in order to assure the required static and dynamic properties of the tree.

**Keywords:** Multicast, overlay, QoS, multimedia distribution, Service Level Specification.

## 1 Introduction

Efficient real-time multimedia distribution over multiple IP domains with support for the required end-to-end (E2E) Quality of Service (QoS) is still an active area of research. Multicast is a resource efficient transport service for multimedia distribution. The development of such a service with QoS enabled in a multi-domain context requires further research. A hybrid multicast service solution, using Overlay Multicast (OM) and IP multicast, where existent, can be attractive. One can benefit of IP multicast [1], where existent, and use OM outside the IP multicast area. IP multicast, despite its two decade age, is not globally deployed [2] [3] due to problems related to group management, needed router capabilities, and QoS addressing problems. OM

G. Pavlou, T. Ahmed, and T. Dagiuklas (Eds.): MMNS 2008, LNCS 5274, pp. 39–51, 2008.

[4]–[9] presents lower efficiency and speed but eases the implementation of multicast services by not relying on network layer multicast capabilities. Therefore, in this paper, a hybrid solution is considered.

An E2E guaranteed QoS capability over multiple domains infrastructure requires an integrated management system to manage the high level services. On the other side, an important requirement is to still maintain the independency, in terms of resource management, in each network domain. The FP6 IST-507637 project *"End-to-End QoS through Integrated Management of Content, Networks and Terminals"* (ENTHRONE)[1] has proposed an architecture that creates Audio/Video (A/V) service distribution chains [11]-[14] with support for content generation and protection, distribution across QoS-enabled heterogeneous networks and the delivery of content to user terminals.

ENTHRONE's key component is the *Integrated Management Supervisor (EIMS)* [11][12]. The EIMS is built on top of a heterogeneous network infrastructure and manages high level services. Examples of such high level services are Video on Demand (VoD), multimedia streaming, E-learning, and IPTV. The EIMS is also responsible for the E2E IP connectivity, but still maintains independence on network resource management and low level QoS mechanisms.

The EIMS assures E2E QoS provisioning by achieving the required coherence between entities, w.r.t. management and control activities. This is based on *Service Level Agreements/Specifications (SLAs/SLSs)* concepts which are used to express inter-entities commitments [12] [13]. In order to transport the SLA/SLS messages, an appropriate set of signalling protocols have been designed. Each EIMS entity, at a Network Provider (NP), cooperates with the local intra-domain Network Resource Manager (RM) in order to ask for resources in the network.

The architecture is flexible, supporting several business models, including scenarios where different entities cooperate to create value-added services for end-users. The main entities considered are: *Service Providers (SP), Content Providers (CP), Network Providers (NP), Content Consumers (CC), and Access Network Providers (ANP)* [11] [14]. The CPs usually own *Content Servers (CSs)* that are used to generate content for the CCs. The SP provides high level services to the end-users. The NPs role is twofold: 1) to cooperate with each others in the E2E chain and 2) to manage their autonomous network domains. The ANPs manage the Access Networks. In practice, several roles can be played by the same business entity.

The EIMS includes a multicast service, offered by a subsystem called E-cast, which was realised in a hybrid form (OM combined with IP multicast, where existent) and including a special component to manage it. In [10],[12] and [14], the principles of the E-cast have been defined and the architecture of the multicast solution was outlined.

The E-cast main objectives are: to provide a scalable multi-domain solution independent of IP multicast capabilities of the core and access networks; to allow a seamless integration of the E-cast in the existing EIMS framework (which used mid-long term QoS enabled transport pipes called pSLS-links); to address the requirements of new services like IPTV; and to be able to take benefit of the IP multicast in IP domains where it is deployed. The multicast tree construction and maintenance is based on inter-domain resource management and signalling protocols between NPs.

---

[1] This work has been supported by IST FP6 038463 ENTHRONE Project.

This work is a continuation of [10]. In Section 2 the general connectivity services framework of ENTHRONE is summarised. The E-cast hybrid multicast service is outlined in Section 3. Section 4 extends the ENTHRONE inter-domain signalling system to support the overlay and IP multicast. The Section 5 introduces the resource management to assure the multicast tree dynamicity. The Section 6 presents the conclusions.

## 2  Connectivity Services Management in ENTHRONE

The EIMS manages an overlay connectivity service based on forecasted information (there exists a Service Planning function) about future users. The SP decides on the construction of logical multi-domain, uni-directional, QoS-enabled aggregated pipes (pSLS-links established prior to real data flows transport). They span over IP core domains crossed by the path from known content servers (CSs) to forecasted regions of expected CCs, which are seen as destination [11], [12]. Each pSLS-link belongs to a given QoS class of service.

The pSLS-link is composed of segments. Each pSLS-link is negotiated and agreed between SP and the first NP placed in the path towards the regions that contain CCs. In its turn, each NP must negotiate and agree on a new segment with the following NP in the path, until the CCs region is reached (*provider pSLS subscription phase*). Each request from a domain is subject to Admission Control (AC) by the requested domain. The EIMS entities performing negotiations and AC are called Network Service Managers (NSM). They are distributed in SP (NSM@SP) and also in the NPs (NSM@NP). Below each NSM@NP there is an Intra-domain Network Resource Manger (RM) whose task is to manage the domain's resources and their links to its neighbours. A negotiation protocol EQoS-pSLS-S/I-NP has been designed [13] to transport the negotiation messages between NSMs.

To avoid inter-domain routing awareness by SP, the forward cascaded mode for inter-domain peering has been selected. Therefore the task of inter-domain path selection from the CS to the CCs regions is performed by each NP. The pSLS request contains all QoS parameters desired (bandwidth, delay, jitter, loss rate). Each NSM@NP is aware of QoS capabilities of its internal paths and also of QoS capabilities of inter-domain links towards the neighbour domains. These capabilities are expressed at overlay level as Traffic Trunks (TT), in terms of bandwidth available, delays, etc. This information has been previously communicated to the NSM@NP by its "lower layer" (RM).

To increase the dynamicity of connectivity services management, the ENTHRONE distinguishes two operations on SLSs [11]-[14]: subscription, by which the necessary resources are logically reserved, and invocation, by which the network resources are actually allocated. The subscription allows EIMS to abstract network resources in terms of end-to-end virtual pipes. After pSLS subscription, SP may later decide on the installation of pSLS-links in the network (*pSLS invocation phase*), by instructing its NSM@NPs to request to the NRM of each domain to perform resource allocation.

After pSLS-link invocation, several individual pipes (cSLS-links), i.e. slices of the pSLS-links, can be agreed and allocated for CCs at their request. The cSLS-links are established by the NSM@SP at request of an EIMS subsystem called *Customer*

*Service Manager at SP (CustSrvMngr@SP)* on behalf of a CC. The cSLS parameters are a mapped version of an agreement established between the *CustSrvMngr@SP* and a CC to reserve the required resources. The cSLS-links pass through the pSLS-links and are extended ("last mile" segment) to the CC's Access Network (AN). Thus, the ENTHRONE solution avoids *per flow* inter-domain signalling. The NSM@SP should communicate with AN Resource Manager to request resource reservation (cSLS subscription phase) and then allocation (cSLS invocation) in the AN for each individual flow.

## 3  Hybrid Multicast System

The E-cast system is built on existing ENTHRONE management infrastructure [10], [12]. E-cast uses overlay multicast (E-cast(o)) for multi-domain multicast and, if available, IP multicast (E-cast(ip)) in the IP core of the leaf domains of the overlay multicast trees. In such leaf domains, numerous branches are expected and thus the E-Cast(ip) trees are grafted on leaf nodes of E-cast(o) trees. The E-cast tree branches are actually the QoS enabled pSLS-links. The set of unicast pSLS-links used to setup an E-cast(o) is named *mcast-pSLS-tree* and is used to transport multiple streams in multicast. The associated multicast pSLS is the group of underlying individual pSLSs contracts. A *mcast-pSLS-tree* holds a set of *mcast-cSLS-trees*, each one representing a subset of the resources available in the *mcast-pSLS-tree*. The *mcast-cSLS-tree* is composed of a set of unicast cSLS-links, each one associated with a single multicast stream (e.g. an IPTV channel). The E-cast system may include intra-domain IP multicast (E-cast(ip)), based on Protocol Independent Multicast - Sparse Mode/Single Source Multicast (PIM-SM/SSM) [16]. Additionally to standard PIM-SM/SSM, the E-cast(ip) provides QoS guarantees by creating at IP level, a single domain tree based on pSLSs.

### 3.1  Overlay Multicast (E-cast(o))

An E-cast tree is composed of several entities called EN nodes. Each one may assume one or more of the following roles [10], [12], [14]: *E-cast root node* - multicast streams entry point for the E-cast(o) tree; *E-cast intermediate nodes* - located in different Autonomous Systems (AS); *E-cast(o) proxy nodes (EPN)* - leaves of the E-cast(o) trees, usually located at the ingress of ANs; *E-cast cross-layer nodes (EXN)* - which terminate the E-cast(o) and act as IP multicast sources by introducing group addresses in the data packets and delivering them to the IP multicast tree. An EN may belong to different E-cast trees, playing different roles in each tree. The number and placement of E-cast nodes are determined by the service planning activities. The management entities for multicast are Multicast Manager at SP (McastMngr@SP) and Multicast Manager at NP (McastMngr@NP). The E-cast(o) tree construction [14] is shortly described next.

Initially, an E-cast(o) mesh is setup by logically interconnecting ENs. To perform the E-cast(o) tree construction, the McastMngr@SP , gets as input information the root and leaves IDs of the tree and also information on the E-cast(o) mesh. The construction of the mesh is based on the *"Locate, Cluster and Conquer"* principle described in [10], and in [15]; this phase is not in the scope of this paper. The algorithm used for the tree construction is a variation of the Dijkstra shortest path algorithm (SPF) that also considers constraints and a composite metric based on delay. Then, the McastMngr@SP subscribes the multicast pSLS to NSM@SP. The invocation of the multicast pSLS may happen at a later time, but never before using the E-cast(o) tree to transport a multicast stream. The subscription and invocation of individual unicast pSLSs that compose the multicast pSLS, and the actions required in each AS, are performed by NSM@SP and NSM@NPs.

Then McastMngr@SP subscribes and invokes the appropriate mcast-cSLS-tree associated to a stream, prior to any packet being replicated and forwarded along a branch of the E-cast(o) tree. Consequently, the McastMngr@SP instructs all EN nodes (root, intermediate, proxies, cross-layer) on how to replicate the packets of the stream along the tree. The E-cast proxy nodes send the packets to access networks. The E-cast cross-layer nodes cooperate with an IP multicast agent to translate unicast address to IP multicast group address, and forward packets to the PIM-SM/SSM tree.

### 3.2  IP Multicast (E-cast(ip))

The ENTHRONE selected PIM-SM/SSM as a significant and largely used protocol at IP layer. In our case it is used in an extended mode, based on multicast pSLSs, to provide IP multicast with QoS guarantees within a leaf domain. The construction of E-cast(ip) tree is performed by the NSM@NP of the leaf domain, upon request of the NSM@SP. At its turn NSM@SP has been requested to do that by the McastMngr@SP. The request parameters are: the QoS class, the stream source (E-cast(o) cross-layer node), and the access networks IDs of prospective consumers.

The E-cast can, in principle, support deployment variations regarding the distribution of flows in the AN. If each AN connected to the leaf AS comprises an E-cast(o) proxy node, then they may receive flows from the egress multicast routers of the leaf AS and distribute them into ANs. If not, the egress routers of the leaf AS can directly distribute the flows in multicast mode, using a group address as destination, into the AN.

## 4  p/cSLS Signalling for Multicast

This section proposes the E-cast(o) signalling support. The identified requirements are: to use ENTHRONE's existing unicast negotiation protocols; to scale in terms of the amount of signalling used per tree branch; to have parallel transaction capability; to support both the E-cast(o) and E-cast(ip).

The solution extends the ENTHRONE signalling framework [13] to enable multicast management. The multicast tree is controlled by McastMngr@SP and is composed of unicast point-to-point pSLS links between E-cast nodes (EN). The McastMngr@SP first determines all the tree elements, namely the root node, the intermediate nodes, the leaf nodes (i.e. topology) and QoS class. Then, it requests NSM@SP to trigger the mcast-pSLS-tree construction. Each negotiated pSLS establishes a virtual link with specific QoS guarantees between two ENs. The NSM@SP reports on the success of the pSLS-links establishment to the McastMngr@SP. Then the McastMngr@SP instructs the ENs to act as root/intermediate/proxy/x-layer nodes on the E-cast tree.

The NSM@SP is tree-topology unaware; it receives a list of pSLS links to be established from the McastMngr@SP. The set of all pSLS-links negotiated by the McastMngr@SP define the overlay tree topology, and, in case of some segments failures, the McastMngr@SP decides upon next actions.

Figure 1 presents an example scenario of the E-cast(o) tree construction that comprises several phases..

First, the McastMngr@SP requests to NSM@SP to construct the {EN1-EN2, EN1-EN4, EN1-EN5, EN2-EN3, EN4-..., EN5-EN6, EN5-EN7} pSLS-links. Then the NSM@SP launches several parallel and independent transactions as shown in the Table 1. Note that, for each pSLS-link request, the forwarding cascade mode is still valid. If required, each intermediate NSM@NP will contact other neighbour NSM@NPs to realize the chain. In step three the NSM@NPs respond to NSM@SP. Finally the NSM@SP returns a list of results to McastMngr@SP which proceeds to the next actions.

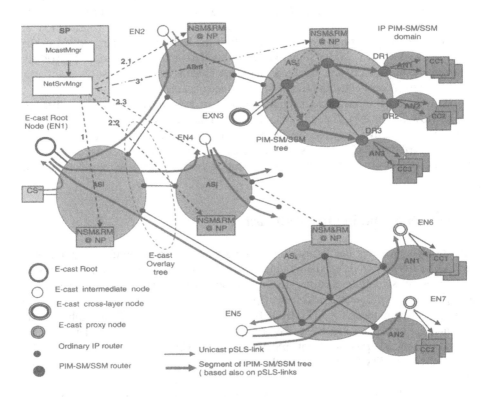

**Fig. 1.** pSLS signalling for E-cast tree construction. NSM – Network Service Manager; RM – Intra-domain Network Resource Manger.

**Table 1.** pSLS requests to construct an example E-cast tree

| pSLS request from NSM@SP # | NSM@NP to solve the pSLS request | pSLS link origin | pSLS-link end | Notes |
|---|---|---|---|---|
| 1 | NSM_i | EN1 | EN2 | |
| | | | EN4 | |
| | | | EN5 | Requests for E-cast(o) tree only |
| 2.1 | NSM_m | EN2 | EXN3 | |
| 2.2 | NSM_j | EN4 | ... | |
| | | EN4 | ... | |
| 2.3 | NSM_k | EN5 | EN6 | |
| | | | EN7 | |
| 3* | NSM_p | EXN3 | DR1, DR2, DR3 | Request for E-cast(ip) tree. |

Figure 2 illustrates a Message Sequence Chart of the signalling used in the mcast-pSLS-tree subscription phase.

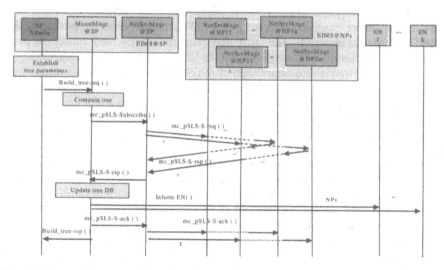

**Fig. 2.** Message Sequence Chart for Build E-cast(o) or E-cast(IP) tree use case, illustrating communication between EIMS entities and EN nodes

The signalling inside a core IP domain for establishing an IP multicast tree will be detailed in another paper. The key issue is that, using the above signalling, the NSM@NP obtains all parameters required for the IP multicast tree. Enabling it to completely control the subscription and invocation of the tree based on PIM-SM/SSM protocol.

For multicast pSLS invocation signalling, the protocols and interfaces are similar to those used for subscription, except for the quantitative parameters. For multicast cSLS signalling we note that, from the point of view of NSM@SP, this invocation only means AC applied at the entrance of the tree in order to see if a given mcast-cSLS request can be accommodated in the current pSLS-link. The result of AC (positive or negative) is stored. Additionally, the first NSM@NP that owns the ingress router is informed about the flow characteristics, allowing it to configure an appropriate police.

## 5  Resource Management

In ENTHRONE the pSLS links are constructed after successfully accomplishing Admission Control (AC) in each IP domain. This is the basis of capability to guarantee the QoS. In multicast case also AC is applied. This check can be applied statically (at pSLS subscription epoch) or dynamically (at invocation time).

### 5.1  Admission Control for E-Cast Tree Subscription

To construct the E-cast(o) tree the list of pSLS-links is asked to be established, by the McastMngr@SP to the NSM@SP. For each pSLS-link the usual AC similar to that applied in unicast case, [13], is performed. A successful multicast tree subscription means that every segment of the tree has successfully passed the AC test.

The NSM@SP response message to the McastMngr@SP indicates a success or a failure. In the failure case, the rejected pSLS links are individually reported by the NSM@SP to McastMngr@SP. The latter may react differently conforming the policies applied by the Service Planning entity of the SP together the McastMngr@SP.

The multicast IP tree is also established at pSLS level but the branches of this tree are intra-domain ones. The intra-domain is governed by an Intra-domain Network Resource Manager at NP (RM@NP). The additional problem in a real deployment is that RM@NP is not always willing to disclose to external parties its internal network topology and traffic load. Such a behaviour will make the AC problem more difficult than in overlay multicast tree case.

In unicast pSLS case AC is performed at NSM@NP based on its knowledge on virtual Traffic Trunks (TT) crossing the respective domain. This information is delivered by the RM@NP to NSM@NP. Performing AC on such a trunk (intra and inter-domain) is sufficient, while it is checked at the entrance of the TT. At NSM level, each TT is independent of other TTs.

In IP multicast tree case the AC should be applied on each branch of the tree. The NSM@NP knows (from the parameters of the request message): the ingress node (router); the list of egress nodes (router); the bandwidth required; the QoS parameters required (e.g. maximum delay).

We make the simplifying assumption that the unicast and multicast pSLS-links are established in two different disjoint "resource planes", i.e. the RM@NP allocate an amount of resources to create multicast trees and this is separated from the resources for unicast pSLS-links. This choice can simplify significantly the management of resources because it decouples the unicast resource management from the multicast one. The unicast TT framework and AC executed at the level of NSM@NP remains not affected. Therefore the following solutions can be applied. Here policies issues may appear.

*A. The RM@NP does not disclose to the NSM@NP the intra-domain topology.*
The NSM only knows the tree root and the leaves, so it cannot make AC. The NSM@NP makes a request for a tree to the RM@NP containing the parameters specified above. Then the RM@NP selects an appropriate tree for this request and performs AC on each tree branch in terms of bandwidth (and maybe delay) - depending on policy applied. The RM@NP returns an answer to the NSM@NP, about acceptance/rejection of the request and also updates its matrices of resources.

While this solution simplifies the task of the NSM@NP, it does not allow it to apply its own policies for AC. In the best case the NSM@NP could pass together with its request, some more additional parameters, to allow RM@NP to apply one of the several options.

*B. The RM@NP discloses the internal tree topology to the NSM@NP.*
The NSM@NP makes a request for a tree to the RM@NP with parameters specified above. In this case the RM@NP selects a possible tree and returns to the NSM@NP information on the available tree in the form: T(V,E), where V is the node set; E is the edge set and we have weights associated to links. Each cost is expressed as a pair (B, d) where the B= max available bandwidth and d = max delay on that link. The NSM@NP performs AC on each tree branch in terms of bandwidth (and maybe delay) - depending on policy. Upon successful AC, the NSM@NP informs the RM@NP about this reservation. The RM@NP updates its matrices of resources.

This solution still makes the AC at NSM@NP level, but the computation of the tree itself is performed by the RM@NP..The advantages of this design are that still NSM@NP is free to apply different policies to accept/reject multicast services requests, independent on how the RM@NP manages its resources. At its turn, the RM @NP can apply its own policies of network dimensioning because it is this entity which offers a given tree to the request of NSM@NP.

*C. The RM@NP discloses the internal graph topology to the NSM@SP.*
This is the most open policy of the RM@NP, based on higher degree of trust and cooperation with EIMS. Initially and at each start of a Resource Provisioning Cycle, [11], [13], the RM@NP sends to the NSM@NP information on an available graph to be allocated for multicast services. The graph is expressed in the form: G(V,E); where V is the node set; E – edge set and we have weights associated to links. Each cost is expressed as a pair (B, d) where the B= max available bandwidth and d = max delay on that link.

Then in the event of a new request for a multicast tree NSM@NP computes a feasible tree. First it constructs a constrained sub-graph eliminating those branches which do not satisfy the bandwidth constraint. Then it computes a spanning tree (even if the tree is bigger than required, the computation algorithm is simpler) having the root in the node indicated in the request. This can be computed depending on policy in several ways: *a.* by only using a concave metric of 1/B where B is bandwidth. The tree is a shortest path one (SPT) in terms of bandwidth wideness and the algorithm can be, e.g. Dijkstra; *b.* by using an additive metric, i.e. delay; *c.* by optimising both bandwidth and delay (more complex solution and less scalable). .On each branch of the required tree the NSM@NP applies AC in terms of delay (remember that the bandwidth constraint has been fulfilled). Upon successful AC, the NSM@NP computes an available graph by subtracting the used resources from the initial ones.

At a new request the NSM@NP uses the updated available graph as an input for tree computation. This solution gives the highest degree of liberty to the NSM@NP in applying different policies in the process of tree computation.

## 5.2 Policy Based Management for Multicast Tree Subscription

The ENTHRONE framework is open and flexible in the sense that it allows the SPs and NPs to apply their own policies for service and resource management. The Policy Based Management related details of ENTHRONE including policy analysis tool and policy decision and enforcement methods are discussed in details in [13].

In multicast service case several policies can be applied at subscription phase. Here are below some examples

Estimated data for future traffic are considered (being generated by the traffic fore-cast block). Therefore, the tree leaves will be defined only for those AN regions where a given minimum number of future users is estimated.

When receiving the answer from NSM@SP about the multicast tree pSLS sub-scription, the McastMngr@SP can react in several ways depending on the policy applied: *P1*. McastMngr@SP can be satisfied with the sub-tree proposed by NSM@SP and ask it to consider installed that sub-tree. The amount/percentage of successful branches is also subject of policies; *P2*. McastMngr@SP is not satisfied and in this case it can ask the cancellation of all sub-trees (i.e. all pSLS-links); *P3*. McastMngr@SP might ask the NSM@SP a new tree with different quantitative pa-rameters (e.g. lower bandwidth, lower QoS, reduced number of branches, etc.).

Also different policies may be applied in the process of making tree computation and AC as shown in the section above.

## 5.3 Dynamic Resource Allocation

The AC for mc_pSLS-tree invocation is performed similarly to that of subscription. The difference is that the tree is already known (computed at subscription phase). Therefore the three cases described in the Section 5 still apply.

In case A, the NSM@NP does not know the tree IP multicast tree topology. The AC should be performed by the RM@ NP.

In case B and C the Admission Control is performed by the NSM@NP because it knows the tree and has the necessary information on previously subscribed trees. Monitoring information can be used in the process of AC if information on the actual load of the tree branches is available.

All policies discussed at multicast pSLS subscription can be applied for invocation also. Additionally policies can be applied for tree maintenance. While not all these policies are included in the current implementation (except some basic ones) the framework is enough flexible to allow different policies to be applied, defined by the SP and also by NPs.

# 6  E-Cast Implementation

The E-cast system is currently under implementation in the ENTHRONE project framework. Figure 3 presents (as an example) a part of the ENTHRONE system, the

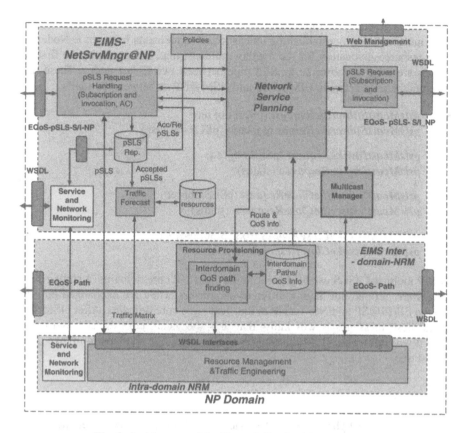

**Fig. 3.** Architecture of the Network Service Manager at NP

overall view of the implemented architecture of the EIMS-Network Service Manager at NP (NSM@NP).

The EIMS@NP subsystem is composed of: Network Service Manager - responsible for service provisioning and pSLS processing; Inter-domain Network Resource Manager –responsible mainly to find inter-domain paths; The Intra-domain Network Resource Manager (Intra-NRM). The latter  does not belong to ENTHRONE EIMS but it is owned by NP.

The details of the NSM@NP subsystem are not given here; they  can be found in [13], [14], [17]. In Figure 3 the Multicast Manager is emphasized and its relationships with other entities are drawn. The Multicast Manager at NP is instructed by the Service Planning block to perform low level multicast related functions (e.g. to  construct the IP multicast tree, etc.).Its  south-bound interface is used to request to the intra-domain resource manager to install the multicast tree.

The implementation solution for the interfaces outside the NSM@NP has been Web-Services based, [17], due to flexibility offered. In particular, *Multicast Manager WSDL interface* –used by the IP Multicast Manager to ask to Intra-NRM to construct a multicast IP level tree composed of pSLS links.

Below it is given an example of a set of messages used for the construction of the overlay multicast tree by establishing unicast pSLS agreements between E-Nodes and also for resource invocation for the overlay multicast tree. For example, the first two messages are used to subscribe a pSLS pipe between two E-cast nodes. These messages could be used between EIMS@SP and NSM@NP or between two NPs.

- *pslsMcastSubscribeRequest* (pSLS obj req)
- *pslsMcastSubscribeResponse* (status, pSLS obj resp)

- *pslsMcastInvokeRequest* (pSLS obj req)
- *pslsMcastInvokeResponse* (status)

- *pslsMcastSubscribeCloseRequest* (pSLS obj req)
- *pslsMcastSubscribeCloseResponse* (status)

- *pslsMcastInvokeCloseRequest* (pSLS obj req)
- *pslsMcastInvokeCloseResponse* (status)

For IP multicast pSLS establishment in the "leaf" IP core domains a similar set of messages are defined but having different parameters. They are exchanged only between the EIMS@SP and NSM@NP in the "leaf" tree core domains. After NSM@NP receives these messages it will know that it is the "leaf" core domain and consequently it will inform the IP Multicast Manager to subscribe and then to invoke the IP multicast tree.

## 7  Conclusions

The work on E-cast hybrid multicast service with QoS guarantees over multiple IP domains, presented previously in [10] is continued with new proposals for a signalling system and scalable solutions (both in the data plane and control/management plane) for resource management, both at overlay level and network level. The overlay multicast solution is independent on the existence of IP multicast in the Autonomous Systems but in our hybrid approach one can benefit of IP multicast in those domains where IP multicast is deployed. The inter-domain multicast signalling is done between managers, at aggregated level, thus exposing good scalability. The resource allocation can be done at aggregated and individual level with distinction between operational phases of subscription and invocation. Separation is achieved between the service management at overlay virtual level and actual resource management at network level. The proposed system is currently implemented in the ENTHRONE project. The implementation results will be soon reported in a future work.

## References

1. Deering, S.: Host Extensions for IP Multicasting, IETF RFC 1112 (1989)
2. Diot, C., et al.: Deployment Issues for the IP Multicast Service and Architecture. IEEE Network 14(1), 78–88 (2000)
3. Asaeda, H., et. al.: Architecture for IP Multicast Deployment: Challenges and Practice. IEICE Transactions on Communications E89-B(4), 1044–1051 (2006)

4. Biersack, E.W.: Where is Multicast Today? ACM SIGCOMM Computer Communication Review 35(5), 83–84 (2005)
5. Zhang, B., Jamin, S., Zhang, L.: Host Multicast: A Framework for Delivering Multicast to End Users. In: Proceedings of the IEEE INFOCOM 2002, New York, USA, vol. 3, pp. 1366–1375 (2002)
6. Lao, L., Cui, J.-H., Gerla, M., Maggiorini, D.: A Comparative Study of Multicast Protocols: Top, Bottom, or In the Middle? In: Proceedings of the IEEE INFOCOM 2005, Miami, USA, vol. 4, pp. 2809–2814 (2005)
7. Li, B., Liu, J.: Multirate Video Multicast over the Internet: An Overview. IEEE Network 17(1), 24–29 (2003)
8. Androutsellis-Theotokis, S., Spinellis, D.: A survey of peer-to-peer content istribution technologies. ACM Comput. Surv. 36(4), 335–371 (2004)
9. Banerjee, S., Bhattacharjee, B., Kommareddy, C.: Scalable application layer multicast. In: Proceedings of the ACM conference on Applications, technologies, architectures, and protocols for computer communications (SIGCOMM 2002), New York, pp. 205–217 (2002)
10. Mehaoua, A., Fang, L.: E-cast: An Overlay Multicast Service Management System for scalable audiovisual services. In: Proceedings of the IEEE-TTTC AQTR Conference, Cluj, Romania (February 2008)
11. ENTHRONE II Deliverables D01: Overall system architecture version 2 (2007)
12. ENTHRONE II Deliverable D03: EIMS for ENTHRONE 2 (2007)
13. ENTHRONE II Deliverable D18: Service management and QoS provisioning (2007)
14. ENTHRONE II Deliverable D21: Multicast provisioning and multicast service management (2008)
15. Kaafar, M.A., Turletti, T., Dabbous, W.: Locate, Cluster and Conquer: A Scalable Topology-aware Overlay Multicast, INRIA, technical report (2005)
16. Fenner, B., et al.: Protocol Independent Multicast - Sparse Mode (PIM-SM): Protocol Specification (Revised). IETF RFC 4601 (2006)
17. Obreja, S.G., Borcoci, E., Lupu, R., Iorga, R.: Web-service solution for inter-domain QoS negotiation, International Conference on Communication Theory, Reliability, and Quality of Service, CTRQ, Bucharest, Romania (2008),
   http://www.iaria.org/conferences2008/CTRQ08.html

# Scalable Multimedia Group Communications through the Over-Provisioning of Network Resources*

Augusto Neto[1], Eduardo Cerqueira[2], Marília Curado[2], Paulo Mendes[3], and Edmundo Monteiro[2]

[1] Institute of Telecommunications, 3810-193 Aveiro, Portugal
augusto@av.it.pt
[2] University of Coimbra, 3030-290 Coimbra, Portugal
{ecoelho,marilia,edmundo}@dei.uc.pt
[3] INESC Porto, 4200-465, Porto, Portugal
pmendes@inescporto.pt

**Abstract.** The efficient management of network resources together with the *Quality of Service* (QoS) control of real-time multimedia group communication sessions in *Next Generation Networks* (NGN) is still a challenging research goal. The unified control of the session quality level, distribution tree allocation and network resources in NGN will increase the user satisfaction, reduce operational costs, optimize network resources and maximize the profits of providers. This paper introduces the *Multi-user Aggregated Resource Allocation* mechanism (MARA), which supports a dynamic control of surplus class-based bandwidth and multicast resources in a scalable way, while assuring the minimal quality level of multimedia group communication sessions. In comparison with existing works, MARA significantly reduces signalling, state and processing overhead. In addition, simulation results present the benefits of MARA by improving the network performance under re-routing conditions.

**Keywords:** Real-time multimedia sessions; Next generation networks; Network resource provisioning; Multi-user communications.

## 1 Introduction

Real-time multimedia sessions are now present in our daily live experience, and will be among the most important applications in next generation networks. The efficient distribution and the quality level control of multimedia sessions, such as IPTV, video streaming and other multimedia multicast-alike sessions, will attract new clients, while increasing revenues to providers. In such real-time session, the content distribution is performed simultaneously to groups of users (multiple users, called multi-user sessions in this paper). In this context, IP multicast seems to be the most attractive

---

* This work was done at the Laboratory of Communications and Telematics of the Faculty of Science and Technology of the University of Coimbra. It is supported by DoCoMo Euro-labs, by the Portuguese Ministry of Science, Technology and High Education, and by European Union FEDER - POSI (projects Q3M and SAPRA).

G. Pavlou, T. Ahmed, and T. Dagiuklas (Eds.): MMNS 2008, LNCS 5274, pp. 52–63, 2008.

solution to control the distribution of multi-user sessions, because it avoids packet duplication and saves network resources. In addition, QoS-aware multi-user sessions can be controlled by using the *Differentiated Service* (DiffServ) model in order to provide scalable traffic differentiation, QoS assurances and overcome the limitations of the current IP best effort approach.

Our previous work proposed the *MultI-Service Resource Allocation* (MIRA) [1] mechanism to allow the distribution of multi-user sessions with QoS support in *Next Generation Networks* (NGN). MIRA supports the coordinated control of *Source-Specific Multicast* (SSM) distribution trees and QoS assurances for multi-user sessions in DiffServ classes. The setup of network resources is deployed by the *Resource Control Function* (RCF) component, through the support of a per-flow edge-to-edge ingress-driven single-pass signalling approach implemented by the *MIRA Protocol* (MIRA-P). MIRA-P defines message-specific flags to control the RCF behaviour in the nodes throughout the network, and uses only two messages for resource requests and operation feedback control, *RESERVE* and *RESPONSE* respectively. The RCF interacts with network elements (e.g., QoS schedulers) for resource allocation, release and update procedures, as well as to detect re-routing events. MIRA state is controlled by soft-state to increase the system robustness. The performance evaluation described in [1] shows that MIRA distinguishes itself from existing solutions by supporting low complex operations, and by controlling multi-user sessions with minimized signalling and state overhead.

However, the per-flow signalling used by MIRA to control the bandwidth required for multi-user sessions in DiffServ classes and the allocation of SSM trees associated with them, poses important issues regarding system performance. While the bandwidth control requires excessive signalling and processing costs in large-scale networks, the SSM trees management (per-flow control) suffers from state overhead. Moreover, unpredictable topology changing detections (e.g., link failures, handovers or new *join/leave* requests) need MIRA operations to restore each affected flow of a multi-user session (scalable session) on a new path that at least fulfils their minimum QoS requirements. Our performance findings in the analysis of MIRA, associated with the strong resource requirements of multimedia group communications, motivated further investigation of strategies to avoid per-flow operations.

In order to overcome the current MIRA limitations, increase the satisfaction of users and optimize resources in multi-user systems, this paper introduces the *Multi-user Aggregated Resource Allocation* (MARA) proposal. MARA provides scalable support of IP multi-user sessions, while minimizing signalling, state and processing costs of MIRA per-flow operations. The MARA contribution is performed by dynamically controlling the over-provisioning of DiffServ classes and SSM trees. Thus, MARA establishes multiple multi-user sessions without per-flow signalling by combining admission control and surplus network resources (bandwidth and SSM trees) procedures in advance. Multicast aggregation is used to optimize multicast state storage. This paper demonstrates the benefits of MARA in comparison with MIRA to control multi-user sessions regarding session robustness operations under re-routing conditions. The MARA performance evaluation was carried out by simulations, which analyzed bandwidth/multicast state and signalling overhead under re-routing events.

The remainder of this paper is organized as follows. Related work is presented in section 2. Section 3 provides a detailed description of MARA, whose performance is evaluated in Section 4. Finally, Section 5 concludes this paper with a summary of our findings.

## 2   Related Work

Over-reservation strategies to over-provision bandwidth resources have been addressed in the literature on a set of proposals. The *Border Gateway Reservation Protocol* (BGRP) [2] and the *Shared-segment Inter-domain Control Aggregation* protocol (SICAP) [3], use a similar two-pass receiver-driven signalling approach to aggregate unicast traffic into sink- and shared trees respectively. However, the multicast trees control is supported by neither of the two approaches. Nevertheless, SICAP demonstrates that the dynamic control of surplus bandwidth reservations is more efficient than the static quantification factor used by BGRP. Furthermore, the *Dynamic Aggregation of Reservations for Internet Services* (DARIS) [4] proposal uses a centralized approach to control resource allocations. DARIS deploys over-reservations based on information about the internal topology, resource capacities and current selected routes. Thus, scalability is the main issue in DARIS proposal, since too much centralization endangers system performance to manage multimedia sessions. For instance, excessive signalling can be required to control resource synchronization and setup.

The creation of multicast trees in advance has been used by some proposals as a means for the over-provisioning of multicast resources. However, there is a lack of solutions focused on allowing a scalable multicast over-provisioning support. Most of the available proposals aim to protect the system against topology changes (e.g., link breaks), instead of reducing signalling overhead, and thus processing overhead, to setup and maintain new multi-user sessions. The solutions presented in [5] and [6] aims to create a pair of trees (a main and a backup tree) for each session request, where the switching procedure from the main tree to the backup tree is controlled dynamically. Thus, the system must be signalled twice whenever a new session request is received, in addition to requiring that each visited router store twice amount of state. In spite of speeding up the restoration of sessions affected by re-routing, scalability (in terms of state and signalling overhead) is a shortcoming in backup-tree based solutions within large-scale systems.

From the related work analysis, none of the above proposals coordinates the over-provisioning of QoS resources/bandwidth and multicast resources. The over-reservation approaches are neither scalable (two-pass signalling protocol) nor efficient for multi-user sessions (no multicast support). In addition, backup-tree based proposals introduce signalling, processing and state overhead to improve reliability. Thus, MARA is proposed to address the above challenges.

## 3   Multi-user Aggregated Resource Allocation

MARA dynamically provides the over-provisioning of network resources (bandwidth and multicast) to establish group communication sessions without per-flow signalling. QoS-aware sessions are controlled based on DiffServ per-class over-reservations, where resources are dynamically re-adjusted according to the bandwidth demand.

SSM trees are over-provisioned in advance (at the system bootstrap) and dynamically controlled based on multicast aggregation. By default, MARA detects re-routing via soft-state operations. In order to improve system robustness, MARA interacts with unicast routing protocols to acquire information also about re-routing events. MARA invokes the restoration of sessions affected by re-routing upon intercepting router advertisements generated as a consequence of topology changes (e.g., OSPF *router Link State Advertisements (LSA)* messages). With MARA, the system is optimized and the satisfaction of the users is increased, because it minimizes the state, signalling and processing overhead of MIRA as well as it reduces the convergence time to setup QoS-aware multi-user sessions on new paths.

MARA re-uses some MIRA components, namely the signalling protocol (MIRA-P) and the resource controller (RCF). MIRA-P provides control information so that RCF can configure the state of network elements to setup network resources associated with multi-user sessions. In relation with MIRA, the common header of MIRA-P messages was extended with two new message-specific flags. Thus, MARA can invoke the initialization of network resources (flag *Initialization* (I)), setup of SSM trees (flag *Multicast* (M)), and the dynamic adjustment of over-reservations according to current demands (flag *Over-reservation* (O)). Moreover, two components ware developed to control the over-provisioning of bandwidth and SSM trees, namely *Advanced QoS Resource Allocator* (ASAC) and *Advanced Aggregation Tree Allocator* (AGTree), respectively. Fig. 1 shows MARA components implemented at the network edges. Interior nodes only implement MIRA-P and RCF. The MARA intelligence is pushed to the edges elements in order to increase the system scalability and robustness.

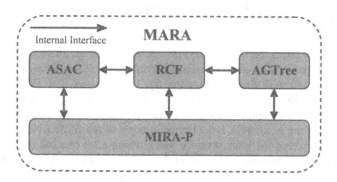

**Fig. 1.** MARA Architecture

ASAC over-provisions bandwidth by assigning per-class over-reservations at the system bootstrap and controlling their dynamic adjustment in an on-demand basis, without generating per-flow signalling. In order to avoid class starvations, each *Class of Service* (CoS) is assigned a *Committed* and a *Maximum Reservation Threshold* (*CRth* and *MRth*, respectively). Moreover, a global initialization factor is also assigned as a fraction of the local link capacity (e.g., ½ or ¼). Whenever realized that a CoS cannot accommodate a multi-user session request (i.e., an overload class), ASAC tries to increase the current CoS's over-reservation based on network utilization ratios and commitments. Moreover, the size of the CoS's *MRth* is also controlled, so that a session can be admitted when the *MRth* of its required CoS is currently congested (procedure not allowed in MIRA).

AGTree over-provisions SSM distribution trees by assigning surplus trees at the system bootstrap. AGTree uses encapsulation to merge multi-user sessions into aggregation trees (instead of source-routing proposals) without any signalling exchange inside the network. Thus, data packets are aggregated at ingress routers and de-aggregated at egress routers of a network accordingly. Moreover, AGTree controls the connectivity of multi-user sessions by dynamically switching sessions from a SSM aggregation tree to another as a consequence of network dynamics (e.g., new *join/leave* requests or re-routing).

## 3.1 MARA Functionalities

This section introduces the functionalities supported by MARA to control the over-provisioning of network resources. It is assumed that all MARA agents have information about whether the local router is an ingress, core or egress router.

### 3.1.1 System Initialization

Ingress routers use a flooding mechanism to request the initialization of bandwidth and to collect information about the available shortest paths until all available edges router of a network. In contrast to end-to-end, the edge-to-edge approach of MARA allows autonomy of each network to control and coordinate resource allocations. Each router within the network initializes the bandwidth resources through multiplying the index factor by the *MRth* of each local CoS. The information about the edge-to-edge paths is used to setup the SSM aggregation trees. An overview of the operations deployed by MARA to initialize network resources is described in the remainder of this Section.

Ingress routers setup the over-reservation of each CoS on all local network interfaces based on the *MRths* and the initialization factor. Afterwards, a *RESERVE(I)* (*RESERVE* message with flag Initialization (*I*)) is composed. The *RESERVE(I)* must carry the initialization factor and the per-class *MRth*, as well as be prepared to collect information about the composition of the resultant distribution path and the CoS's characteristics of the bottleneck link. Hence, a copy of the *RESERVE(I)* is sent in all interior routers (except the inter-network link), where each one has the IP address of the associated local *outgoing interface* (Oif) filled in the *Reserved Path* (RSVPATH) object. The current QoS capabilities are filled in the *QoS Specifications* object (QSPEC) as proposed in the NSIS suite. As a consequence of the flooding schema, each router must do some verification before setting up resources aiming at: 1) ensuring that per-class over-reservation is initialized only once (when the CoS has no reservation state); 2) avoiding infinite signalling loops (by dropping messages already carrying the IP address of a local network interface in the *RSVPATH* object). As a result of 2), long trees are avoided by dropping *RESERVE(I)* messages that return to ingress routers. The signalling used by MARA, and its composition, to initialize the bandwidth resources in a generic scenario is shown in Fig. 2.

After initializing the bandwidth resources, ingress node *I1* composes a *RESERVE(I)* carrying the initialization factor, the *MRths* and  the *RSVPATH* object

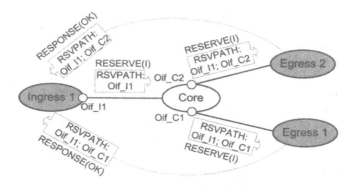

**Fig. 2.** Signalling events for the initialization of bandwidth resources in each network router

(filled with the *Oig_I1* IP address), which is then sent downstream. Upon visited by the *RESERVE(I)*, core node *C1* initializes the local bandwidth resources (as in *I1*) and sends a copy of the *RESERVE(I)* (with the *RESVPATH* object of each one correctly updated) to all local network interfaces (*Oif_C1* and *Oif_C2* in this case), except the one in which it was received. In the case of an edge router (egress nodes *E1* and *E2* in Fig. 2), a *RESPONSE(OK)* message is composed with the information derived from the associated *RESERVE(I)* after concluded the local bandwidth initialization. The *RESPONSE(OK)* is sent to the IP address found in the first entry of the *RSVPATH* object (i.e., *Oif_I1*), allowing the ingress router to store information about the edge-to-edge path and about the characteristics (per-class bandwidth and thresholds) of the CoS of the bottleneck link of all paths.

After successfully accomplished the initialization of CoS bandwidth, MARA set-ups the SSM trees along each collected communication path. As a first step, a SSM tree is assigned to each communication path composed by a pair of ingress and egress routers (called un-branched). Each tree is composed/identified by the IP address of the ingress router (*I1* in the case) and a multicast group IP. The latter is locally created by *I1* via a dynamic multicast address allocation solution [7]. After that, a *RESERVE(M)* (notation used to a *RESERVE* message with flag Multicast (*M*)) is sent downstream, being forwarded based on the *RSVPATH*. In order to allow the support of QoS-aware multicast trees under environments with asymmetric routing, each visited router configures the *Multicast Routing Information Base* (MRIB) with information derived from the *RSVPATH* object and propagates the message downstream. At the egress routers *E1* and *E2*, PIM-SSM is triggered to build the SSM tree, and a *RESPONSE(OK)* message is sent to *I1*, confirming the successful operation.

After the creation of the un-branched trees, MARA uses a combinatorial algorithm to create a set of branched trees, simultaneously supplying multiple egress routers. At first, all possible combinations between the available un-branched trees are generated in n-1 interaction, where n is the number of un-branched trees. In order to optimize the large number of resultant branched trees, filters are used to retain the best ones. One selection criterion is based on the fact that a distribution tree demands more network resources (e.g., bandwidth) as branching points get close to the root. Based on this criterion, SSM trees with branching point in the ingress routers are discarded. Furthermore, combinations with multiple paths converging to the same node are also discarded. Optionally, MARA can be configured with a maximum on-tree hops (which can derive from network historical or measurement tools). After generating all SSM aggregation trees, the ingress routers signal the identified egress routers so that PIM-SSM can build the created SSM trees.

The combinatorial algorithm used to create the branched SSM aggregation trees can pose performance overhead to MARA, where the processing cost is overloaded with the increasing number of combinations (which increases with the number of links/nodes in the network). Other combinatorial algorithms can be used. The specification of an efficient combinatorial solution is out of the scope of this paper.

### 3.1.2 Dynamic Resource Allocation

The combination of over-provisioning and admission control allows MARA to dynamically establish multi-user sessions without per-flow signalling. Whenever required the establishment of a session, MARA must be triggered at an ingress router with a session request ($Ri$) carrying the QoS requirements within the QSPEC (at least the CoS, the required bandwidth ($Brq(i)$) and user IP). Based on the egress router IP associated to the interested user (retrieved via intra-domain routing approaches, such as BGP), MARA selects one (the first matching) of the previously created SSM aggregation trees. Afterwards, the packets association with multi-user sessions are encapsulated (aggregation) in the selected SSM aggregation tree. At the egress router(s) associated to the selected SSM aggregation tree, the original IP header information is restored (de-aggregation) and forwarded towards its destination.

If succeeding the information that the ingress router has about the current usage of the required CoS $i$ in the bottleneck link of the required SSM tree (i.e., the bandwidth required by $Ri$ is available in the current over-reservation of CoS $i$), the session is admitted without further processing or signalling. In addition, whenever the required CoS $i$ experiences unavailable bandwidth, ASAC attempts to re-adjust its current over-reservation. The amount of bandwidth to re-adjust the over-reservation of CoS $i$ ($Bov(i)$) is given by (1). The Equation 1 is based on the utilization ratio ($Bu(i)$) of the CoS and the amount of bandwidth which will be available after the session setup. The information used in (1) is related to the bottleneck link of the selected SSM aggregation tree. After the computation of a positive $Bov(i)$ (in case of failure the equation returns a negative value), MARA updates the current reservation of CoS $i$, $Brv(i)$, where $Brv(i) \leftarrow Bov(i) + Brq(i)$), and sends a $RESERVE(O)$ (notation used to a $RESERVE$ message with flag Over-reservation ($O$)) in the selected communication path.

$$Bov(i) = \underbrace{\frac{Bu(i)}{MRth(i)}}_{\text{Utilization}} + \underbrace{(MRth(i) - Bu(i) - Brq(i))}_{\text{Bandwidth available after setting up } Ri} \tag{1}$$

All routers along the communication path update the local $Brv(i)$ with the $Brq(i)$ derived from the QSPEC transported in the $RESERVE(O)$ message. Upon receiving the $RESPONSE(OK)$, the ingress router re-processes $Ri$, which is now supposed to succeed (available bandwidth) and be admitted without signalling. If the amount of resources requested by $Ri$ exceeds the current $MRth(i)$, (1) does not succeed ($Bov(i) < 0$), and so the adjustment of the CoS over-reservation fails. In this congestion case,

MARA invokes the re-adjustment of the CoSs so that $Ri$ can be admitted. For this propose, (2) provides a bandwidth index ($B\_Idx(j)$) of any other CoS $j$, except the congested one ($i$). The bandwidth index of a CoS is the ratio between the amount of bandwidth that is currently available and reserved by CoS $j$.

$$\forall j \in c, B\_Idx(j) = \left( \frac{Brv(j) - Bu(j)}{Brv(j)} \right) \qquad (2)$$

Furthermore, the threshold index ($Th\_Idx(j)$) of any CoS $j$, except the congested one ($i$), is provided by (3) as being the ratio between the $MRth$ and a bandwidth reference ($Bref(j)$). The bandwidth reference can be the bandwidth currently reserved for CoS $j$ (if the $Bu(i)$ is lesser than the $CRth(i)$), otherwise the $CRth$ is used. Thus, MARA ensures at least the minimal QoS commitment of the CoSs.

$$\forall j \in c, Th\_Idx(j) = \left( \frac{MRth(j) - Bref(j)}{MRth(j)} \right) \qquad (3)$$

The results of (2) and (3) are used to compute, by means of (4), the amount of bandwidth by which the $MRth$ of each CoS $j$ ($Brl\_MRth(j)$) will be reduced. Equation 4 computes $Brl\_MRth(j)$ based on the average between the sum of bandwidth and threshold indexes of CoS $j$, multiplied by its amount of bandwidth currently available.

$$\forall j \in c, Brl\_MRth(j) = \left( \frac{B\_Idx(j) + Th\_Idx(j)}{2} \right) * (MRth(j) - Bref(j)) \qquad (4)$$

After computation of (4), MARA adds $MRth(i)$ with the sum of the $Brl\_MRth(j)$ of the selected CoS ($j$). The $MRth(j)$ of each CoS ($j$) is decreased by the computed value accordingly. After successfully accomplished the CoS re-adjustment, $Ri$ is re-processed again and the over-reservation is expected to be successfully updated now. If the re-adjustment of the CoSs fails $Ri$ is rejected. As occurs with MIRA, MARA also allows explicit releasing of resources, which is done by signalling the network with a $RESERVE(T)$ ($RESERVE$ message with flag $Tear$ (T)).

### 3.1.3  Session Connectivity Control
MARA ensures the continuity of on-going multi-user sessions during their entire lifetime by automatically switching them between available SSM aggregation trees. This operation is deployed at the ingress router associated with the required session. This way, MARA prevents waste of resources (by avoiding sending packets to leaf nodes without active member users) and session quality degradation is controlled due to re-routing (e.g., link failures, new *join/leave* events or handovers).

In the case of receiving new *join/leave* events (or handovers) and detecting that a session has no leaf nodes in some of the egress routers of its current SSM aggregation tree, MARA performs the following operations: (*i*) selects another SSM aggregation tree leading to the right set of egress routers and supporting the required QoS (as upon receiving the $Ri$); (*ii*) switches the session to the selected SSM tree (by controlling the aggregation accordingly). In the case that none of the available SSM aggregation trees can support the QoS required by the affected session, MARA tries to re-adjust the current resource configuration. If the switching fails (unavailable resources), the request is denied.

In what concerns re-routing detections due to link-failures, the same set of operations described above is deployed by MARA. Based on the local *router LSA*, generated by OSPF upon detecting that the state of a network interface changes (*down* or *up*), a copy of a *RESPONSE(Failure)* (*RESPONSE* message with a failure report) must be sent to each ingress router (locally stored in the reservation data base). After received the *RESPONSE(Failure)*, MARA locally matches (session state) all flows established in the SSM aggregation tree(s) affected by the failure condition to further re-route them into another one(s). The sessions can be restored in the previous path when the link is *up* again, if the new path cannot fulfil all requirements.

## 4  MARA Performance Evaluation

The benefits of MARA over MIRA, to setup multi-user sessions in a dynamic environment, from the network and the user expectation, are verified by using the *Network Simulator-2.29* (NS-2.29). The simulation model considers a network topology composed by 14 routers, interconnected by links with different capacities and propagation delay randomly generated by BRITE. As suggested in [8], the simulation model supports one *Expedited Forwarding* alike CoS (Premium), two *Assured Forwarding* alike CoSs (Gold and Silver), and one Best Effort class. The initialization factor and the *MRth* are respectively 25% and 20%, and the *CRth* is 50% of the *MRth* for each one of the four CoSs. In order to achieve all functionalities required to accomplish the evaluation, the NS-2.29 was extended with the WFQ discipline (for QoS scheduling), PIM-SSM (for IP multicast), as well as MIRA and MARA agents accordingly.

The experiments were repeated 10 times to simulate a large number of multi-user UDP sessions (1,000) sent from the same ingress router to different receivers, with confidence interval of 95%. The sessions have a lifetime that varies from 20s (short-live) to 120s (long-live), and have a constant bit rate of 224Kb/s to emulate a scalable session with three flows are used by common multimedia CODECs, such as MPEG4 (flow 1 32Kb/s, flow 2 64Kb/s and flow 3 128Kb/s) [9]. The session requests (establishing and releasing) take place from the beginning up to the end of the simulation (120s), being generated by a Poisson distribution. Furthermore, MARA is configured to over-provision SSM trees with a maximum limited number of 6 hops, as justified in the following. Our previous study [10] revealed that only 5.4% of all available trees, selected in average, comprise a maximum of 5 hops. Moreover, other researches [11], [12], attested that 80% of intra-network shortest paths have 4 hops or less.

The performance evaluation is composed by three experiments, which aims to examine the impact that MIRA and MARA takes to establish multi-user sessions, and re-route them, from the perspective of both network and user. Hence, re-routing conditions are introduced by setting the state of a potential link to *down* and *up* at random instants. Regarding network perspective, it is examined the signalling load throughout the simulation and, in the users perspective, it is studied the throughput in the receivers. In the first set of tests, the QoS support is provided by DiffServ without the presence of a solution to implement admission control (without MIRA or MARA). In the next set of tests, whereas DiffServ provides QoS support, MIRA and MARA implement resource allocation and admission control.

Additionally, background traffic sources are placed in the environment in order to achieve data losses by exceeding in 20% the overall link capacity of the new communication path. For simplification, only the results measured for one receiver that has joined a multi-user session (denoted as *R1* and *M1* respectively) is considered due to the similar results of all the remaining receivers. The simulation results expose that *M1* starts at instant 5.84s, and the events for link-down and link-up take place at instant 33.75s and 74.8s respectively. Moreover, OSPF averages 5.88s to generate a router LSA after detected the link-down event, and 5.11s after detected the link-up event.

The numeric results reveal that MARA minimizes in 66.35% the signalling load taken in MIRA tests. The per-flow basis of MIRA is the reason for the excessive signalling load, where the twice re-routing events (when the network interface goes down and come up again) has triggered per-flow signalling to restore all affected multi-user sessions. Thus, MIRA exchanged approximatelly11.10 times more data for *RESERVE* messages than MARA.

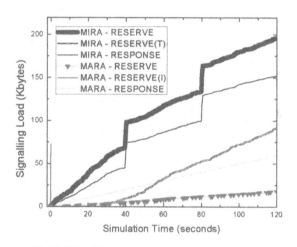

**Fig. 3.** Signalling load of MIRA and MARA tests

The traced results show a signalling load averaging 448.15KB (MIRA) and 150.76KB (MARA). The per-flow resource allocation signalling of MIRA is the reason for its large signalling load. In contrast, MARA signalling occurs mostly during the system initialization phase (73.42KB for *RESERVE(I)*), being the signalling load during the simulation resultant of the dynamic update of over-reservations (17.64KB for MARA, while MIRA generates 195.89KB). As a consequence, MIRA also generates more *RESPONSE* messages (102.80KB) than MARA (59.85KB). Furthermore, per-flow releasing operations (triggered by *RESERVE(T)* messages, and invoked whenever a multi-user session ends) introduce an average of 91.51KB in MIRA experiments. MARA has no *RESERVE(T)* messages, since the end of multi-user sessions grants the associated CoS with surplus resources, instead of releasing them (as occurs with MIRA). Hence, MARA minimizes in 66.35% the signalling load of MIRA.

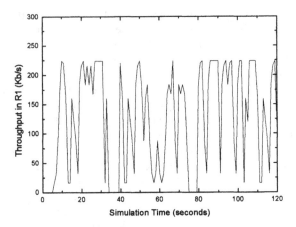

**Fig. 4.** Throughput at mobile user *R1* with DiffServ

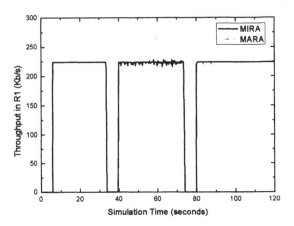

**Fig. 5.** Throughput at mobile user *R1* with MIRA and MARA

It can be clearly noted the degradation experienced by *M1* in the DiffServ tests, in which only during ~24% of the simulation its content is propagated with full rate. In the new path (from ~39 seconds up to ~75 seconds), the degradation of *M1* is even worse due to the congestion caused by background traffics. In the MIRA and MARA tests, a lightly variation in the throughput is noted in the new path due to the presence of congestion. However, this variation does not endanger the quality of *M1*, since no packet loss is noticed. Thus, MIRA and MARA are perfectly suitable to support multimedia content to groups of users.

## 5   Conclusions

This paper introduces the *Multi-user Aggregated Resource Allocation* mechanism (MARA) to coordinate the over-provisioning of bandwidth and SSM trees to be used by multimedia multi-user sessions. The proposed mechanism aims to mitigate the scalability problems of per-flow signalling approaches, such as the *MultI-service Resource Allocation* mechanism (MIRA) previously proposed by the authors. The combination of over-provisioning of resources (bandwidth of DiffServ classes and SSM trees) with admission control allows MARA to setup a significant number of sessions (74.9%) without any signalling in the network. Moreover, the performance limitations of IP multicast (state and maintenance signalling) are overcome by using multicast aggregation. Finally, waste of resources due to over-reservations is prevented by dynamically re-adjusting resources and controlling session connectivity on-demand. Simulation results prove the benefits of MARA in relation to MIRA. Although MARA performs all over-reservations in-advance, after the system bootstrap, simulation results show that system initialization takes only 0.04s and consumes no more than 8% of the link capacity. During the simulation, MARA reduces in 60.33% the signalling load in relation to MIRA. In what concerns state overhead, MARA reduces the state of the ingress router (the most problematic point) in 67.5% in comparison to MIRA, and generate signalling to control SSM trees no longer. The future work prompted in this paper consists in providing efforts to evaluate MARA through prototyping. Thus, it is expected to examine the accuracy of the benefits of MARA described in this paper in real scenarios.

# References

1. Neto, A., Cerqueira, E., Rissato, A., Monteiro, E., Mendes, P.: A Resource Reservation Protocol Supporting QoS-aware Multicast Trees for Next Generation Networks. In: 12th IEEE Symposium on Computers and Communications, Aveiro, Portugal (2007)
2. Pan, P., Hahne, E., Schulzrinne, H.: BGRP: A Tree-Based Aggregation Protocol for Inter-domain Reservations. J. Com. and Net. 2, 157–167 (2000)
3. Sofia, R., Guerin, R., Veiga, P.: SICAP, a Shared-segment Inter-domain Control Aggregation Protocol. In: Conf. in High Performance Switching and Routing, Turin, Italy (2003)
4. Bless, R.: Dynamic Aggregation of Reservations for Internet Services. In: 10th Conference on Telecommunication, Monterey, pp. 26–38 (2002)
5. Braun, T., Arya, V., Turletti, T.: A Backup Tree Algorithm for Multicast Overlay Networks. In: Networking, Waterloo (2005)
6. Kodialem, M., Lakshman, T.: Dynamic routing of bandwidth guaranteed multicasts with failure backup. In: IEEE INFOCOM, New York (2002)
7. Hanna, S., Patel, B., Shah, M.: Multicast Address Dynamic Client Allocation Protocol (MADCAP). IETF RFC 2730 (1999)
8. Di, Z., Mouftah, H.: Performance Evaluation of Per-Hop Forwarding Behaviours in the DiffServ Internet. In: IEEE Symposium on Computers and Communications, Antibes-Juan les Pins (2001)
9. Rose, K., Regunathan, S.: Toward optimality in scalable predictive coding. IEEE J. on Image Processing 7, 965–976 (2001)
10. Neto, A., Cerqueira, E., Curado, M., Monteiro, E., Mendes, P.: Scalable Resource Provisioning for Multi-user Communications in Next Generation Networks. IEEE Globecom, New Orleans, USA (submitted 2008)
11. Wong, T., Katz, R.: An analysis of multicast forwarding state scalability. In: 8th Int. Conf. on Network Protocols, Osaka (2000)
12. Shaikh, A., Tewari, R., Agrawal, M.: On the Effectiveness of DNS-based Server Selection. IBM Research Report (2000)

# Comparative Study of Real-Time Multimedia Transmission over Multi-homing Transport Protocols

Changqiao Xu[1,2], Yuansong Qiao[1,2], Enda Fallon[1], Gabriel-Miro Muntean[3], Paul Jacob[1], and Austin Hanley[1]

[1] Athlone Institute of Technology, Athlone, Ireland
[2] Institute of Software, Chinese Academy of Sciences, Beijing, China
[3] School of Electronic Engineering, Dublin City University, Dublin, Ireland
{cqiaoxu,ysqiao,efallon}@ait.ie, munteang@eeng.dcu.ie,
{pjacob,ahanley}@ait.ie

**Abstract.** The availability of multimedia applications suitable for deployment using 3G and GPRS networks has led to a requirement for end-to-end quality of service. More efficient mechanisms are needed in order to provide the required end user quality of service in wireless data networks. This paper investigates the performance implications of transmitting real-time multimedia content over a multi-homed transport protocol in a manner which is tolerant of network failure. It evaluates video quality with different retransmission policies combined with various path failure detection thresholds, path bandwidths, delays and loss rate conditions through Partial Reliable Stream Control Transmission Protocol (PR-SCTP). A solution called Evalvid-SCTP, which is a trace driven simulation of MPEG-4 video over SCTP, was designed to achieve the performance evaluation.

**Keywords:** PR-SCTP, Multi-homing, MPEG-4 Video, Congestion Control Algorithm, Network simulation.

## 1 Introduction

In recent years the number of mobile and wireless networks available to devices have increased to the extent that there is a near pervasive deployment of networks capable of supporting IP communication. The availability of such networks creates significant technical opportunities for real time distribution of multimedia content. There are technical challenges however, as the networks available to a mobile device can have significantly differing performance characteristics in terms of signal propagation and bandwidth. In such an environment where the availability and capability of network changes dramatically in a short period of time it is logically to employ a seamless network migration strategy which can select the most appropriate network type at a given point in time. Seamless handover between heterogeneous networks can be achieved by using multi-homing technologies [1, 2, 3]. Currently, two multi-homing transport protocols have been proposed. They are Stream Control Transmission Protocol (SCTP) [4] and Datagram Congestion Control Protocol (DCCP) [5]. Especially with the SCTP, an extension named mobile SCTP (mSCTP), which facilitates mobility has been drafted in [2]. DCCP is an unreliable transport protocol with congestion

G. Pavlou, T. Ahmed, and T. Dagiuklas (Eds.): MMNS 2008, LNCS 5274, pp. 64–76, 2008.

control, SCTP is a reliable transport layer protocol and employs a similar congestion control mechanism to TCP, Multi-homing feature of SCTP provides a basis for mobility support since it allows a mobile node (MN) to add a new IP address, while holding the old IP address already assigned to itself. On top of SCTP multi-homing feature, mSCTP utilizes ADDIP and DELETEIP functions which enables dynamically adding and deleting an IP addresses to and from the list of association end points in the middle of association [1].

The Partial-Reliable SCTP (PR-SCTP) [6] is an unreliable data mode extension of SCTP, PR-SCTP allows an SCTP sender to assign different levels of reliability to data so that lost data can be retransmitted until a predefined reliability threshold is reached. When the reliability threshold is reached for unacknowledged data, the sender abandons that retransmission of the data and notifies the receiver (with Forward TSNs) to neglect the outstanding data and move the cumulative ACK point forward. The authors of [7] investigated MPEG-4 video transmission by partial reliable transmission in SCTP in GPRS network and studied QoS interactions between SCTP, RTP and application. This paper investigates the capability of partial-reliability scheme defined by PR-SCTP to support the real time distribution of multimedia content.

## 2  Handover and Retransmission Algorithms in SCTP

SCTP is designed to tolerate network failure and therefore provides a mechanism to detect path failure. The path failure detection time is determined by SCTP parameters *Path.Max.Retrans* (*PMR*) and *Retransmission Timeout* (*RTO*). For an idle destination address, the sender periodically sends a heartbeat chunk to that address to detect if it is reachable and update the path *Round Trip Time* (*RTT*). The heartbeat chunk is sent per path *RTO* plus SCTP parameter *HB.interval* with jittering of +/- 50% of the path *RTO*. The default value of *HB.interval* is 30s. *RTO* is calculated from *RTT* which is measured from non-retransmitted data chunks or heartbeat chunks. For a path with data transmission, it can be determined if it is reachable by detecting data chunks and their SACKs. When the acknowledgement for a data chunk or for a heartbeat chunk is not received within a *RTO*, the path *RTO* is doubled and the error counter of that path is incremented. For a data chunk timeout, the sender retransmits data chunks through the timeout retransmission algorithm. For a heartbeat chunk timeout, the sender sends a new heartbeat chunk immediately. When the path error counter exceeds *PMR*, the destination address is marked as inactive and the sender sends a new heartbeat chunk immediately to probe the destination address. After this, the sender will continuously send heartbeat chunks per *RTO* to the address but the error counter will not be incremented. When an acknowledgement for an outstanding data chunk or a heartbeat chunk sent to the destination address is received, the path error counter is cleared and the path is marked as active. If the primary path is marked as inactive, the sender will select an alternate path to transmit data. When the primary path becomes active, the sender will switch back to the primary path to transmit data.

The SCTP congestion algorithms [4] are inherited from SACK TCP [8], which include slow start, congestion avoidance and fast retransmit. In [9], the authors present a detailed comparison between the congestion algorithms of SCTP and TCP. SCTP defines two retransmission algorithms: fast retransmission and timeout retransmission. SCTP sends all lost data chunks first before sending new data chunks to ensure that multiple paths are not used in parallel.

When an SCTP sender discovers a data chunk is lost on the primary path through the fast retransmission algorithm, it will enter fast recovery phase. The sender will adjust Congestion Window (*cwnd*) and Slow Start Threshold (*ssthresh*) of the primary path and then fast retransmit the data chunk immediately via a selected path, no matter what the current congestion window size of that path is. If multiple data chunk losses are detected simultaneously, the sender will only send one packet via the fast retransmission algorithm. The rest of the lost data chunks will be retransmitted when the path *cwnd* allows. After all the lost chunks have been retransmitted, the sender will send new data chunks on the primary path if the primary path *cwnd* allows. As long as the congestion window is not full and the receiver window size (*rwnd*) maintained in the sender is not zero, the sender can continuously send new data.

According to path selection strategies during retransmissions, three retransmission policies have been proposed and investigated in [10]. They are:

**AllRtxAlt.** All Retransmissions to an Alternate Path;

**AllRtxSame.** All Retransmissions to the Same Path;

**FrSameRtoAlt.** Fast Retransmissions to the Same Path, Timeout Retransmissions
, to an Alternate Path.

The authors of [10] evaluated these three retransmission policies with different extensions and the default SCTP parameters in various lossy environments. The results show that *FrSameRtoAlt* with the Multiple Fast Retransmission algorithm and the Timestamp or the Heartbeat after *RTO* extension performs best amongst the three policies and their respective extensions. *AllRtxAlt* performs worst because of the stale *RTO* problem [10].

In [11], the authors studied the performance of different *PMR* settings with *FrSameRtoAlt* and the Multiple Fast Retransmission extension [10]. The results show that *PMR*=0 can achieve best throughput in various path failure or non-failure situations. The authors of [12] investigate SCTP's throughput performance in different path scenarios and proposed a change to the protocol's heartbeat mechanism to improve the performance. The effect of path delay on SCTP performance was studied in [13]. [14] indicates that retransmission of all data on the same path with the path failure detection threshold set to one or zero gives the most stable performance in all path configurations. However, all of above researches focus on the performance of "FTP over SCTP".

This paper investigates real-time multimedia transmission performance of SCTP's retransmission policies with different *PMR* values, path bandwidths, delays and loss rates in various symmetric and asymmetric path conditions. In the simulations, 3G and GPRS link parameters are used as the references for network configurations. Although SCTP is designed to provide transport services over connectionless packet networks, not merely over IP, this paper assumes the underlying network is IP. In this way, the simulation scenarios are IP over 3G and GPRS. For symmetric path conditions, this paper focuses on the situations where a computing node has two 3G connections. For asymmetric path conditions, the tests cover different path delay, bandwidth configurations and the situations where a computing node has a hybrid 3G or GPRS connection. Uniform loss is used to simulate network congestion.

The rest of this paper is structured as follows. In Section 3, we propose the solution for evaluating quality of MPEG-4 video transmission over SCTP. Section 4 compares different retransmission policies with various *PMR* settings in symmetric and asymmetric path conditions, and then gives the analysis of the results. The conclusions are presented in Section 5.

## 3  Evalvid-SCTP

With the increasing deployment of real-time applications over 3G and GPRS networks, end-to-end delay and packet loss are vital QoS requirements for these applications. In order to investigate the behavior and quality of such applications under heavy network load, it is therefore necessary to create genuine traffic patterns, both at network/transport layer and application. To setup true multimedia test networks is expensive and offer little flexibility. Instead network simulations using tools like the NS-2 [15] enable building customized effective networks at a low cost at their testing in details.

In recent years, many papers have studied multimedia delivery through simulations. In [16], MPEG-4 trace files are used to calibrate a Transform Expand Sample (TES) mathematical model, and rate adaptation is incorporated by adjusting the frame size output by a scalar (from rate-distortion curve). The simulation model however has no on-line rate controller, and since the traffic is synthetic, perceived quality cannot be investigated. H.263 video trace files are used in [17], and the sending rate is controlled by DCCP TCP-like. In [18] models are derived for pre-recorded media streaming over TFRC and compared to simulations. The models focus on the impact of the TFRC rate changes to the probability of rebuffering events, i.e. events where the receive buffer is emptied. Authors of [19] proposed a tool-set called Evalvid-RA to support rate adaptive MPEG-4 VBR video simulation. Evalvid tools-set [20] is an open-source project, and supports trace file generation of MPEG-4 as well as H.263 and H.264 video. Using Evalvid together with the NS-2 interface code suggested by C.-H. Ke [21], perceived quality and objective measure like Peak Signal-to-Noise Ratio (PSNR) calculation can be obtained after network simulation.

The quality of a video transmission depends on the impression a human observer receives of the delivered video. The subjective video quality test results are expressed by means of e.g. the mean opinion score (MOS) as defined by the ITU. The MOS is a scale from 5 (excellent) to 1 (bad). In contrast, objective video quality metrics are calculated by computers. Basically, these can be divided into pixel-based metrics, like SNR or PSNR, and psycho-visual metrics.

Based on related work, we designed Evalvid-SCTP, a solution for MPEG-4 video investigation over SCTP in NS-2, it is based on modifications to Evalvid and Delaware University's SCTP module [22] for NS-2 [15], and then Evalvid is integrated into SCTP.

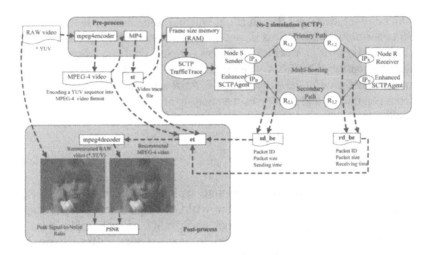

**Fig. 1.** The pre-process, NS-2 simulation and post-process of the Evalvid-SCTP framework

**Table 1.** The Evalvid-SCTP Tools Overview: Pre-process, NS-2 simulation, Post-process

| Tool | Purpose |
|---|---|
| mpeg4encoder.exe | Pre-process: Encode video file into MPEG-4 video |
| mp4.exe | Pre-process: Create frame size trace file of encoded file from previous step |
| SCTPTrafficeTrace | Ns-2 simulation: A extended Agent which send data to the enhanced SctpAgent following the trace file from previous step |
| Enhanced SctpAgent | Ns-2 simulation: Modified sctp.h and sctp.cc in where sender trace file is written, including sending time, packet type, id, size, and receiver trace file is written, including receiving time and packet type, id, size. |
| et.exe | Post-process: From Evalvid to reconstruct video after transmission. |
| fixyuv.exe | Post-process: Inserts missing frames due to drop or late arrival so that sent and received video has the equal number of frames |
| psnr.exe | Post-process: calculate the PSNR |
| mos.exe | Post-process: Map MOS values from PSNR |

Evalvid-SCTP enables simulation of multimedia transfer based on the generation of MPEG-4 video trace files. The trace files consist of real compressed video characteristics including frame number, frame type, size, fragmentation into segments and timing for each video frame. These characteristics can be utilized to construct mathematical traffic models and traffic generators for network simulators since they determine the packet sizes and time schedules. The simulation utilises pre-generated media trace files. While running SCTP, NS-2 records packet throughput at each node including the receiver. Using this information and the original compressed video file, Evalvid-SCTP reconstructs the video as if it were received on a real network. This reconstruction enables the video to be inspected visually as well as allowing for the calculation of PSNR and Mean Opinion Score (MOS) for the transferred video.

As figure 1 shows, the framework of Evalvid-SCTP has three stages namely: pre-process, NS-2 simulation and post-process. In pre-process, the original YUV format video is compressed into MPEG-4 format video, then video trace file is generated which includes information about each frame (I-frame, P-frame, B-frame) in the video. In the NS-2 simulation, the Agent SCTPTrafficeTrace sends data to SCTP network following video trace file, the enhanced SCTPAgent records the sender trace file including sending time, packet type, packet id, size. It also records the receiver trace file including receiving time, packet type, packet id and size. In the post-process phase, the video is reconstructed and converted in to raw video (YUV), the video quality evaluation is given by the calculation of PSNR. Table 1 lists some primary tools used by Evalvid-SCTP.

## 4   Simulation-Based Assessment

### 4.1   Simulation Setup

The simulations in this section consider different network path conditions. The simulation topology is shown in Figure 2 and includes node S and node R which are the SCTP sender and receiver respectively. Both SCTP endpoints have two addresses. $R_{1,1}$, $R_{1,2}$, $R_{2,1}$ and $R_{2,2}$ are routers. The implementation is configured with no overlap between the two paths. The Maximum Transmission Unit (MTU) of each path is 1500B. The queue length of bottleneck links in both paths is 50 packets. The queue length of other links is set to 1000 packets.

The SCTP parameters are the default ones [4]. The initial slow start threshold is set large enough to ensure that the full primary path bandwidth is used. SCTP is set as PR-SCTP, the default reliability level of PR-SCTP is set to 1. Only one SCTP stream is used and the data is delivered to the upper layer in order. For simulations with an infinite receive buffer, the receiver window (*rwnd*) is set to 100 MB as this size is larger than the data size transmitted by the sender. Network congestion is simulated by varying the path loss rate (2%, 4% and 8%).

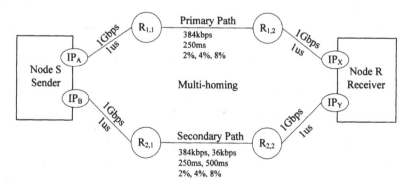

**Fig. 2.** Simulation network topology

A YUV video sequence is used with a QCIF format (resolution 176x144 pixels) and 2000 frames. After pre-processing in Evalvid-SCTP, a MPEG-4 video trace file is produced. In NS-2 node S sends data from this video trace file at 30 frames/sec to node R at t=5 sec. 10 random seeds are used for simulation and testing results are calculated by averaging the results of 10 runs.

## 4.2 Symmetric Path Bandwidth and Path Loss Rate

This section studies the performance of retransmission policies and *PMR* settings in symmetric path conditions. A computing node has two 3G connections and an infinite buffer. The bandwidth of both bottleneck links is set as 384kbps. The delays on the primary and secondary path are 250ms, and the paths loss rates are set to 2%, 4% and 8%. Aggressive (*PMR*=0) and less aggressive (*PMR*=1) failover settings are set respectively. The results for *PMR*=2, 3, 4, 5 are not shown in this paper. One reason for this omission is that the path failure detection time is long, such as for *PMR*=5, it means that SCTP needs 6 consecutive transmission timeouts to detect path failure. *RTO* will be doubled for each transmission timeout and ranges between the SCTP parameters *RTO.Min* and *RTO.Max*. The default values for *RTO.Min* and *RTO.Max* are 1s and 60s respectively. If *RTO* is 1s (*RTO.Min*) in the case of a path failure, the minimum time for detecting path failure is 1+2+4+8+16+32=63s. However, the initial *RTO* could be 60s (*RTO.Max*). Therefore, the maximum path failure detection time is 6*60=360s! Another reason is that the data transmission time for *PMR*>0 is similar.

Table 2 and 3 show the comparison results of average PSNR (dB) values and the numbers of different lost frames (I-frame/P-frame/B-frame) after transmission, which

**Table 2.** Post-processing results (*PMR*=0)

|  | Path loss rate =2% | | Path loss rate =4% | | Path loss rate =8% | |
|---|---|---|---|---|---|---|
|  | Average PSNR (dB) | Frames dropped (I/P/B) | Average PSNR (dB) | Frames dropped (I/P/B) | Average PSNR (dB) | Frames dropped (I/P/B) |
| *AllRtxSame* | 35.20 | 8/17/49 | 33.02 | 42/85/252 | 26.60 | 115/229/686 |
| *AllRtxAlt* | 35.39 | 6/11/32 | 33.39 | 34/69/204 | 27.17 | 108/216/647 |
| *FrSameRtoAlt* | 35.20 | 8/17/49 | 33.02 | 42/85/252 | 25.82 | 122/243/728 |

**Table 3.** Post-processing results (*PMR*=1)

|  | Path loss rate=2% | | Path loss rate =4% | | Path loss rate =8% | |
|---|---|---|---|---|---|---|
|  | Average PSNR (dB) | Frames dropped (I/P/B) | Average PSNR (dB) | Frames dropped (I/P/B) | Average PSNR (dB) | Frames dropped (I/P/B) |
| *AllRtxSame* | 35.06 | 11/21/62 | 33.02 | 42/85/252 | 26.60 | 118/235/705 |
| *AllRtxAlt* | 34.55 | 19/37/110 | 31.08 | 70/139/416 | 25.05 | 128/256/766 |
| *FrSameRtoAlt* | 34.94 | 13/25/74 | 33.42 | 35/69/206 | 25.59 | 125/250/749 |

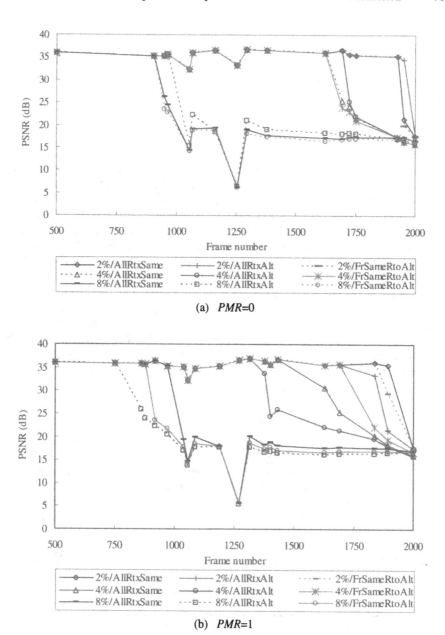

(a)  *PMR=0*

(b)  *PMR=1*

**Fig. 3.** PSNR (dB) for symmetric paths (primary path: 384kbps & 250ms; secondary path: 384kbps & 250ms; paths loss rate change with 2% , 4%, 8%)

employed different retransmission policies: *AllRtxSame*, *AllRtxAlt* and *FrSameRtoAlt* with *PMR* 0 and 1 respectively. Figure 3 shows the corresponding PSNR values frame-by-frame (only the last 1500 frames are shown). As the tables and figure illustrate, with the increasing path loss rate PSNR decreases and the numbers of lost frames increase in all cases. However, in most cases, setting *PMR*=0 performs better than setting *PMR*=1. Retransmission of all data on an alternate path with *PMR*=0 performs best; however, its performance degrades with *PMR*=1. Retransmission of all data on the same path with the *PMR* set to zero or one performs in a more stable manner than other configurations.

### 4.3 Asymmetric Path Bandwidth and Path Loss Rate

This section studies the performance of retransmission policies and *PMR* settings in asymmetric path conditions. A computing node has a hybrid of 3G or GPRS connections and an infinite buffer. The primary path bandwidth is 384kbps and the secondary path bandwidth is 36kbps. The delay on the primary path is 250ms, the delay of secondary path is 500ms, and the loss rates of both paths are set to 2%, 4% and 8%. Other settings are the same as for previous tests. Table 4 and 5 illustrate the comparison results for average PSNR (dB) values as well as lost frames (I-frame/P-frame/B-frame), for different retransmission policies: *AllRtxSame*, *AllRtxAlt* and *FrSameRtoAlt* with *PMR* 0, 1 respectively. Figure 4 shows the corresponding PSNR values frame-by-frame (only the last 1500 frames are shown). As the table and figure show, with the increasing of path loss rate the PSNR decreases and the number of slipped frames increase in all the cases. The total average video quality degrades compared with symmetric path conditions. In most cases however, *PMR*=1 performs better than *PMR*=0. Retransmission of all data on an alternate path performs worst. Retransmission of all data on the same path with the *PMR* set to zero or one performs in a more stable manner than other configurations.

**Table 4.** Post-processing results (*PMR*=0)

|  | Path loss rate =2% | | Path loss rate =4% | | Path loss rate =8% | |
|---|---|---|---|---|---|---|
|  | Average PSNR (dB) | Frames dropped (I/P/B) | Average PSNR (dB) | Frames dropped (I/P/B) | Average PSNR (dB) | Frames dropped (I/P/B) |
| *AllRtxSame* | 34.06 | 23/45/136 | 32.96 | 44/87/262 | 24.72 | 131/262/785 |
| *AllRtxAlt* | 33.83 | 25/49/217 | 32.69 | 46/91/274 | 24.66 | 137/275/822 |
| *FrSameRtoAlt* | 34.06 | 23/45/136 | 32.69 | 46/91/274 | 24.72 | 133/266/796 |

**Table 5.** Post-processing results (*PMR*=1)

|  | Path loss rate=2% | | Path loss rate =4% | | Path loss rate =8% | |
|---|---|---|---|---|---|---|
|  | Average PSNR (dB) | Frames dropped (I/P/B) | Average PSNR (dB) | Frames dropped (I/P/B) | Average PSNR (dB) | Frames dropped (I/P/B) |
| *AllRtxSame* | 35.06 | 11/21/62 | 33.02 | 42/85/252 | 26.60 | 115/229/686 |
| *AllRtxAlt* | 33.83 | 25/49/148 | 32.96 | 44/87/262 | 24.90 | 129/257/770 |
| *FrSameRtoAlt* | 34.58 | 18/35/105 | 32.88 | 44/89/264 | 26.08 | 119/239/714 |

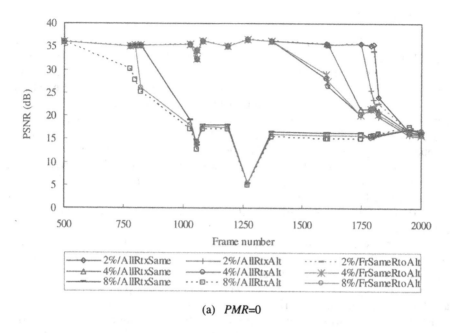

(a)  *PMR*=0

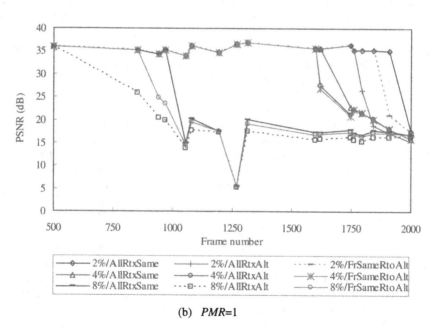

(b)  *PMR*=1

**Fig. 4.** PSNR (dB) for asymmetric paths (primary path: 384kbps & 250ms; secondary path: 36kbps & 500ms; paths loss rate change with 2%, 4%, 8%)

## 4.4 Analysis of the Results

The test results illustrate that in most cases, aggressive failover setting (*PMR*=0) performs better than less aggressive failover setting (*PMR*=1) regardless of the path loss rates in symmetric path conditions. As we know, the underlying advantage of aggressive failover is that handover occurs with less time blocked during failure detection. With *PMR*=0, a single timeout migrate new data transmission to the alternate path quickly while the primary destination is probed with heartbeats. Though aggressive failover setting could increases the possibility of spurious failover where a small number of lost packets is interpreted to mean that the destination address is no longer reachable and sender mistakenly concludes a failure has occurred, however the alternate path has the same good path conditions with the primary path, which avoids negative impact by unnecessary failovers. So this scenario of symmetric paths with *PMR*=0 is actually a concurrent multi-path transmission, then it achieves better performance.

However, the investigation revealed that when a bandwidth asymmetry did exist, setting *PMR*=0 was not good advice. Less aggressive failover setting (*PMR*=1) generally outperforms aggressive failover setting (*PMR*=0) in asymmetric path conditions. As the secondary path conditions are worse than primary path with less bandwidth and larger delay. In this scenario, as it is discussed in [12], there is a substantial advantage to sticking with the higher speed primary path, despite the fact that it is not functioning, and waiting for it to be restored, rather than switching over to the lower speed alternate path. The reason for this is that when SCTP stays with the primary path, it will more quickly discover when the path is again functional (by retransmitting user data using exponential back-off) than if it fails over to the alternate and relies upon the slower heartbeat (HB) mechanism to probe for the primary's recovery. So with *PMR*=1, the worse secondary path is seldom used, which achieves better performance than that of *PMR* setting to 0.

The results show that all retransmissions to an alternate path with *PMR*=0 performs best in symmetric path conditions and degrades seriously in asymmetric path conditions. For *AllRtxAlt*, the lost data will be retransmitted on the secondary path, even for *PMR*=0. Therefore, the performance will be degraded when the secondary path conditions are significantly worse than the primary path conditions. For *PMR*>0, *AllRtxAlt* performs worst because the stale *RTO* problem as indicated in [10] and can be explained as follows. A retransmission timeout on the alternate path will double the *RTO*, whereas a successful retransmission will not refresh the *RTO* which can only be updated by the heartbeat chunks. Consequently, the *RTO* on the alternate path is usually a large value which causes the data loss detection time to become very long and degrades the performance. However, SCTP can avoid the stale *RTO* problem with *PMR*=0. Every time a packet is lost, the destination address is marked as inactive. The sender will transmit a heartbeat chunk to the inactive destination address immediately, which can get a new measurement for the path *RTT* and *RTO*. The HeartbeatAfterRTO extension proposed in [10] can be achieved automatically through *PMR*=0. *AllRtxAlt* retransmits all lost data on an alternate path. In the fast retransmit phase, the lost data are retransmitted immediately irrespective of the current path *cwnd*. This is actually a concurrent multipath transmission. Therefore, *AllRtxAlt* with *PMR*=0 in symmetric path conditions gives the best performance.

# 5 Conclusions

This paper proposed a solution called Evalvid-SCTP to analyse the performance of real-time multimedia transmission over multi-homing transport protocols utilizing network failure tolerant mechanisms. In particular, we focus on the extension of SCTP, Partial Reliable Stream Control Transmission Protocol (PR-SCTP). The three PR-SCTP retransmission policies: *AllRtxSame*, *AllRtxAlt* and *FrSameRtoAlt* were evaluated using a number of path failure detection threshold values in various symmetric and asymmetric path conditions through SCTP simulations. Uniform loss is used to simulate network congestion. The results indicate that an aggressive failover setting (*PMR*=0) performs better in symmetric path conditions, however a less aggressive failover strategy (*PMR*=1) performs better in asymmetric path conditions. Retransmission of all video on an alternate path with *PMR*=0 performs best in symmetric path conditions but with *PMR*=1 performs worst among all retransmission policies and *PMR* settings. Retransmission of all video on the same path with the path failure detection threshold set to zero or one is recommended since it gives the most stable performance in all path situations.

# References

1. Stewart, R., Xie, Q., Tuexen, M., et al.: Stream Control Transmission Protocol (SCTP) Dynamic Address Reconfiguration. IETF draft, draft-ietft-tsvwg-addip-sctp-20.txt, draft-ietf-tsvwg-addip-sctp-15.txt (2007)
2. Riegel, M., Tuexen, M.: Mobile SCTP. IETF Draft, draft-riegel-tuexen-mobile-sctp-05.txt (2005)
3. Dutta, A., Das, S., Famolari, D., et al.: Seamless Handoff across Heterogeneous Networks - An 802.21 Centric Approach. In: Proc. IEEE WPMC, Aalborg Denmark (2005)
4. IETF RFC 2960: Stream Control Transmission Protocol (2000)
5. IETF RFC 4340: Datagram Congestion Control Protocol (DCCP) (2006)
6. Stewart, R., Ramalho, M., Xie, Q., et al.: Stream Control Transmission Protocol (SCTP) Partial Reliability Extension. IETF RFC 3758 (2004)
7. Huang, H., Ou, J., Zhang, D.: Efficient Multimedia Transmission in Mobile Network by using PR-SCTP. In: Proc. of Communications and Computer Networks, CCN, Marina del Rey, USA (October 2005)
8. IETF RFC2018: TCP Selective Acknowledgement Options (1996)
9. Fu, S., Atiquzzaman, M.: SCTP: State of the art in Research, Products, and Technical Challenges. IEEE Communications Magazine 42(4), 64–76 (2004)
10. Caro, A., Amer, P., Stewart, R.: Retransmission Policies for Multihomed Transport Protocols. Computer Communications 29(10), 1798–1810 (2006)
11. Caro, A., Amer, P., Stewart, R.: Rethinking End-to-End Failover with Transport Layer Multihoming. Annals of Telecommunications 61(1-2), 92–114 (2006)
12. Grace, K.H., Pecelli, D., Amelia, J.D.: Improving Multi-homed SCTP Mobile Communication Performance. Technical Papers, The MITRE Corporation (2006)
13. Qiao, Y., Fallon, E., Murphy, L., et al.: SCTP Performance Issue on Path Delay Differential. In: Boavida, F., Monteiro, E., Mascolo, S., Koucheryavy, Y. (eds.) WWIC 2007. LNCS, vol. 4517, pp. 43–54. Springer, Heidelberg (2007)

14. Qiao, Y., Fallon, E., Murphy, L., et al.: Performance Analysis of Multi-homed Transport Protocols with Network Failure Tolerance. IET Communications 5(2), 336–345 (2007)
15. UC Berkeley, LBL, USC/ISI, and Xerox Parc ns-2 documentation and software, Version 2.29 (2005), http://www.isi.edu/nsnam/ns
16. Liew, C.H., Kodikara, C., Kondoz, M.A.: Modelling of MPEG-4 Encoded VBR Video Traffic. IEE Electronic Letters 40(5) (2004)
17. Xu, C., Liu, J., Zhao, C.: Performance analysis of transmitting H.263 over DCCP. In: Proc. of IEEE Int. Workshop VLSI Design and Video Technology (2005)
18. Xu, L., Helzer, J.: Media Streaming via TFRC: An Analytical Study of the Impact of TFRC on User-Perceived Media Quality. In: Proc. of IEEE Infocom (2006)
19. Lie, A., Klaue, J.: Evalvid-RA: Trace Driven Simulation of Rate Adaptive MPEG-4 VBR Video. ACM/Springer Multimedia Systems Journal (2007)
20. Klaue, J., Rathke, B., Wolisz, A.: Evalvid - A Framework for Video Transmission and Quality Evaluation. In: Proc. of the 13th International Conference on Modelling Techniques and Tools for Computer Performance Evaluation, Urbana, Illinois, USA (2003)
21. Ke, C.H.: How to evaluate MPEG video transmission using the NS2 simulator. [Online], http://hpds.ee.ncku.edu.tw/smallko/ns2/Evalvid in NS2.htm
22. Caro, A., Iyengar, J.: ns-2 SCTP module, Version 3.5, http://www.armandocaro.net/software/ns2sctp/

# L-CAN: Locality Aware Structured Overlay for P2P Live Streaming

Nikolaos Efthymiopoulos, Athanasios Christakidis, Spyros Denazis,
and Odysseas Koufopavlou

Department of Electrical and Computer Engineering
University of Patras
Patras, Greece
{nefthymiop,schristakidis,sdena,odysseas}@ece.upatras.gr

**Abstract.** A p2p streaming system must be able to exploit the locality information between peers, in order to deliver a stream quickly to all peers with high
level of bandwidth utilization. In this paper we propose a locality aware and
balanced overlay for p2p live streaming which can adapt to the dynamic behavior of the participating peers and the underlying network. Our overlay is created
and maintained through the use of two algorithms, called the placement and the
swapping algorithm that we consider as the major contributions in this paper.
These are responsible for the insertion of a node and the dynamic and distributed optimization of the overlay in order to reflect the underlying network. The
proposed overlay is evaluated through extensive simulations that show that the
bandwidth utilization of the peers and the set-up time are significantly improved
through locality between peers.

**Keywords:** P2P live streaming, DHT, locality aware overlay.

## 1 Introduction

P2P streaming is a real time application with strict delivery time constraints and very
demanding in terms of the aggregate bandwidth required for the delivery of the stream
to the participating peers. In general, a server generates a video stream at a given service rate which is then divided into blocks followed by their delivery to a small subset
among the participating peers. As a final step, all peers exchange these blocks in order
to reproduce the whole video stream.

Peers involved in these systems, may have heterogeneous upload bandwidth capabilities while the average upload bandwidth capability of the participating peers
constrains the maximum service rate of the video stream that can be delivered successfully to all peers [12]. An efficient P2P streaming system must be able to deliver a
video stream with service rate as close as possible to the average upload capability of
the participating peers with the smallest possible delay, called *setup time*. With the
term setup time we define the time interval between the generation of a block from
the origin server and its distribution to every peer in the system.

Several approaches that have been recently proposed for creating P2P streaming
systems may fall into two categories.

G. Pavlou, T. Ahmed, and T. Dagiuklas (Eds.): MMNS 2008, LNCS 5274, pp. 77–90, 2008.

The first is based on a formation of forests of trees whereby each node is a leaf in every tree but one. Blocks are assigned equiprobably into a number of stripes equal to the number of the formed trees. Each tree distributes (pushes) one stripe by propagating each one of its blocks from parent to its children. In this category blocks are pushed according to the overlay topology. SplitStream [4] is a distributed implementation of this approach that is based on a locality aware DHT called Pastry [10]. Split-Stream and systems alike have the advantage of being topologically aware (trees are formed according to the network distance between nodes) leading to small setup time as the propagation of a block from the root of the tree to the leaf nodes is done through nodes which are physically close in the underlying network. However these systems suffer from two main drawbacks: a) they don't take into account the heterogeneous upload capacities of the peers [17], and b) they can't cope up with the dynamic behavior of the participating peers as well as the underlying network as observed in commercial P2P streaming systems [18],. When a peer leaves the overlay, the path between it and its descendants is broken resulting in idle descendants during the reconstruction phase of the tree.

The second category described in [2],[12],[15]. Each node maintains connections with a relatively small number of nodes which are considered as its neighbors in the overlay. The overlay is constructed randomly or according to the upload capacities of the nodes that participate in it. Blocks that are generated by a server have playback deadlines. Each peer exchanges and maintains a number of lists (buffers), one per neighbor. Each one of these buffers contains those blocks of its neighbor that their playback deadline has not expired yet. To this end, a peer is capable at any time of making a decision about which block should be transmitted to which neighbor. This decision process is implemented by a scheduler running in every node. The characteristic of these systems is that the block transmissions are agnostic to the overlay topology.

Due to their architecture the main advantage of them is their flexibility which allows them to take advantage of the heterogeneity of the participating peers and deal with the dynamic behavior of the system leading to higher levels of bandwidth utilization. However, these systems can't exploit the network proximity among the peers that exchange blocks. This means that the time required for a block to be transferred from one node to another and hence the required time for all nodes to acquire the block (setup-time) could reduced if the overlay exploits the locality between peers. Another drawback of overlays agnostic to locality is that buffer exchanges between neighbors performed with high network latency. This effect leads duplicate block transmissions and so to wasted upload bandwidth.

The primary contribution of this paper is the creation of an overlay where each node discovers and exchanges blocks with the nodes physically close to it in the underlying network. The physical network distance is captured by means of a novel, locality aware structured P2P graph which is reconfigured dynamically according to the latencies between nodes in the underlying network. This overlay can approximately be seen as a self-organized d-dimensional grid where the position of each node in the overlay reflects its position in the underlying physical network. There are two algorithms that every node runs. The first is the placement algorithm that each node runs only once when it enters the system and is responsible for finding a suitable neighborhood of the overlay for this node. The second one, called the swapping algorithm, aims at the distributed and dynamic optimization of the neighborhoods in order to reflect the underlying network.

The rest of this paper is organized as follows. In section 2 we present our proposed overlay and we describe in detail the placement and the swapping algorithm in Section 3 we describe briefly the scheduler that we use in order to evaluate our overlay and in Section 4 we evaluate its performance. At last in section 5 we conclude and we point our future work.

## 2 The Proposed System

### 2.1 Locality Aware P2P Overlay Architecture

For creating a locality aware P2P overlay where each node has as neighbors the nodes in the underlying network that are physically close to it, we have used structured P2P overlay, in particular we have use the neighbor table maintenance mechanism from CAN [1], CAN is a distributed self-organized overlay, which intuitively approximates a d-dimensional grid. In CAN each node holds a random portion of a d-dimensional space. It offers three major advantages that explain our architectural decision to use it as a substrate for our streaming system. The first is that is guarantees that each node will have at least 2*d incoming neighbors and so at least 2*d nodes will provide blocks to it. The second is the balanced properties of the overlay (are demonstrated in the evaluation section) that means that there are no nodes with a large number of outgoing neighbors and so as we will see later that feature reduces the control overhead of live streaming. The third and most important feature of this overlay is that between any two nodes there are at least 2*d paths where in each one a different set of nodes participates. Given this attribute and by the creation of the appropriate scheduler no point of the graph is a bottleneck in live streaming. At last offers a mechanism to formulate our distributed optimization algorithm as we will analyze in section C.

In contrast, locality aware DHTs proposed so far, lead to overlays where nodes have highly unbalanced number of neighbors [8] and so are unsuitable to be used as overlays in P2P streaming.

In order to reflect the underlying network in the d-dimensional space of CAN, thus capturing locality, we have developed two algorithms. The first, influenced from [16], is called *placement algorithm*. This is responsible for navigating and placing each node that enters our system next to its closest node in the physical network. The second called *swapping,* is responsible for the distributed and dynamic optimization of the overlay according to the network latencies between nodes. These two algorithms constitute the extension of the original CAN leading to a locality aware overlay called L-CAN.

### 2.2 The Placement Algorithm

The placement algorithm is a distributed algorithm responsible for finding a suitable neighborhood for each node which enters the system. Its high accuracy is not a critical issue, because we do not rely entirely on this algorithm to provide an optimal placement of the nodes (neighbors that are also physically close to each other) in the

L-CAN. This is the job of our swapping algorithm that is responsible for an optimal dynamic and stable solution.

Each node, already part of the overlay, must be capable of navigating each new node closer to its final position. To do so, each node i in the L-CAN must maintain some kind of information about the structure of the overlay. The first source of information comes from the neighbors of i as through the exchange of control messages with them, node i can get an estimate of the corresponding STTs. In addition to communicating with its neighbors, each node communicates with a number of nodes $R_i$ uniformly spread in all d dimensions of L-CAN (Figure 1). We call these nodes *ring nodes*.

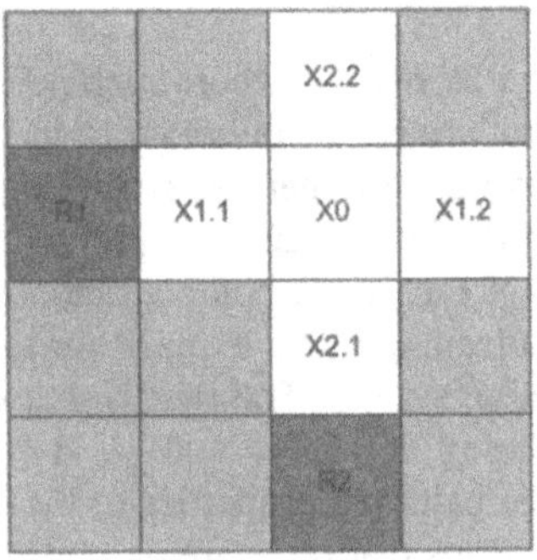

**Fig. 1.** Node X0 is already placed in a two dimensional CAN. Its neighbors are nodes {X1.1, X1.2, X2.1, X2.2} and communicates with one additional node in each dimension ($R_i=1$), namely, its ring nodes {R1,R2}.

Every node N, which is already placed in L-CAN, has a structure (called `topology_list(N)`) that holds the values of the estimated STTs with its neighbors and its ring nodes. Methods and algorithms which provide STT estimates through many RTT measurements are described analytically in [21].

When a node X is to be inserted in our system it makes use of two lists. The first one, called `closer_list`, contains those nodes which our placement algorithm has found upon completion of an iteration to be closer to node X up to a maximum number `closer_num`. The second one, called `check_list`, is used and updated at every step of the placement algorithm in order to infer from the `topology_list` of those nodes in the `check_list` additional nodes that happen to be close to X. The maximum size of `check_list` is set to `check_num`. (Figure 2).

In order to bootstrap the placement algorithm, the new node X randomly selects a node N already in the L-CAN and places it in both lists. Then, the new node performs the following iterative steps until its `closer_list` remains the same for a number of `stop_check` steps.

For each node $N_i$ in X's `check_list` the new node X takes a pre-defined number of nodes (`cl_num`) from $N_i$'s `topology_list` which are potentially closer to X. This is done by calculating the absolute difference between the STT from $N_i$ to X and the STT from $N_i$ to the node which was present in $N_i$'s topology list 16. Then X probes these `cl_num*check_num` nodes and if it finds that some of these nodes are closer to X than those in its `closer_list`, it substitutes those nodes in the `closer_list` with the new nodes with smaller STTs. Finally, `check_list` is assigned the contents of the `closer_list` and the process is repeated until convergence.

When the algorithm terminates, the first node in the `closer_list` is the nearest to X in the physical network. The pre-defined numbers `closer_num`, `check_num`, `cl_num` and `stop_check` define the trade-off between accuracy and speed of convergence of our placement algorithm.

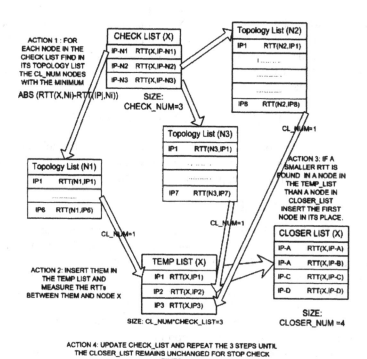

**Fig. 2.** At each step 4 actions are performed. The data structures which the new node X maintains during its entry in the DHT. $N_i$ denotes the nodes which X asks at each step.

After the discovery of the physically closest node to X, node K, X sends to K a request for insertion. At this point we face another challenge: to create a balanced overlay, namely, the number of neighbors of every node must be similar in size. To this end, X checks whether a neighbor of K has a zone bigger than K's zone. If such a neighbor exists then the new node will be inserted in the overlay between K and the neighbor of K with the bigger zone, otherwise, it will be inserted in the zone of K. By doing this we still ensure that nodes K and X will also be neighbors in L-CAN, while we avoid the possibility of a node having a relatively big zone compared with another one close to it. In this way the requirement for a balanced overlay in terms of the size of neighbors is guaranteed.

### 2.3  The Swapping Algorithm

The swapping algorithm, aims at keeping L-CAN dynamically updated and optimized with respect to locality as opposed to the placement algorithm which is responsible for maintaining a balanced overlay during initial node insertion.

Two events may trigger the need for such a reconfiguration: a) the arrival or departure of a node, and b) any change in network conditions. Both events result in new STT values maintained by L-CAN, which, in turn, invokes the swapping algorithm to rearrange the "neighborhoods" in L-CAN.

The L-CAN swapping algorithm is based on a function, we call *energy function*, denoted as E(i,j), where i is a node in L-CAN and j is the zone that this node occupies, $i \in N$ *and* $j \in Z$ where N,Z the sets of the nodes and the zones in L-CAN respectively. Additionally each zone j in L-CAN is adjacent with a set of zones noted as Zneigh(j) and the nodes that hold these zones defined as Neigh(i). Accordingly, the energy function of a node i that holds a zone j is defined as:

$$E(i,j) = \sum_{k=1}^{k=|Neigh(i)|}[Stt(i,k) \mid k \in \{Neigh(i)\}] \tag{1}$$

This small subset Neigh(i) of N is the nodes that i uses in order to exchange blocks. If we assume that links between neighbors are used with equal probability in streaming the performance of the streaming application is based on the metric:

$$E_{all} = \sum_{i \in N}[E(i,j) \mid \forall i1 \neq i2 \ \rightarrow j1 \neq j2] \tag{2}$$

If we minimize $E_{all}$ the overlay would minimize the average latency and consequently it would also minimize the average probability for duplicates The algorithmic complexity of such problem is O(|N|!) provided that we apply an exhaustive search of all possible combinations among  all nodes and zones of L-CAN. To this end, there is a need for a distributed algorithm that will minimize $E_{all}$ or at least it will converge in a good sub-optimal value for $E_{all}$. So we propose an algorithm that dynamically rearranges "neighborhoods" in L-CAN. Accordingly our swapping algorithm starts from a node that we called as the initiator. In a swapping process the nodes that participate is the initiator and all of its neighbors. The goal of our swapping algorithm is an optimal assignment between these nodes and their zones that we denote with the set Nswap and Zswap respectively. As optimal assignment we define the assignment that results in the minimum sum of energy of the participating nodes in the swapping process. In order to reduce the complexity of such an assignment that is O(|Nswap|!) we formulate this process as a linear integer programming problem that solved with a polynomial complexity. In the rest of this section we describe this formulation in detail.

More specifically, Figure 3 illustrates an example of swapping among 5 neighboring nodes, Nswap={x0,x1,x2,x3,x4} that occupy zones Zswap ={p0,p1,p2,p3,p4} respectively, in a 2-dimensional L-CAN. x0 is considered the initiator of a swapping process.

Initially, nodes x0-x4 exchange with each other the set of their own neighbors. For instance, node X1 and X3 exchange Neigh(x1) = {a1,a7,a8,x0}, and Neigh(x3) = {a3,a4,a5,x0}, respectively. After all nodes that belong to Nswap have been notified of all these neighbor sets in each position, each one measures its STT in the nodes that

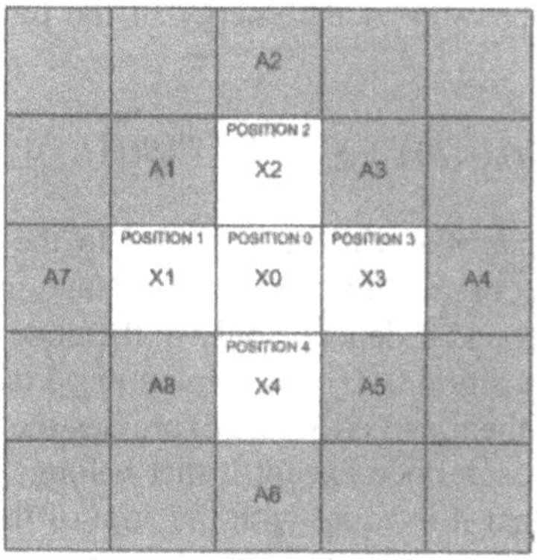

**Fig. 3.** A two-dimensional CAN where nodes {X0, X1, X2, X3, X4} perform a concurrent swapping, where X0 is the initiator

presented in every set Neigh(i) where i∈Nswap and send the measurements to the initiator as this is the node that carries out the execution of the swapping algorithm. Now the initiator is capable of calculating the optimal assignment between nodes Nswap and positions Zswap. In order to formalize the swapping process we note now as Zneigh(i) the set of nodes that are adjacent with a zone i and do not participate in the swapping process (Ex. Zneigh(P2) ={a1,a2,a3}).For the calculation of energy in every zone except the central one (P0 in our example) we use the set Zneigh this set excludes the node that will be moved to the central position as it is unknown yet. For instance, the energy of x1 to position P2 is calculated for the needs of the swapping as:

$$E(x1,p2)=Stt(x1,a1)+Stt(x1,a2)+Stt(x1,a3) \qquad (3)$$

The problem with (3) is that we do not know which of the x0, x2, x3, and x4 moves to the central position P0. Four outcomes are possible, but we will describe later how we tackle this problem.

The case where a node moves to the central position P0, is simpler as each node of the calculation of its energy uses the set Nswap that participate in the swapping process except itself. That's because as we observe from the Figure 3 if this node moved to the central position will have as its neighbors these nodes. Again, if X1 moves to P0 its energy function becomes:

$$E(x1,p0)=Stt(x1,x0)+Stt(x1,x2)+Stt(x1,x3)+Stt(x1,x4) \qquad (4)$$

We are now able to determine the energy of each node in a more abstractive way in order to formulate the swapping algorithm. In order to find the optimal assignment of the nodes∈ *Nswap* and their zones∈ *Zswap* we have to calculate the energy of each node in each potential position.

So for the zone of the initiator, noted as position 0, the node i that will be swapped there will have energy:

$$E(i,0) = \sum_{j=1}^{j=|Nswap|-1}[Stt(i,j)| \, j \in Nswap, i \neq j] \qquad (5)$$

For the other zones $k \in \{Zswap-0\}$ the energy of the potential node i that will be swapped there is:

$$E(i,k) = Stt(i,j0) + \sum_{j=1}^{j=|Zneigh|}[Stt(i,j)| j \in Zneigh(k)] \qquad (6)$$

With j0 we note the node that will be swapped to the central position after the swapping process. As we observe the first term of this equation $Stt(i,j0)$ is independent from the position k and it depends only in the node that will take the position of the initiator that noted position 0. If we examine these factors we will observe that there will be $|Nswap|-1$ of them and each one expresses the Stt between the node that will placed in zone 0 and each node except it that belongs to Nswap. If now we observe $E(i,0)$ we will find that it is equal with the sum of these factors as we observe from the equation 5. After this observation we have prove that by the selection of a node for the central position we determine a factor:

$$E'(i,0) = 2 * E(i,0) \qquad (7)$$

While the selection of a node for the other positions k determines a factor:

$$E'(i,k) = \sum_{j=1}^{j=|Zneigh|}[Stt(i,j)|j \in Zneigh(k)] \qquad (8)$$

After these calculations in order to perform the swapping process we want to minimize:

$$\sum_{i}^{|Nswap|} \sum_{j}^{|Zswap|} a(i,j) * E'(i,j) \qquad (9)$$

Where $a(i,j) \in \{0,1\}$ and for each node i and each position j holds that:

$$\sum_{j=1}^{j=|Zswap|} a(i,j) = 1 \text{ and } \sum_{i=1}^{i=|Nswap|} a(i,j) = 1 \qquad (10)$$

These are the constraints of the problem and intuitively express that each node will be placed in exactly one position and also in each position j will be placed exactly one node. As the nodes and the positions are equal this is an integer linear programming problem always feasible. After its solution for each a(i.j)=1 node i will be placed in position j. If it will moved in the central position t will take as neighbors the set {Nswap–i} and in the other positions j the set Zneigh(j) and the node that will move to the central position. This is a well know problem of linear programming and we refer to [20] for its solution.

There is an analytical proof that our algorithm converges but due to the restricted space we just describe that each time that the algorithm is executed to a neighborhood the energy of this neighborhood is reduced and so the total energy of the system. As a result of this property and the fact that the total energy is a positive number the whole system will converge to an assignment between nodes and positions will the low total energy and as we observe for our simulations it converges to a very attractive suboptimal.

## 3  P2P Live Streaming Systems

Without loss of generality we assume that in a P2P streaming system there is a boot-strap node which is used for the entrance of the nodes in the system while it acts as a source for providing the video stream. Furthermore, the video stream is divided into blocks. The block size depends on the service rate, say $\mu$ (measured in bps that the video playback requires), and the number of blocks in which the bootstrap node divides one second of video. We define this number as $N_b$ *blocks/sec* representing also the frequency of new blocks generated by the source. So each block is generated every $1/N_b$ *seconds* at the bootstrap node, with a size equal to $L_b=\mu/N_b$ *bits*.

Every block is also associated with a time stamp indicating the time of its generation. All peers reproduce (play) the video with a delay called *set-up* time which we denote it as $t_s$. As mentioned previously, setup time is the time that elapses from the generation of a block at the source until its distribution (propagation) to every node in the P2P system. Accordingly, at every time instant every peer plays the block that was generated $t_s$ times before in the origin server, provided of course that this block has eventually reached its destination.

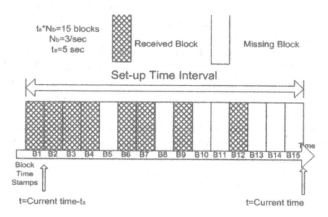

**Fig. 4.** Snapshot of a buffer in a node with the states of the blocks

During this setup time a number of blocks have been generated, equal to $N_b*t_s$, the first of which will be played by every node after $t_s$ seconds. Therefore, at every instant every node is required to keep track of all $N_b*t_s$ blocks generated within a sliding window of $t_s$ seconds. For this reason every node maintains a buffer of size $N_b*t_s$ that holds the state of these blocks. Two states are of interest: received blocks and missing blocks (not delivered yet). Figure 4 provides a snapshot of the states of blocks of a buffer in a node.

More specifically, each node upon reception of a new block, propagates this information to all of its neighbors. Therefore, every time that a node wants to transmit a new block knows the blocks that it has and the blocks that their neighbors have. A scheduler, described in [2], proposes the transmission of a block to the neighbor that misses the largest number of blocks among those that the transmitting node has. According to it, each node i has to decide which neighbor j must serve first, by calculating the difference(i,j) of the blocks that each neighbor j misses and are present in node i. The node with the largest difference is the one selected for block transmission while ties are resolved arbitrarily. Finally, the block to be transmitted is selected randomly with a uniform distribution.

## 4  Evaluation

For the evaluation of our P2P streaming system we have used OPNET Modeler [24] in order to avoid the imperfections of a custom made simulator. We have tested our proposed system under various underlying network topologies. Here we present its performance based on a topology from [5], where the provided round trip time measurements were gathered using the King method between globally distributed DNS servers. We have opted for this particular real data set in order a) to avoid inaccurate conclusions which a network model may introduce, and b) to use a real topology of globally distributed nodes and so have a fair benchmark for a locality aware overlay. In the rest of this section we present a system with 2000 nodes.

Before examining our system and its performance in live streaming, we present the results that show the cumulative density function of the number of neighbors that each node has for a random mesh and for our overlay. As we observe in Figure 5 our overlay is more balanced than a mesh although the nodes are placed according to their position in the underlying network. At this point we want to clarify that we don't claim that nodes have similar zone sizes (ex. In network regions with high density of nodes the zones of LCAN may be smaller) as we don't want to use L-CAN as a DHT in order to store keys in it. In contrast we want to have a balanced overlay in terms of the neighbors that each node has. We achieve this goal due to our placement algorithm as described earlier.

Now in Figure 6 we demonstrate the performance of our overlay in live streaming compared with the performance of a randomly created mesh. We examine two scenarios: a) all the participating nodes have homogeneous upload capacities, and b) the upload capacities of the nodes conform to those in [3] that have been collected from users of a real P2P system and they are heterogeneous.

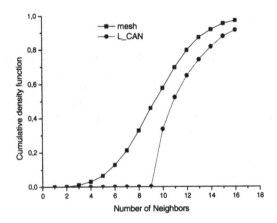

**Fig. 5.** Cumulative density function of the number of neighbors that each node has in a random mesh (black line) and in L-CAN (red line)

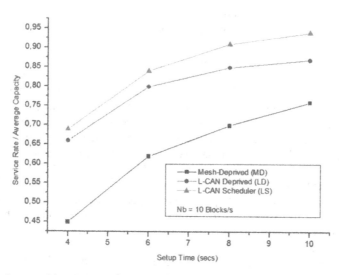

**Fig. 6a.** Maximum achievable service rate (as a percentile of the average upload bandwidth) of each system under various setup time intervals. Nodes contribute equal upload bandwidths.

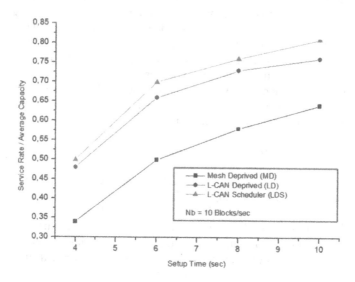

**Fig. 6b.** Maximum achievable service rate (as a percentile of the average upload bandwidth) of each system under various setup time intervals. Nodes contribute heterogenous upload bandwidths.

Based on these two scenarios we have evaluated three different systems. The first system, denoted as MD, is a mesh overlay where each node has 10 neighbors, while the exchange of blocks among nodes is performed according to the most deprived node scheduler [2] as described earlier. The second system, denoted as LD, uses the same scheduler as MD, but it relies on our topology aware overlay L-CAN with

5-dimensions (each node has approximately 10 neighbors) which replaces the mesh overlay. In the third system, denoted as LS, we have maintained the L-CAN overlay and we have substituted the scheduler in MD with our own.

This new scheduler we propose, though simple, exploits in its logic the existence of a locality aware overlay and in particular every node's likely network position reflected in the L-CAN. According to it, each node keeps an incremental list of its neighbors according to STT between them. The probability with which each one of its neighbor is selected for a block transmission is proportional to its rank in the list. Figure 6 shows the ratio between the maximum achievable service rate that each system can deliver and the average upload bandwidth of the participating nodes, for various setup time values given a constant rate for block generation ($N_b$=10 blocks/sec). For the first graph we have used homogenous upload capacities whereas the later is based on heterogeneous. Inspecting the two graphs in figure 6, we observe that the same performance trend emerges from either case i.e. homogeneous and heterogeneous upload capacities. Furthermore, all systems perform slightly worst in case of heterogeneous upload capacities.

As predicted by our analysis applying a locality aware overlay, L-CAN, results in a significant increase in the achievable service rate (LD), as opposed to a mesh overlay (MD), because of the smaller STT values that exist between the neighbors in L-CAN. Further improvement especially for not very small set-up time values is obtained when we apply our scheduler in (LDS) as we see observe from the blue line in figure 6.

Finally, the control overhead of our scheduler is trivial. Every time that a node receives a new block it sends to all of its neighbors a control packet with the contents of its buffer. The frequency of this transmission is equal to $N_b$ by the definition of the scheduler. Additionally the size of the buffer is $t_s*N_b$ and is modeled with one bit of information for each block (ex. One for its presence and zero for its absence). So the control bandwidth that is consumed in each node in order to update the other nodes for the new block arrivals is approximated by:

$$C.B.=(Header\_size+t_s*N_b)*N_b*Number\_of\_neigh$$

where Header_size+$t_s*N_b$ is the size of each control packet Nb is the frequency that this is transmitted and Number_of_neigh is the number of neighbors in which the control packets are send. By the value of $N_b$=10 blocks/sec as, $t_s$=5sec and Number_of_neigh=10 the control bandwidth that consumed in each node is has a value around 30 kbps and its independent from the upload capacities. This means that with higher upload capacities of peers the overhead that is consumed from the buffer exchange lowers as a percentage of the upload bandwidth.

## 5  Conclusions and Future Work

As we have observed though our evaluation L-CAN greatly improves the set-up time and the bandwidth utilization in live streaming. Additionally combined with our previous work in [22] enables locality in CAN and the whole system can be used in other applications such as multi-attribute range queries. Furthermore we will modify and apply our algorithms in other overlays in order two evaluate them in these.

In live streaming our future work is focused in two major areas. The first is the creation of a sophisticated scheduler that exploits locality and the information that is infused in any node during the buffer exchanges by selecting the appropriate block for transmission and not only the appropriate node. The second is the selection of the appropriate number of neighbors and the adjustment of the block size in order to further improve the performance of our system. At last we plan to evaluate our system in dynamic network conditions to demonstrate its adaptive behavior.

# References

1. Ratnasamy, S., Francis, P., Handley, M., Karp, R., Shenker, S.: A Scalable Content-Addressable Network. In: ACM Sigcomm, San Diego (2001)
2. Massoulie, L., Twigg, A., Gkantsidis, C., Rodriguez, P.: Randomized decentralized broadcasting algorithms. In: 26th IEEE International Conference on Computer Communications (INFOCOM), pp. 1073–1081. IEEE Press, Anchorage (2007)
3. Bharambe, A., Herley, C., Padmanabhan, V.: Analyzing and improving bittorrent performance, Technical Report, Microsoft Research (2005)
4. Castro, M., Druschel, P., Kermarrec, A.M., Nandi, A.: Antony Rowstron, Atul Singh, SplitStream: High-Bandwidth Multicast in Cooperative Environments. In: SOSP, New York (2003)
5. Meridian, A.: Lightweight Approach to Network Positioning,
   http://www.cs.cornell.edu/People/egs/meridian/data.php
6. MIT Parallel and Distributed Operating Systerms Group,
   http://pdos.csail.mit.edu/P2Psim/kingdata/
7. Ng, T.E., Zhang, H.: A network positioning system for the Internet. In: USENIX Conference, Boston (2004)
8. Castro, M., Druschel, P., Hu, Y.C., Rowstron, A.: Exploiting network proximity in distributed hash tables. In: International Workshop on Future Directions in Distributed Computing (FuDiCo), Bologna (2002)
9. Stoica, I., Morris, R., Liben-Nowell, D., David, R., Karger, M., Kaashoek, F., Frank Dabek, F., Balakrishnan, H.: A Scalable Peer-to-Peer Lookup Protocol for Internet Applications. IEEE/ACM Transactions on Networking 11(1), 17–32 (2003)
10. Rowstron, A., Druschel, P.: Pastry: Scalable, Distributed Object Location and Routing for Large-scale Peer-to-peer Systems. In: Guerraoui, R. (ed.) Middleware 2001. LNCS, vol. 2218, pp. 329–350. Springer, Heidelberg (2001)
11. Gkantsidis, C., Rodriguez, P.: Network coding for large scale content distribution. In: 24th Annual Joint Conference of the IEEE Computer and Communications Societies. Proceedings (INFOCOM), pp. 2235–2245. IEEE Press, Miami (2005)
12. Kumar, R., Liu, Y., Ross, K.W.: Stochastic Fluid Theory for P2P Streaming Systems. In: 26th IEEE International Conference on Computer Communications (INFOCOM), pp. 919–927. IEEE Press, Anchorage (2007)
13. Zhang, X., Liu, J., Li, B., Yum, T.-S.P.: CoolStreaming: A Datadriven Overlay Network for Peer-to-Peer Live Media Streaming. In: 24th Annual Joint Conference of the IEEE Computer and Communications Societies. Proceedings (INFOCOM), pp. 2102–2111. IEEE Press, Miami (2005)
14. Castro, M., Druschel, P., Hu, Y.C., Rowstron, A.: Exploiting network proximity in distributed hash tables. In: International Workshop on Future Directions in Distributed Computing (FuDiCo), Bologna (2002)

15. PPLive, http://www.pplive.com
16. Wong, B., Slivkins, A., Sirer, E.G.: Meridian: A Lightweight Network Location Service without Virtual Coordinates. In Proceedings of ACM SIGCOMM, Philadelphia (2005)
17. Magharei, N., Rejaie, R., Guo, Y.: Mesh or Multiple-Tree: A Comparative Study of Live P2P Streaming Approaches. In: 26th IEEE International Conference on Computer Communications (INFOCOM), pp. 1424–1432. IEEE Press, Anchorage (2007)
18. Hei, X., Liang, C., Liang, J., Liu, Y., Ross, K.W.: A Measurement Study of a Large-Scale P2P IPTV System. IEEE Transactions on Multimedia 9(8), 1672–1687 (2006)
19. Magharei, N., Rejaie, R.: PRIME: Peer-to-Peer Receiver-drIven MEsh-based Streaming. In: 26th IEEE International Conference on Computer Communications (INFOCOM), pp. 1415–1423. IEEE Press, Anchorage (2007)
20. Dimirti, P.: Bertskeas, Network Optimization: Continuous and Discrete Models. Athena Scientific (1998)
21. Pietzuch, P., Ledlie, J., Seltzer, M.: Supporting Network Coordinates on PlanetLab. In: Proceedings of WORLDS (2005)
22. Efthymiopoulos, N., Christakidis, A., Denazis, S., Koufopavlou, O.: Enabling locality in a balanced peer-to-peer overlay. In: IEEE Global Telecommunications Conference (GLOBECOM), San Fransisco, pp. 1–5 (2006)
23. Hei, X., Liu, Y., Ross, K.W.: Inferring Network-Wide Quality in P2P Live Streaming Systems, Technical Report (2006), http://eeweb.poly.edu/faculty/yongliu
24. Opnet Technologies, http://www.opnet.com

# ACME: An Automated Tool for Generating and Evaluating the Quality of VoIP Calls

Leandro C.G. Lustosa, André A.D.P. Souza, Paulo H. de A. Rodrigues, and Douglas G. Quinellato

Laboratório de Voz Sobre IP – Núcleo de Computação Eletrônica
Universidade Federal do Rio de Janeiro (NCE/UFRJ)*
Caixa Postal 2324 – 20001-970 – Rio de Janeiro – RJ – Brasil
leandro@instant.com.br, {andreabrantes,aguiar}@nce.ufrj.br,
douglas@las.ic.unicamp.br

**Abstract.** ACME, an automated tool for generating and evaluating the quality of VoIP calls, is presented. ACME examines the availability of bandwidth and processing capacity to determine the largest number of simultaneous calls that a node can operate in a given topology, besides supporting pre-programmed schedule of VoIP experiments. Demos of ACME usage as a capacity estimation tool and as an instrument for monitoring of an IP telephony production service show its effectiveness and versatility.

**Keywords:** monitoring tool, VoIP call generation, capacity determination.

## 1 Introduction

ACME (Automatic Call Measurement Environment) is a tool capable of performing two basic activities: generation of VoIP calls and measurement of the quality of the generated calls. The tool uses the potential of these two activities to build an automated environment supporting two classes of experiments. The first class, called stress experiment, is primarily used for determining the ability (in number of simultaneous calls) that a medium (wired or wireless) or VoIP system (service or set of servers) can support without compromising voice quality below a previously established level. The second class, called periodic experiment, is used to check the change in call quality over time, even allowing VoIP service availability monitoring.

ACME development was based on a voice quality evaluation infrastructure proposed by [13] which assumes that VoIP clients (IP phones or gateways) are able to assess the quality of the incoming voice flow and provide a specific call detailed record named VQCDR (Voice Quality Call Detail Record) . VQCDR contains several voice quality indicators, besides parameters for call and involved terminals identification. Additionally, it may include a report with the history of quality indicators status

---

* Partially funded by the Brazilian National Education and Research Network (RNP). Paulo Rodrigues is also a professor at DCC/UFRJ. Douglas Quinellato is a member of LASS at IC/UNICAMP. Leandro Lustosa is presently at Instant Solutions (www.instant.com.br).

G. Pavlou, T. Ahmed, and T. Dagiuklas (Eds.): MMNS 2008, LNCS 5274, pp. 91–103, 2008.

throughout the call. VQCDR quality indicators are computed according to the E-Model and its extensions [9, 6, 7].

Voice degradation can be caused by several factors [12] such as network packet losses, losses due to late arrival in jitter compensation buffer, extreme large end-to-end round trip delay (influencing interactivity), factors related to codec (inherent quantization errors, robustness to single or multiple losses, loss compensating algorithms, voice activity detectors, etc), among others. E-model output is a scalar factor R, which can be correlated to MOS (Mean Opinion Score) [10]. MOS is a voice quality score representing the average opinion of a group of unbiased testing listeners and varies from 1 (poor) to 5 (excellent).

E-model computation and MOS determination is performed by a library called VQuality (Voice Quality Library) [14]. VQuality was developed in C + + and has been integrated to IP clients to enable VQCDR generation. The use of VQCDR allows ACME to analyze a call in detail and plot timely graphics of results.

Evaluating a system or transmission technology for voice capacity is a more complex task than the evaluation of a simple call. To determine the capacity of a link in carrying good quality VoIP calls, for example, several rounds of calls are needed. ACME uses an automatic mechanism for dynamic call generation and achieves an estimate of VoIP call capacity when overall MOS for the increasing number of simultaneous calls falls below an acceptable level. Sizes of confidence intervals are used as stopping times for the call generation process.

Several commercial tools enable the evaluation of VoIP call quality [17, 5, 2, 16], but none can be found that enables automatic capacity determination of links and servers. With the cited tools it is possible to get somehow the capacity of a medium, but it would require that all calculations and call executions be carried out manually, what would be laborious and prone to human error when large numbers are involved.

This paper is organized into eight sections. In Section 2, the infrastructure and architecture for evaluation of VoIP calls is described. In Section 3, the architecture of ACME and its components are presented. In Sections 4 and 5, the concepts of stress and periodic experiments are discussed. Section 6 shows how experiments are carried out concurrently. In Section 7, the use of ACME is demonstrated and, finally, Section 8 presents the conclusions and future work

## 2   Architecture for Evaluating VoIP Calls

According to the architecture proposed in [13], VQCDRs are collected by an entity called VQCDR Server, which is in charge of interpreting, authenticating and forwarding VQCDRs to a data base storage. The VQCDR server has three modules:

*Collector Module (CM)*: responsible for collecting and interpreting the VQCDR, besides acting on the Authenticator Module (AM) and the Storage Module (SM).

*Authenticator Module (AM)*: responsible for validating VQCDRs received by CM. For testing and measurements in basic experiments or controlled environments, VQCDR server offers a simple access list based on IP addresses. However, in production environments, where a more sophisticated and flexible validation mechanism is required, the AM module is the solution.

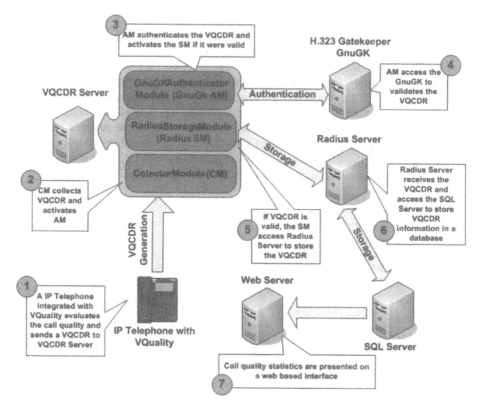

**Fig. 1.** UFRJ VoIP Call Quality Evaluation Architecture

*Storage Module (SM):* responsible for storing VQCDRs collected by CM. The storage can be deployed in a SQL data base or Radius Server.

Fig. 1 illustrates general operation of the architecture: At the end of a call, an IP phone integrated to VQuality evaluates the received voice quality and then generates a VQCDR, which contains voice quality indicators and call identifiers (Fig. 1-1). The CM module of the VQCDR Server collects the VQCDR (Fig. 1-2) and instructs the AM module to check its legitimacy (Fig. 1-3). In case of H.323 architecture using GnuGK [8], authentication is performed by a specific module (Fig. 1-4). If VQCDR validation is successful, module SM is instructed to store the VQCDR. When using RADIUS, VQCDR is sent to a RADIUS Server (Fig.1-5). The RADIUS server stores VQCDR data in a database, for example an SQL server (Fig. 1-6). A Web interface then allows displaying graphics and statistics reports (Fig. 1-7). ACME uses the whole VQCDR collecting architecture and adds new elements described in section 3.

# 3   ACME Architecture

ACME has a master-slave type architecture. A central element called ACME Master (or simply master) coordinates a series of peripheral ACME Slaves (or simply slaves), instructing them to initiate (said an active slave) or get ready to receive calls (said a passive slave). An active slave can start a call to a non slave destiny as an IP phone to check VoIP system availability and operational status.

A passive slave has two elements: a VoIP client softphone (VC) with VQuality integration, and an interpreter for interacting with the master through the ACMEp protocol (to be described in section 3.2). It is expected a slave being able to generate multiple simultaneous calls. However, slave hardware has limited memory and processing power what limits the maximum number of calls that can be generated without impairing voice quality, which is named slave capacity. Over a threshold, longer delays are incurred in the coding/decoding process and discards in jitter buffers start to happen. How to determine a slave capacity is addressed in section 3.1.

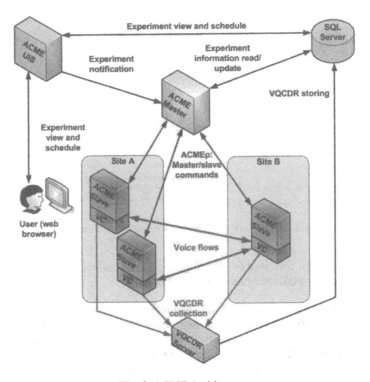

**Fig. 2.** ACME Architecture

To determine the capacity of a system or slow speed communication link, at least one active and one passive slave are needed. The site concept allows using a set of slaves of inferior hardware to generate a larger number of simultaneous calls to stress a superior hardware system or a very high speed link. Experiments are always realized between two sites hosting one or more slaves.

ACME has a Web interface running in an HTTP server called User Interface Server (UIS), allowing user to schedule experiments and visualization of outputs.

ACME architecture and its components are shown in Fig. 2. When a user schedules a new experiment via Web interface, the experiment data is stored in an SQL database

(PostgreSQL is used) and the master is informed that a new experiment has been filed. When starting the experiment at the programmed time, the master reads experiment configuration parameters and orders slaves in the two sites involved in the action to perform calls and collect VQCDRs.

UIS enables the user to receive via e-mail status reports about its experiment, when certain events occur: an error is detected; there is an unreachable slave; or measured voice quality is in an alarming level, possibly indicating that a system being monitored by a periodic experiment (fired in pre-scheduled times) is in critical condition.

ACME core was developed in C++ and UIS in PHP. ACME is aimed toward Linux, but any other Unix systems may be used. Voice streams are prerecorded and have three minute duration, long enough for detecting voice degradation in all situations. Nevertheless, prerecorded messages of any length can be used.

## 3.1 Slave Capacity Determination

Stress experiments must be performed to determine slave capacity and avoid getting imprecise results. In capacity determination, the number of simultaneous calls is gradually increased while call quality is kept at maximum optimal value. The stopping condition is the start of call degradation. There are three possible scenarios: *two slaves with equivalent computational power hardware* - quality degradation occurs symmetrically, and capacity is valid for both slaves; *one superior slave and one inferior slave* - quality degradation occurs asymmetrically and only the inferior slave capacity is determined; *one slave S with much superior capacity and a set of slaves with overall capacity higher than S* - degradation occurs asymmetrically and only S has its capacity determined. In capacity determination experiments, available network bandwidth has to be enough to force slave hardware to be the limiting factor.

## 3.2 ACMEp Protocol

ACMEp is the protocol used in the communication between master and slave. Master commands passive slaves to get them ready to receive a certain number of calls, or order active slaves to start calls to specific destinations. In this process, call configuration data is also informed: codec, duration and destination (IP address and port, E.164 number or user alias). Master can also instruct slave to register in a specific server, making it possible to test a server or an environment associated to a server. In this last case, server address and account/password for registration are also passed to the slave. The protocol has only three messages:

*Start:* From master to slave. It commands slave to get ready for receiving calls, initiating calls or registering to a server.

*Status:* From slave to master. It allows a slave to inform its master if a call was successful or not. Passive slaves also use status message to inform when they are ready to receive calls.

*Cancel:* From master to slave. It allows a passive slave to inform that an active slave call is canceled. Basically, *Cancel* cancels a *Start* message previously sent.

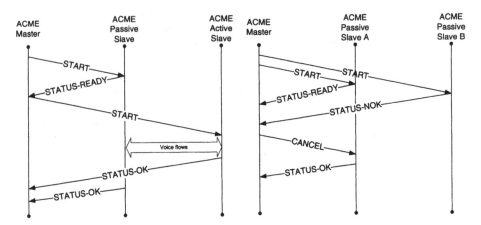

**Fig. 3.** Successful slave to slave exchange      **Fig. 4.** Failed slave to slave exchange

Fig. 3 shows an experiment between two slaves. Master commands passive slave to get ready to receive calls (START). Passive slave informs master it is ready to receive calls (STATUS-READY, STATUS message with ready indicator). Master commands active slave to start calls (START). Calls are established and media flows start. If everything goes right, both slaves send to master a STATUS with an OK indicator, otherwise a STATUS with NOK (NOT OK) indicator is sent. It is important to mention that if any call fails, the whole experiment fails and must be restarted, because it is essential that the correct number of simultaneous calls is executed.

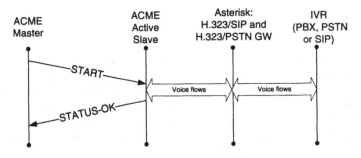

**Fig. 5.** Slave to gateway

Fig. 4 also shows an experiment between two slaves. However, in this example an error occurs in the active slave: Master commands passive slave to get ready to receive calls (START). Passive slave informs master it is ready to receive calls (STATUS-READY). Master commands active slave to start calls (START), but, for some reason, active slave cannot initiate calls and send master a STATUS-NOK. Master then sends CANCEL to passive slave, informing that for some reason slave will not get the calls it was waiting for.

Fig.5 shows an experiment between an active slave and a gateway. The gateway can forward calls to PBX or PSTN. In this case, master just needs to send START to the active slave and wait for a STATUS-OK. This operation is useful when monitoring gateway availability and its capability to establish calls to a certain network or destination.

ACMEp runs over TCP and uses port 8000 by default (configurable). No cryptography is available, but security aspects are being considered for the future. To avoid a non authorized master to command a slave, access lists can be configured in each slave. However, the START message is critical, since it carries a non ciphered password. TLS [4] must be used for secure operations.

# 4 Stress Experiments

The goal of a stress experiment is capacity determination of a target. Capacity is the number of concurrent VoIP calls that can be performed (using a specific codec, e.g., G.711), without getting the average MOS (see section 1) over all calls to fall below a minimum value. Target can be a link, a network, a system or even a VoIP service.

Slave capacity determination evaluates hardware via a stress experiment which demands that the average MOS is not less than the maximum MOS in ideal conditions. It is important to say that the maximum MOS depends on type of codec. For example, G.711 reaches a 4.41 maximum MOS score.

A stress experiment is made of tests. Each test has a certain number of concurrent calls. So, if test 1 which handles N simultaneous calls obtains an average MOS equal or above the established average MOS, a new test, test 2, is executed. Test 2 on its hand will handle N + X simultaneous calls. If test 2 reaches equal or better result compared to the established average MOS, a new test (test 3) is performed now with N + X + X simultaneous calls. And so on. The initial number N of concurrent calls and the number X of calls increment are configurable parameters.

When the user configures a required average MOS for an experiment, he also configures a target percentage, as, e.g., 10%, to be greater or equal the size of the confidence interval divided by the center value of the interval. Any test is required to achieve a confidence interval of size equal or less than the target percentage of the center of the interval. The center of the confidence interval is the average MOS estimator.

To reach the target confidence interval, a test has to be repeated many times. Each repetition is called a round and may require a minimum number of rounds per test, before considering the restriction on the size of the confidence interval. This procedure avoids situations where a few number of rounds with similar MOS values gives an average which satisfies the target percentage but does not guarantee MOS convergence indeed. It is important to say that the average MOS and associated confidence interval at each round is calculated over the MOS values of all calls of all rounds (current and previous) of a test.

Table 1 shows the structure of an experiment. Three tests are presented, where test 1 (with three concurrent calls) is expanded to show details of the executed rounds. The target percentage for this test is 10%. It can be noted that the target percentage is met after five rounds, when the size of the interval is 0.32 and the average MOS is

**Table 1.** Experiment structure

| |
|---|
| **Test 1 → 3 concurrent calls** |
| • *Round 1 – average MOS = 4.10, conf. int. size = 0.81, target = 0.41 (10%)* |
| • *Round 2 – average MOS = 4.03, conf. int. size = 0.71, target = 0.40 (10%)* |
| • *Round 3 – average MOS = 4.08, conf. int. size = 0.58, target = 0.41 (10%)* |
| • *Round 4 – average MOS = 4.07 conf. int. size = 0.42, target = 0.41 (10%)* |
| • *Round 5 – average MOS = 4.08 conf. int. size = 0.32, target = 0.41 (10%)* |
| **Test 2 → 4 concurrent calls** |
| **Test 3 → 5 concurrent calls** |

4.08. Round 5 gives a percentage around 8% (0.32/4.08), which is less than 10%. Round 4 gives a percentage that is slightly greater than 10%. After test 1 reaches the target percentage, test 2 with 4 concurrent calls is started.

## 5  Periodic Experiments

There are three basic types of periodic experiments:

*Availability Experiment*: In regular time intervals, a destination is called to monitor its reachability and availability. Presently, only H.323 protocol is directed by ACME, but using a gateway H.323/SIP allows monitoring of SIP destinations. Similarly, a voice gateway allows monitoring a PBX system and PSTN destinations reached through the PBX. In this kind of experiment, destinations are answering machine or IVR (*Interactive Voice Response*), as calls are answered automatically on these systems.

*Quality Experiment:* By default, all availability experiments also evaluate the received call quality. The difference with quality experiments is that alerts can be set. Then, as MOS values are obtained below a certain level, the user is notified. Availability and authentication experiments only emit alert in case of error.

*Authentication Experiment*: In regular time intervals, a slave tries to authenticate in a given server to monitor the correctness of the authentication operation. At present, only H.323 is supported.

## 6  Concurrency of Experiments

Slaves are experiment resources. After registered in ACME, slaves can be included in sites and be used by any experiment. Slaves can be included in more than one site at the same time, but the sites of an experiment cannot share the same slave.

A test is the granularity in experiment concurrency. Thus, two experiments A and B can be executed concurrently and have slaves and even sites in common. However, tests never occur simultaneously, as ACME executes one test at a time.

Fig. 6 shows the finite state machine (FSM) for a quality periodic experiment. When the experiment is scheduled, it enters the Scheduled state and remains in this state until the programmed starting time is reached and there is not other experiment ahead waiting for execution. When the first test starts execution, FSM changes to Running. At the end of a test, Ready-OK state is entered, in case the MOS is above the required value. If MOS is below required value, the state Ready – Low MOS is entered. Another possibility is the test not finishing because of an error. If an expected error occurs, as destination unreachability, the FSM enters Ready- Can't connect to host, or another state which represents a defined error. If an undefined and irreversible error occurs, Undefined error state is entered. The state of an experiment always returns to Running when a next test is run. Although, Undefined error state does not allows transition out of the state.

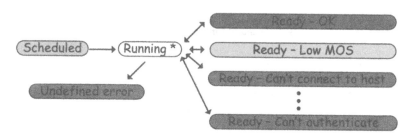

**Fig. 6.** Finite State Machine for a Quality Experiment

All experiments have similar state machines. A periodic experiment only ends if its FSM enters Undefined error. On the other hand, stress experiments end when the required target MOS is reached, when available slaves are unable to support more increment in the number of calls, or, finally, when slave goes to Undefined error.

Experiment execution is performed as a kind of circular round-robin scheme. Two lists for experiments in Ready state are kept, one for periodic and another for stress experiments. The scheduler (ACME module for concurrency management) always dispatches the next experiment in the periodic experiment ready list. If this list is empty, next experiment in the stress experiment ready list is taken. Periodic experiments are prioritized because they have time constraints.

## 7 Demonstrations

Fig. 7 shows a 500 kbps serial PPP link interconnecting two Cisco routers (not pictured) for the stress experiment. UDP generator [11] was configured to generate 200 kbps constant rate large packet background traffic towards the reflector. Slaves 1 and 2 send G.711 VoIP media packets marked with DSCP EF [1], generating around 80 kbps at the link level per call. Two router queue disciplines were tested: WFQ (weighed fair queue); and a 320 kbps guaranteed rate priority queue (PQ) [3] for voice flow.

Fig. 8 shows the stress experiment output. The target percentage for confidence interval was set at 10%. Confidence intervals are automatically plotted. With PQ, up to 4 concurrent calls cause no degradation and MOS is maintained at 4.41 (maximum value for G.711). From the fifth simultaneous call on, as PQ only supports four calls

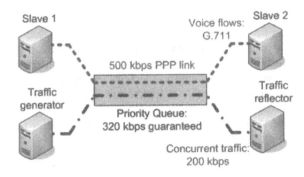

**Fig. 7.** Scenario for Stress Experiment

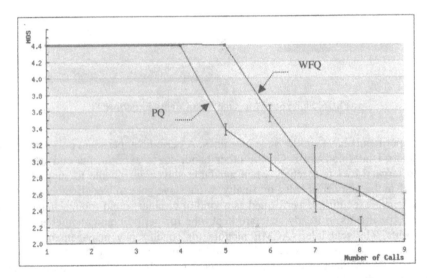

**Fig. 8.** Stress Experiment Output. The vertical axis represents the average MOS and the horizontal axis is the number of simultaneous calls per test.

with no degradation, MOS degrades abruptly and confidence intervals also increases, indicating variability in call quality. If minimum acceptable MOS is 3.0, the maximum number of simultaneous VoIP calls should be 5 with PQ. On the other hand, when a WFQ queue is used, up to 6 simultaneous calls can be accepted. WFQ inherently prioritizes small packets (like voice) over large packets. However, large confidence intervals with increasing number of calls show that MOS begins to vary randomly among voice calls.

The fone@RNP VoIP service [15] was used as a scenario for periodic experiments. Fone@RNP uses a heterogeneous H.323 and SIP architecture which, besides interconnecting academic institutions PBXs, it allows IP softphone usage and PSTN interconnection. The objective of the demo was to monitor the service at a local institution (UFRJ) and fictitious institution established in the same manner as a real institution (called Institution 1). As shown in Fig. 9, each monitored institution represents a site and has a local slave. The central slave in the figure represents a third site that will interact with the other two sites. According to fone@RNP, each institution has a gate-keeper to attend H.323 clients, an OpenSER proxy for SIP clients registration, and a gateway Asterisk for H.323/SIP interoperability and PBX interconnection. Six peri-odic experiments were designed for each institution:

*SIP Phone*: Monitors SIP service availability via regular calls from central slave to
    SIP softphone with auto-answer. Local gateway converts from H.323 to SIP.
*H.323 Phone*: Monitors H.323 service availability via regular calls to local slave;
*PBX Phone*: Monitors call routing to PBX via regular calls from central slave to an
    IVR PBX extension PBX;

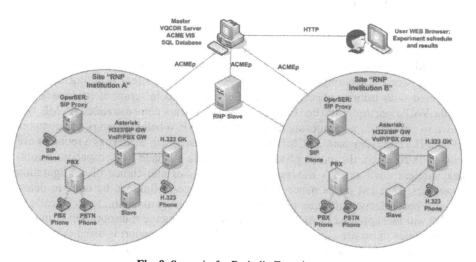

**Fig. 9.** Scenario for Periodic Experiments

| Group | Experiment | Type | Status | |
|-------|-----------|------|--------|---|
| *Institution 1* | SIP Phone | availability | Ready - Ok | Delete |
| | H.323 Phone | availability | Ready - Ok | Delete |
| | PBX Phone | availability | Ready - Can't complete call | Delete |
| | PSTN Phone | availability | Ready - Can't complete call | Delete |
| | H.323 Authentication | authentication | Ready - Ok | Delete |
| | Voice Quality | quality | Ready - Low MOS (2.30) | Delete |
| *UFRJ* | SIP Phone | availability | Ready - Ok | Delete |
| | H.323 Phone | availability | Ready - Ok | Delete |
| | PBX Phone | availability | Ready - Ok | Delete |
| | PSTN Phone | availability | Ready - Ok | Delete |
| | H.323 Authentication | authentication | Ready - Ok | Delete |
| | Voice Quality | quality | Ready - Ok (4.41) | Delete |

**Fig. 10.** ACME Monitoring Panel

*PSTN Phone*: Monitors PSTN routing via regular calls from central slave to an 800 IVR service;

*H.323 Authentication*: Monitors H.323 authentication via periodic authentications of local slave to the gatekeeper;

*Quality*: Monitors quality of periodic calls between central and local slaves.

Fig. 10 shows ACME monitoring panel: experiments with positive status are shown in green; experiments with problems are shown in red, indicating failure; experiments in critical condition, as with MOS below some acceptable level, are in yellow. Panel configuration allows yellow and red indicators to trigger alerts via e-mail.

## 8  Conclusions and Future Work

An automated tool for the generation and quality evaluation of VoIP calls is presented and its effectiveness and versatility are demonstrated in real environments. Dynamic automated experiment execution and graphics output with confidence intervals is an advantage when comparing to other tools. As a demo of stress experiment, a link configured with priority queuing and WFQ is analyzed in terms of its capacity to handle VoIP concurrent traffic. For periodic experiments demonstration, ACME was shown to perform as a monitoring tool for fone@RNP, a heterogeneous and complex SIP and H.323 environment. ACME has also been used with success as a tool in VoIP courses. In research, the tool is planned to be used to evaluate VoIP capacity in complex wireless environments mixing priority disciplines and choice of configuration parameters. Detailed performance studies in slow access link can be done to determine the best selection of router parameters and disciplines to maximize VoIP calls.

TLS will be supported in ACMEp for the future, as secure transport will eliminate vulnerabilities in master-slave communication. SIP native support is being developed, what will permit SIP availability monitoring without any signaling gateway in place.

## References

1. Babiarz, J., Chan, K., Baker, F.: Configuration Guidelines for DiffServ Service Classes, IETF. RFC 4594 (2006)
2. Brix: BrixCall (December 2007), http://www.brixnet.com/products/
3. Cisco Systems: VoIP over PPP Links with Quality of Service. (access in December 2007), http://www.cisco.com/warp/public/788/voice-qos/voip-mlppp.html
4. Dierks, T., Rescorla, E.: The Transport Layer Security (TLS) Protocol Version 1.1. IETF. RFC 4346 (2006)
5. Empirix: VoIP and IMS Hammer Call Analyzer(access in December 2007), http://www.empirix.com/products-services/v-hca.asp
6. ETSI TS 101 329-5 v1.1.2: Telecommunications and Internet Protocol Harmonization Over Networks Release 3, End-to-end Quality of Service in TIPHON systems; Part 5: Quality of Service (QoS) measurement methodologies (2002)
7. ETSI TS 102 024-5 v4.1.1. (2003). Telecommunications and Internet Protocol Harmonization Over Networks Release 4, End-to-end Quality of Service in TIPHON systems; Part 5: Quality of Service (QoS) measurement methodologies.

8. GnuGK: The GNU Gatekeeper (Access in December 2007),
   http://www.gnugk.org/
9. ITU-T G.107: The E-Model, a computational model for use in transmission planning (2003)
10. ITU-T P.800: Methods for subjective determination of transmission quality (1996)
11. Leocadio, M.A.P., Rodrigues, P.H.A.: Uma Ferramenta para Geração de Tráfego e Medição em Ambiente de Alto Desempenho. In: Proceedings of XVIII. SBRC (2000)
12. Lustosa, L.C.G., Carvalho, L.S.G., Rodrigues, P.H.A., Mota, S.E.: Utilização do Modelo E para avaliação da qualidade da fala em sistemas de comunicação baseados em voz sobre IP. In: Proceedings of XXII SBRC. pp. 603–616 (2004)
13. Lustosa, L.C.G., Rodrigues, P.H.A., David, F., Quinellato, D.G.: A Voice over IP Quality Monitoring Architecture. In: Dalmau Royo, J., Hasegawa, G. (eds.) MMNS 2005. LNCS, vol. 3754, pp. 168–178. Springer, Heidelberg (2005)
14. Lustosa, L.C.G., Rodrigues, P.H.A., David, F., Quinelato, D.G.: VQuality: Uma Biblioteca Multiplataforma para Avaliação de Qualidade de Chamadas Telefônicas IP. In: Proceedings of XXIII SBRC. pp. 1185–1188 (2005)
15. RNP: fone@RNP (access in December 2007), http://www.rnp.br/voip/
16. Solarwinds: VoIP Monitor (access in December 2007), http://www.solarwinds.com
17. Telchemy: SQmon (Access in December 2007),
    http://www.telchemy.com/products.html

# Live Video Streaming Using P2P and SVC

Tsung-Chieh Lee[1], Pin-Chuan Liu[2], Woei-Luen Shyu[1], and Chen-Yih Wu[1]

[1] Industrial Technology Research Institute
Bldg. 14, 195, Sec. 4, Chung Hsing Rd., Chutung, Hsinchu, Taiwan 31040, R.O.C.
{cjlee,wlshyu,Kevin_Wu}@itri.org.tw
http://www.itri.org.tw
[2] National Tsing Hua University
101, Sec. 2, Kuang-Fu Rd., Hsinchu, Taiwan 30013, R.O.C.
flash@rtlab.cs.nthu.edu.tw
http://www.nthu.edu.tw

**Abstract.** The research of Video Streaming has often focused on the methodologies of P2P protocols, such as peer selection, network structure, group organization, etc. In addition, streaming mechanism and system deployment are significant to provide a Video Streaming service. Research in this field, however, is scant. On the other hand, the layered video codec provides scalability when environment is divergent due to different transmission rate, computational power, and so on. Recently, Scalable Video Coding (SVC), which is a layered video codec, has been standardized and caught much attention. The study is to explore how to provide Video Streaming service by employing P2P and SVC. A system architecture which involves video layering, dynamic Segment seeding and scheduling, and Segment downloading and sharing is developed. To provide high quality Live or On-demand P2P Video Streaming service, a Video Streaming system, GaiaSharp, is implemented and deployed, and the experience is shown to explain the importance of layered video codec.

**Keywords:** P2P, SVC, Video Streaming.

## 1 Introduction

With the innovation of transmission technology and improvement of hardware, services used to rely on specific devices are now available in computers; for example, composing a song is not always done in studio, because computer software helps musician accomplish their work at any place. In the mean while, new services are proposed or combined across different domains, and applications which were stand alone are connected to each other. The computer and Internet have been changing our life style rapidly. From desktop to invisible equipment, information is exchanged with our friends or transmitted to someone we do not know. Recently, Digital Home has become a hot topic, and to watch TV is major entertainment. Computers were able to convert analog signal with a TV adapter plugged and configured correctly - this is not convenient for most people. Is there any way to achieve this goal without additional requirement? Traditional

G. Pavlou, T. Ahmed, and T. Dagiuklas (Eds.): MMNS 2008, LNCS 5274, pp. 104–113, 2008.

Video Streaming protocols have been designed, but nowadays, they cannot afford the growth of users and higher video quality because of hardware overload or transmission bandwidth. P2P has been caught much attention for data delivery in large scale overlay; although P2P solves the bottleneck (e.g. the maximum concurrent connections), it brings up new issues and makes many applications re-designed. In the mean while, a standard of layered video codec, Scalable Video Coding (SVC), is published. The layered structure of video codec yields flexible quality and is configurable based on computation power, transmission bandwidth, and monitor size, etc. Different from research in P2P protocol and SVC structure, we propose a mechanism to provide a Video Streaming system by taking advantages of P2P and SVC. As P2P which is an unstable network, this article describes issues of deploying live P2P Video Streaming system and provides dynamic configuration to support better service quality.

In this article, we introduce P2P Video Streaming applications, systems, and Scalable Video Coding in Section II. In Section III, we present our work to build a Video Streaming system based on P2P and SVC. The system deployment and configuration of GaiaSharp, a live Video Streaming system we are developing, is shown in Section IV. The conclusion and future work are described in the last section.

## 2   Related Work

Peer-to-peer (P2P) overlay networks is a kind of promising architecture to scalability share files [1][2], and audio streams [3]. Recent research further focus on transmitting video streams via p2p. Those works can be divided into two categories: live and recorded. The latter one, e.g. Video-on-dement (VoD), in fact transfers video data in the form of files so existing p2p transmission mechanisms [1][2] can be applied. As any regular files, video files are first split into equal-size pieces and then uploaded to interested peers. These peers further exchange acquired pieces in parallel, known as the swarming procedure. Once enough continuous pieces from the beginning of a video file are downloaded, these pieces are appended and played [4]. However, swarming exchanges pieces randomly, rather than in sequence, and may cause long initial waiting time. To overcome this problem, pieces needed in near future should be downloaded first. Both Vlavianos et al. [5] and Shah and Paris [6] proposed similar piece selection mechanisms. The former category further integrates p2p and video streams by temporally splitting video files into chunks [7][8], e.g. each chunk contains one-second video and/or audio data. Thus, if a chunk is not downloaded in time, video playing can skip or wait for this chunk [9] and provide better user experience than the latter category. They take much effort on the mechanism of P2P protocol to improve the performance of Video Streaming. Layered encoding and multiple description coding are suitable for many applications over heterogeneous networks. SVC, a layered video codec, is an extension of H.264/MPEG-4 AVC [10]. Venkata et al. [11] present a tree-based algorithm to find out path diversity, and a framework for multiple description codec. Pierpaolo et al. [12] implement SPPM protocol, a prioritized mechanism, to construct a multicast tree with six-way handshake process. Mubashar and Toufik [13] provide smooth media streaming by peer selection methodology. Devices can partially download decodable stream based on their capabilities, such as computation power and network bandwidth. Our work is going to provide a solution for Video Streaming service, and focuses on how to make use of SVC and P2P features to deployment a streaming system. That is, our mechanism can be applied with any P2P protocol.

## 3   Proposed Mechanism

Relative to other transmission protocol, P2P network is more un-stable. In this section, in order to provide stability of Video Streaming service in an unstable environment, we present a mechanism to take advantage of P2P and SVC, and configure parameters dynamically while downloading video segments. The mechanism is divided into *Channel Server*, and *Client Engine* (Fig. 1).

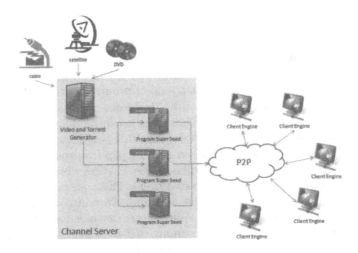

**Fig. 1.** The mechanism of Channel Server and Client Engine

### 3.1   Channel Server

In our mechanism, Channel Server receives video signal from different source, and splits signal into Segments and Crumbs with layers based on SVC information; moreover, torrents are made, scheduled and dispatched into Program Super Seed for streaming out. Figure 2 shows main modules and steps from processing video signal to share Crumbs. There may be more than one Program Super Seed to enhance sharing performance. Client Engines download Crumbs with P2P protocol from Program Super Seeds or other Client Engines. With Crumbs,

**Fig. 2.** Main modules from video signal to torrents

users watch video which is composed by SVC. The main steps and modules are shown in the following:

1) **Segment Splitter:** The video signal is received, converted, and split into Segments by GOPs (Fig. 3). According to SVC specification, a Segment is

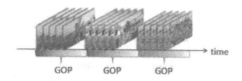

**Fig. 3.** Video is split into Segments by GOPs

organized with a Header, a Base Layer, and several Enhancement Layers [10] which is various via different video qualities (Fig. 4). Moreover, one Enhance-

**Fig. 4.** A Segment is organized according to SVC specification

ment Layer could be partitioned by SVC into dimensions. Let $v$ be the video with $n$ Segments, $s_i$ be the $i$th Segment of $v$, and for $s_i$, let $H_i$ be Header, $B_i$ be Base Layer, and $E_{il}$ be Enhancement Layer $l$ ($l$ is no more than 3 [10]), we know

$$v = \sum_{i=1}^{n} s_i = \sum_{i=1}^{n} \left( H_i + B_i + \sum_{l=1}^{3} E_{il} \right). \tag{1}$$

Different with other protocols, P2P network is an unstable environment, because the behavior of a peer to join and leave the service network in P2P environment may cause service unstable to another peer. On the other hand, buffer time is an important factor of sharing performance in P2P Video Streaming [14]. The more the buffer time is, the more delay-live the Video Streaming is, but the more served users and better streaming quality are. As a result, *dynamic amount of GOPs of a Segment* is required. Let $|G_{max}|$ and

$|G_{min}|$ be the maximum and minimum amount GOPs of a Segment respectively, and $|G_i|$ is the amount of GOPs of $s_i$, so $|G_{min}| \leq |G_i| \leq |G_{max}|$; let $\rho_i$ denotes the ratio of *successful downloading* $s_i$ among all Client Engines, and we set

$$|G_i| = \begin{cases} |G_{i-1}| + 1, \text{ if } \rho_i \text{ is greater than a threshold} \\ |G_{i-1}| - 1, \text{ else} \end{cases}$$

Based on this dynamic configuration, if $|G_i|$ is smaller, the Client Engine watches TV programs approximate live. However, the Segment which is too small causes an overhead of sharing in P2P, and that is the reason why a lower bound $|G_{min}|$ is required. In Section 3.2, we will define what *successful downloading* is.

2) **Torrent Maker:** Let the dimension of $E_{il}$ is $|E_{il}|$, and the $j$th dimension of $E_{il}$ is $e_{ilj}$, $v = \sum_{i=1}^{n} \left( H_i + B_i + \sum_{j=1}^{|E_{i1}|} e_{i1j} + \sum_{j=1}^{|E_{i2}|} e_{i2j} + \sum_{j=1}^{|E_{i3}|} e_{i3j} \right)$ is derived from Equation 1. Because the amount of Enhancement Layers is various with different video qualities, $dil$ might be 0 if Enhancement Layer $l$ does not exist. Additionally, SVC is able to compose a video segment as long as both Header and Base Layer exist, so we break borders between Enhancement Layer 1, Layer 2, and Layer 3; in other words, the Enhancement Layers are regarded as a set of dimensions of Layer 1, Layer 2, and Layer 3, and the dimension of Enhancement Layers is $|E_{i1}| + |E_{i2}| + |E_{i3}|$. Since Header and Base Layer are essential for a Segment composition, we group Header and Base Layer as an atomic element, called Crumb, and view each dimension of $E_i$ as a Crumb, too; hence, there are $1 + |E_{i1}| + |E_{i2}| + |E_{i3}|$ Crumbs for $s_i$. Let $c_{ik}$ be $k$th Crumb of $s_i$, we know

$$v = \sum_{i=1}^{n} s_i = \sum_{i=1}^{n} \left( \sum_{k=1}^{1+|E_{i1}|+|E_{i2}|+|E_{i3}|} c_{ik} \right). \tag{2}$$

We make every Crumb into a torrent. Figure 5 is an example to make Crumbs of Segment No.78, $s_{78}$, into torrents: There are 2 Enhancement Layers in $|s_{78}|$, and dimension of Enhancement Layer 1 and Enhancement Layer 2 is 3 and 5 respectively. Torrent Maker makes 9 Crumbs into 9 torrents.

3) **Program Scheduler:** Channel Server maintains a window which keeps tracks on sequence numbers of available Segments which imply the buffered Segments in Channel Server and Client Engine for P2P sharing. Let $|w|$ be the windows size, and $x$ be the sequence number of the latest Segment, the sequence numbers of available Segments range from $x - |w| + 1$ to $x$. In other words, only $s_{x-|w|+1}, s_{x-|w|+2},...,$ and $s_x$ are available live Segments. Besides, Channel Server maintains another incremental sequence number, $x'$, which is an initial index, for every Client Engine that once connects to this streaming service network. Note that it is a bad idea to set $x' = x$ in Channel Server, because every Client Engine tends to download the same Segment, and the

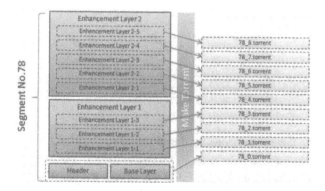

**Fig. 5.** Crumbs of Segment No.78 are made into torrents

performance of sharing cannot be obvious, but to set $x' = x - |w| + 1$ decreases successful downloading rate as well.

4) **Crumb Seeding**: Initially, only Program Super Seeds have Crumbs of Segments of video. By downloading torrents of Crumbs, Client Engines exchange information with the tracker to download and share Crumbs. After several Client Engines download successfully, the loading of Program Super Seeds is spread, and the advantage of P2P is amplified.

### 3.2   Client Engine

The idea of P2P network is sharing; on the other hand, the most important feature of live Video Streaming is timing. As a result, to setup a live P2P Video Sreaming system, which is also a timely sharing system, is going to face a trade-off between delay and efficiency of P2P. We design a schema for Client Engines to execute downloading tasks, and the schema comes up with two selection models: a) Segment Selection, and b) Crumb Selection.

a) **Segment Selection**: As mentioned in *Program Scheduler*, Channel Server maintains $x'$ for every Client Engine connecting to this service network, and $x - |w| + 1 < x' < x$. Let $|s_i|$ be the playback time interval of $s_i$. In initial stage, the Client Engine starts downloading $s_{x'}$ at time $t_{x'}$, $s_{x'}$ has to be downloaded successfully by $t_{x'} + |s_{x'}|$ to make sure the downloaded Segment is live. That is, Client Engine has $|s_{x'}|$ to download $s_{x'}$. After $t_{x'} + |s_{x'}|$, $s_{x'}$ will be expired no matter it is downloaded successfully or not, even Client Engine is sharing $s_{x'}$ with others. Note that the Segment which Client Engine is downloading is the most urgent than any other Segments, so Client Engine focuses on downloading a single Segment at a time. Two situations are separately discussed as follows:

  – If $s_{x'}$ is downloaded successfully at time $t_{x'+1}$, Client Engine starts to download $s_{x'+1}$. Because the previous Segment is downloaded successfully, Client Engine earns a *Time Extension* $t_{x'} + |s_{x'}| - t_{x'+1}$ for current

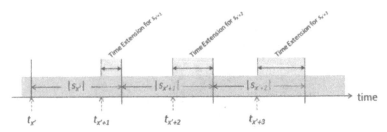

**Fig. 6.** Time Extensions for downloading $s_{x'+1}$, $s_{x'+2}$, and $s_{x'+3}$

Segment to be downloaded; that is, Client Engine has $|s_{x'+1}| + (t_{x'} + |s_{x'}| - t_{x'+1})$ to download $s_{x'+1}$, and so on for the following Segments. Figure 6 illustrates Time Extensions for downloading $s_{x'+1}$, $s_{x'+2}$, and $s_{x'+3}$. The downloading sequence number $x' + k$ keeps looking forward until it reaches $x$ which is the upper bound of available Segments. This racing behavior makes as many Client Engines synchronize Segments with Program Super Seeds as possible (Note that for a Client Engine, Segments are not always downloaded from Program Super Seeds). Therefore, more and more Client Engines which sharing the same Segments as Program Super Seeds do come up, and can be regarded as new Program Super Seeds.

- If Segment $s_i$ is not downloaded successfully at time $t_i$, the Client Engine goes back to initial stage and refresh the sequence number $x'$ from Channel Server.

b) **Crumb Selection:** In our mechanism, the definition of a *successful downloading task* is refined due to the characteristic of SVC. As mentioned in *Torrent Maker*, SVC is able to compose a video segment as long as Header and Base Layer exist; hence, if Header and Base Layer downloaded, the downloading task is *successful*. Comparing with a successful downloading task, a *complete downloading task* means all required dimensions of a Segment are downloaded. There are $1 + |E_{x'1}| + |E_{x'2}| + |E_{x'3}|$ Crumbs for Segment $s_{x'}$, and let $c_{x'1}$ denote Crumb of Header and Base Layer. For a particular Client Engine in initial stage, transmission rate between Program Super Seed is evaluated, said $\mathbb{R}$, and dimensions that are required for $s_{x'}$ are from 1 to $\mathbb{D}_{x'}$, where $\mathbb{D}_{x'}$ is the max $d$ satisfying

$$\frac{\sum_{k=1}^{d} c_{x'k}}{\mathbb{R}} \leq |s_{x'}| + TimeExtension(s_{x'}). \tag{3}$$

Any $\mathbb{D}_i$ for $s_i$ sustains $1 < \mathbb{D}_i \leq 1 + |E_{i1}| + |E_{i2}| + |E_{i3}|$. If all $\mathbb{D}_{x'}$ Crumbs are downloaded (which means *completely*), $\mathbb{D}_{x'+1}$ is set to $\mathbb{D}_{x'} + 1$; otherwise, $\mathbb{D}_{x'+1}$ is set to $\mathbb{D}_{x'} - 1$. This *dynamic dimensions* for Crumb downloading is suitable for Video Streaming in P2P network, because $\mathbb{R}$ of every Client Engine is not the same, and a Client Engine is not always in poor transmission rate, not to mention that Segment can be downloaded from any other Client

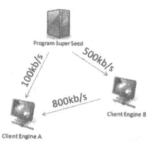

**Fig. 7.** The downloading rate of a Client Engine is not unchangeable

Engine. Figure 7 illustrates a scenario that Client Engine A tries to download two Segments $s$, and $s'$ in the same size 256KB from Program Super Seed and Client Engine B separately; theoretically, it takes 20.48 seconds for $s$, but takes only 6.656 seconds for $s'$ after Client Engine B gets $s'$.

# 4   System Deployment and Configuration

In this section, how our Video Streaming system, GaiaSharp, is deployed and configured is presented. Figure 8 is a snap shot of Client Engine of GaiaSharp, which downloads Segments and EPG (Electronic Program Guide) to provide Live or On-demand Video Streaming service.

The P2P engine of GaiaSharp is MonoTorrent, which is an open source of Mono Project [15]. We develop two systems in different video codecs: Windows

**Fig. 8.** A snap shot of Client Engine of GaiaSharp

Media Codec (without layered structure) and H.264 (with layered structure by SVC). Firstly, Channel Server generates every Segment in WMV format 640x480 resolution, 600kbps, and 29.97 fps. Every Segment size is about 20 seconds, and 1.5MB; based on [14], piece size of torrent are made in 256KB to perform better P2P sharing efficiency. The window size $|w|$ is 5, which means there are 5 Segments seeding at the same time; $x'$ is $x-3$ to act as a buffer for P2P sharing. In LAN, the video displayed smoothly and works fine, but in WAN with one Super Seed of upload bandwidth 2MB/s, it performance is unacceptable. For watching live TV, the lower bound of transmission rate between a Super Seed and a Client Engine is 600kbps which is the minimum requirement to display video without downloading any Segment failed; that is not a workable requirement for our Channel Server and most Client Engines in practice. According to the experiment result, we apply the proposed mechanism and split video into Segments in H.264 format, the resolution is 640x480, and Enhancement Layers are partitioned into 30 Crumbs; the bit rate is 128kbps for Base Layer, 512kbps for Enhancement Layer 1, 2048kbps for Enhancement Layer 2; for a Segment of 20 seconds, the Crumb of Base Layer is about 360KB, Enhancement Layer 1 is partitioned into 4 Crumbs in 320KB, and Enhancement Layer 2 is partitioned into 10 Crumbs in 512KB; we set $G_{max}$ and $G_{min}$ about 20 and 5 seconds respectively. As a result, the best quality is bettered from 600kbps to 2688kbps, and more importantly, the minimum requirement to display video is lowered from 600kbps to 144kbps which is acceptable even for ADSL clients with bandwidth in 256/64.

## 5    Conclusion

Although P2P file sharing applications have become popular, previous research seldom investigates streaming mechanism and system deployment. A Channel Server and Client Engine strategy for Live Video Streaming based on the advantages of P2P and SVC is developed. By breaking and re-organizing layers of Segments into Crumbs, a successful and complete downloading task is re-defined. Moreover, due to the un-stability of P2P network, GaiaSharp dynamically configures Segment seeding and scheduling to provide scalability for live P2P Video Streaming system. Making use of SVC, the requirement of transmission rate is much smaller than un-layered video codec. There is still much work to be done. For example, there are Channel Management algorithms to reduce the waiting time during switching and provide better user experience, and is it possible to provide Video Streaming service in HD quality?

## References

1. Saroiu, S., Gummadi, K.P., Gribble, S.D.: Measuring and analyzing the characteristics of Napster and Gnutella hosts. Multimedia Systems 9(2), 170–184 (2003)
2. Cohen, B.: Incentives build robustness in BitTorrent. In: The First Workshop on the Economics of Peer-to-Peer Systems, Berkeley (2003)
3. Baset, S.A., Schulzrinne, H.G.: An analysis of the Skype peer-to-peer Internet telephony protocol. In: IEEE INFOCOM 2006, Barcelona, Spain, pp. 1–11 (2006)

4. Dana, C., Li, D., Harrison, D., Chuah, C.-N.: BASS: BitTorrent Assisted Streaming System for Video-on-Demand. In: IEEE 7th Workshop on Multimedia Signal Processing, Shanghai, pp. 1–4 (2005)
5. Vlavianos, A., Iliofotou, M., Faloutsos, M.: BiToS: Enhancing BitTorrent for Supporting Streaming Applications. In: INFOCOM 2006, Barcelona, Spain, pp. 1–6 (2006)
6. Shah, P., Paris, J.-F.: Peer-to-Peer Multimedia Streaming Using BitTorrent. In: IPCCC 2007, New Orleans, LA, pp. 340–347 (2007)
7. Xie, S., Li, B., Keung, G.Y., Zhang, X.: Coolstreaming: Design, Theory, and Practice. IEEE Trans. on Multimedia 9(8), 1661–1671 (2007)
8. Pplive, http://www.pplive.com
9. Hei, X., Liang, C., Liang, J., Liu, Y., Ross, K.W.: A Measurement Study of a Large-Scale P2P IPTV System. IEEE Transactions on Multimedia 9(8), 1672–1687 (2007)
10. Schwarz, H., Marpe, D., Wiegand, T.: Overview of the Scalable Video Coding Extension of the H.264/AVC Standard. IEEE Transactions on Circuits and Systems for Video Technology (2007)
11. Padmanabhan, V.N., Wang, H.J., Chou, P.A.: Resilient peer-to-peer streaming. In: 11th IEEE International Conference on Network Protocols, Atlanta, USA, pp. 16–27 (2003)
12. Baccichet, P., Schierl, T., Wiegand, T., Girod, B.: Low-delay Peer-to-Peer Streaming using Scalable Video Coding. Packet Video, Lausanne, Switzerland, pp. 173–181 (2007)
13. Mushtaq, M., Ahmed, T.: Smooth Video Delivery for SVC based Media Streaming over P2P Networks. In: 5th IEEE Consumer Communications and Networking Conference, Las Vegas, NV, pp. 447–451 (2008)
14. Tewari, S., Kleinrock, L.: Analytical Model for BitTorrent-based Live Video Streaming. In: 4th IEEE Consumer Communications and Networking Conference, Las Vegas, NV, USA, pp. 976–980 (2007)
15. Mono Project, http://monotorrent.com/

# Peer-to-Peer Overlay Multicast for Scalable Audiovisual Services over Converging Wired and Wireless Networks

Ahmed Mehaoua[1], Li Fang[1], George Kormentzas[2], and Dominique Seret[1]

[1] University Paris Descartes - Faculty of Mathematics and Computer Science
45 rue des Saints Pères 75006 Paris – France
Tel.: +33 1 39 25 40 59; Fax: +33 1 39 25
{mea,fang,seret}@math-info.univ-paris5.fr
[2] National Center for Scientific Research 'Demokritos',
Institute of Informatics & Telecommunications,
15310 Aghia Paraskevi Attikis, POB 60228, Athens, Greece
gkorm@iit.demokritos.gr

**Abstract.** The deployment of scalable audiovisual multicast services over heterogeneous core and access networks is a challenging problem. In this article we propose E-Cast, an efficient, source-specific, scalable, overlay multicast system based on the peer-to-peer system Kademlia. This novel overlay multicast system enables IPTV multicast to be deployed as a service level infrastructure to overcome IP network multicast discontinuity in converging wired and wireless network domains. E-cast consists of a set of edge devices called E-Cast Service Node (ESN) and one managing device called E-Cast Service Manager (ESM). ESNs are distributed in the network and provide efficient video distribution services. They not only transport the media-streaming but also can cache the media files according to some given criteria. Performance evaluation using simulation and features comparison with existing proposals are also proposed.

**Keywords:** Overlay multicast, IPTV streaming, Peer-to-peer communication, Scalability.

## 1 Introduction

Although the concept of IP multicast was introduced in 1989 and it is now enabled in many routers, many network providers are still not willing to deploy multicast services today. The IP multicast model allows scalable and efficient multi-party communication, particularly for groups of large size. However, deployment of IP multicast in a multi-operator environment requires substantial infrastructure modifications and coordination. The advantage of overly multicast is that it is able to bypass these issues and network layer complexity. However, the performance of overlay multicast might not be as good as plain IP-based multicast. The deployment of scalable audiovisual multicast services over heterogeneous and converging core and access networks is a challenging problem.

In this article, a novel overlay multicast system, named E-cast, is proposed to enable multicast to be deployed as a service level infrastructure to overcome IP network

G. Pavlou, T. Ahmed, and T. Dagiuklas (Eds.): MMNS 2008, LNCS 5274, pp. 114–126, 2008.

multicast shortcoming. E-cast is setting up a virtual topology constructed on top of multiple network domains and involving a set of distributed application-level multicast service nodes called E-Cast Service Nodes. These E-Cast Services Nodes communicate with terminals and with each other using a set of unicast signalling and forwarding mechanisms. To ensure scalable audiovisual service operations, E-cast is based on the peer-to-peer system Kademlia, where E-cast Service nodes act as peer proxies that forward and replicate AV data packets on behalf of the senders. The data paths among E-Cast Service Nodes within an E-Cast session form a virtual multicast tree, where each tree branch is a QoS-enabled unicast connection pre-established. The association between a terminal and its delegated E-Cast Service Node for a particular multicast service request is decided by an E-Cast Service Manager and based on pre-defined policies.

The reminder of the paper is as follows: Section 2 provides the related works and features comparison of the E-cast system. Sections 3 and 4 present the overall architecture and related protocols. Section 5 then describes the performance evaluation of the system and results analysis using three simulation scenarios. Finally, future works and conclusion are provided in Section 6 and 7 respectively.

## 2  Related Works

Many projects have explored implementing multicast at the application layer. Some of them offered some ideas for the design of E-Cast. We will describe them briefly and compare them at last.

Narada[1] is one of those first projects. It constructs multicast trees in a two-step process: firstly, it constructs efficient meshes among participants, and secondly, it constructs spanning trees basing on the mesh. The mesh-based approach supports well multi-source applications. Narada serves specially among end-to-end system and wants to know the global state of a system. In this case, its control is central and not scalable for serving a large number of terminals. It isn't suitable to construct the whole architecture of E-cast, but its mesh-based approach is the base of the construction of E-cast's intra-cluster.

OMNI[3] is a two-tier infrastructure to efficiently implement large-scale media streaming applications on the internet. Different to Narada, OMNI is a proxy-based system. Service providers deploy a set of service nodes (called MSNs) in the network and these MSNs are organised into an overlay and act as proxies to serve a lot of clients. In order to have a good use of bandwidth and distribute a fair charge among MSNs, OMNI gives a dynamic priority to different multicast service nodes based on the size of their service set respectively. Moreover, an approach which iteratively modifies the overlay tree using localized transformations was proposed to adapt with changing distribution of MSNs, clients and network conditions. ESNs of E-Cast system are similar to MSNs of this infrastructure.

Bayeux[4] and Scribe[5] are two overlay multicast system basing on peer-to-peer architecture protocols called Tapestry[6] and Pasty[7] respectively. Bayeux utilizes a prefix-based routing scheme which it inherits from Tapestry, a wide-area location and routing architecture. On top of Tapestry, Bayeux provides a simple protocol to organize the multicast receivers into a source-rooted distribution tree. In addition, Bayeux leverages the Tapestry infrastructure to provide simple load-balancing across replicated root nodes and reduced bandwidth consumption by clustering receivers by identifier. Finally, Bayeux provides a variety of protocols to leverage the redundant routing structure of Tapestry. Scribe is another overlay multicast architecture similar to Bayeux. It builds a multicast tree per group on top of a Pastry overlay, and relies on Pastry to optimize the routes from the root to each group member based on some metric, like latency. Compared to Bayeux, the expected amount of group membership information kept by each node in Scribe is smaller because this information is distributed over the nodes. And group join and leave requests are handled locally. Additionally, the multicast tree in Bayeux consists of the routes from the root to each destination, while in Scribe the tree is composed of the routes from each destination to root. Consequently, messages traverse less long links near the root in Scribe. These two architectures show us the benefit of distributed-hash table (DHT) to locate node and values. That spurs us to develop content advertisement protocol and content discovery protocol on kademlia, a peer-to-peer information system based on the XOR metric.

The two last above architectures can find neighbour nodes (in logic) and files quickly but they don't take consider of the underlying network structure. Two nodes near in logic ID can be very far each other. As a result, that will cause long latency and degrade the quality of a media streaming service. Recently, some researchers attribute to exploit underlying network topology data to construct efficient overlays. LCC [8] is one of these projects. It consists of two phases: a locating phase and an overlay construction phase. The first one is based on an accurate and scalable global position technique. Using partial knowledge of location-information for participating nodes, the algorithm consists in locating the closest existing set of nodes (cluster) in the overlay for a newcomer. Secondly, the multicast overlay construction phase builds and manages a topology-aware clustered hierarchical overlay so as to optimize the average end-to-end delay. This scheme shares the same idea of E-Cast topology construction protocol among ESNs to avoid initially randomly-connected structures and construct a topology having less latency.

Finally, Table1 provides a comparison of the main features of the discussed P2P systems and protocols. The criteria are chosen in order to suit live media applications.

**Table 1.** Features comparison of P2P systems and protocols for the support of live media streaming

| Protocols | Narada | OMNI | Bayeux | Scribe | LCC | Ecast |
|---|---|---|---|---|---|---|
| Underlying network topology-aware | Y | N | N | N | Y | Y |
| Distributed control (scalable) | N | Y | Partial | Y | Y | Y |
| Proxy-based | N | Y | Y | Y | Y | Y |
| Content advertisement protocol | N | N | Y | Y | N | Y |
| Content discovery protocol | N | N | Y | Y | N | Y |

## 3   E-CAST System Architecture

In this paper we propose E-Cast, an efficient, source-specific, scalable, overlay multicast system. This system consists of a set of devices called E-Cast Service Node (ESN) and one managing device called E-Cast Service Manager (ESM). ESNs are distributed in the network and provide efficient data distribution services. They not only transport the media-streaming but also can cache the media files according to some given criteria. The ESM coexists with service provider and manages the service of those ESNs. Four actors are connected by ESNs or ESM in E-Cast: Content Consumer (CC), Content Provider (CP), Service Provider (SP) and Network Provider (NP). A CC subscribes with SP to get media-streaming transported or cached by ESNs. A CP publishes its hot and new media information at SP and distributes the information to ESNs, and sends the media packets to a large number of CCs through ESNs. An SP is in charge of the management of the services delivered from CP to CC through an ESM. An SP establishes one or several agreements previously with many CPs. Moreover, a CC can pass the information of a media file which it wants by SP to execute a searching among ESNs to find it. NPs provide physical support to CCs, CPs and SP, for example, the placement of ESNs. The E-Cast overall architecture is depicted in Figure 1.

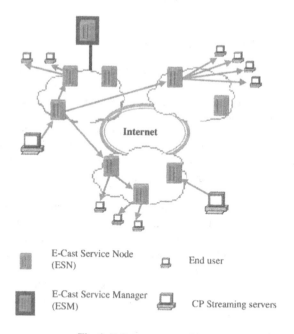

**Fig. 1.** E-Cast system architecture

## 4   E-CAST Overlay Protocols

Four protocols cooperate in E-Cast system to realise a resilient, efficient, source-specific and scalable media overlay multicast. *E-Cast topology construction protocol* is in charge of helping a new ESN to find a proper ESN cluster to bootstrap E-Cast service and clustering the ESNs which are close to each on considering underlying network condition. *E-Cast content advertisement protocol* is carried on by the content providers. They publish the information not only on the service provider but also on ESNs. However, the information on ESNs is different from that on the list of service provider. The core of this information is a hash value of the real information, and this value serves for a rapid, effective searching of content based on the kademlia [9] protocol. This searching procedure is carried on *E-Cast content discovery protocol.* This protocol takes effects when one content consumer joins E-Cast system. The CC can choose a media file information from its subscribed SP or find a media file information distributed on ESNs by the searching procedure. This search can even be applied on the E-Cast deployment of another SP, which has already established the cooperation relationship previously with the scribed SP. On the basis of the information published by content advertisement, content discovery protocol locates the media file either on the source (CP streaming server) or on one of the ESN which has cached it to provide a high quality and rapid transporting. Finally, *E-Cast overlay multicast routing protocol* is in charge of constructing and maintaining a reliable, fault-tolerant, efficient multicast tree for a content session facing a large number of dynamic content consumers. Moreover, it is responsible to construct a tunnel between the content consumer and the ESN of another E-Cast system.

### 4.1  E-Cast Topology Construction Protocol

E-Cast topology construction protocol takes the underlying network condition in considering, clusters the ESNs which are close to each other and classifies them into two levels. This way can reduce the latency from the source to ESNs and balancing the consummation of network bandwidth.

In E-Cast system, we adopt a similar approach of LCC protocol [8] to cluster ESNs so as to provide a resilient and low-latency topology to bootstrap the E-Cast system. There is a previously given active node called Rendezvous Point (RP) for a new ESN, say node A. RP can be the ESM or the ESN cluster leader recently or often connected by the new ESN. In general, the information of the two nodes is both known for A, A contacts firstly with the known ESN cluster leader. If the ESN cluster leader is still alive and can still accept new ESNs, A joins to its cluster. If the ESN cluster leader has already left or is already saturated, A contacts to the ESM to obtain the identity of a randomly selected boot cluster leader, B. A measures the distance (delay) from itself to B, $d(A,B)$, and then compares it with the given limited delay, $R_{max}$. If $d(A,B) < R_{max}$ A joins B's cluster. Otherwise, B queries its all neighbour cluster representative nodes to locate closest clusters for A and then it sends a candidate list to A. A chooses the closest to measures the delay and compares, all like to B. This procedure is repeated until A finds a proper cluster to join or a give searching time T is reached, A creates its own cluster. Then A will get a cluster ID (CID) which is unique in one E-Cast and a local ID (EID) which is only unique in its cluster. If A has joined to a cluster, the CID is given by the cluster leader. If A creates its cluster, the CID will be generated randomly. The combination of CID and EID of an ESN is unique in an E-Cast system and will be used until it leaves the system. To be resilient, A will conserve also the information of the second closest ESN cluster leaders and the edge node which is in several clusters' scope. The

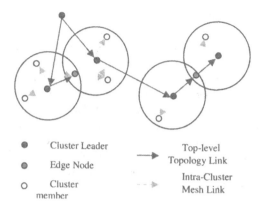

| | | | |
|---|---|---|---|
| ● | Cluster Leader | → | Top-level Topology Link |
| ● | Edge Node | | Intra-Cluster |
| ○ | Cluster member | - -▸ | Mesh Link |

**Fig. 2.** E-Cast topology construction involving ESNs

multicast tree construction on the clusters' leaders and interior of one cluster will be organised and managed by *overlay multicast routing protocol*. The figure 2 depicts the cluster structure after running E-cast topology construction protocol.

## 4.2  E-Cast Content Advertisement Protocol

The procedure of content advertisement consists of two parts. Shortly, Content provider publishes its media information to service provider and distributes the information of contents to ESNs to support the searching procedure of the *E-Cast content discovery protocol*.

The first part is between CPs and SP. CP updates regularly the information of its media contents database and sends it to the SP so that content consumers can look for and then choose what they want in the available contents at a moment. The depiction of each media file is complete: name, quality of media, published date, etc. At the bootstraps step, CP sends a complete description of the whole media content database. After that, CP sends regularly just the modification of its database: new media files, out of date files and etc. It is to avoid bandwidth waste.

Moreover, CP distributes the information of contents to ESNs. That's the second part of advertisement protocol. The principle of this part is similar to the STORE procedure of protocol Kademlia [9]. This step guarantees that SP can find a media file efficiently even if this file isn't in SP's local list. In this step, the depiction of a media file is a set of <sID, sValue, SP@, CP@, QoC, n >, called *key* of a media content. "sValue" can be the name or a short description of a media file. "sID" is a 160bits hash value of sValue, uniquely identifying a media file in a E-Cast system. SP@ is the address of SP (or the address of ESM coexisting with SP) which has the right to manager this file. Since one CP can probably have contact with more than one SP. This value is used to distinguish different SPs and will be useful for the cooperation between SPs. The "CP@" is the address of a content provider server. "QoC" is the quality of content, a description of quality of this media file in terms of resolution. This description can be just a degree number, like (1 to 10), the higher resolution a media file has, the higher degree it should be set. The norm which evaluates a content quality should be unified for all the content providers previously. A media file quality is evaluated automatically on basis of the norm and then a QoC degree corresponding is set in the *key*. "n" is a caching start switch counter for registering the amount of downloading of this file. This value is very important for start ESN caching function. It is initialized to 0 and augmented by 1 if and only if when this file is downloaded and also the ESN is in the multicast tree of this file downloading. When "n" reaches to a given value, which means that this file is enough "hot" for this ESN, this ESN begins to cache this media. The caching start value can be set manually. For the ESNs which have great storage capacity, the caching start value can be set very small. "n" starts to decrease if the content doesn't pass any more for a given time. When a maximum limited time reached, the content will be removed from the ESN for save the space for other new hot media files. One *key* is stored on ESNs with EIDs "close" to the sID in their exclusive or value.

### 4.3  E-Cast Content Discovery Protocol

A CC can acquire the media information by two ways. The simpler case is to choose the content which has already had the information in a list of the SP. In this case, a client will be redirected to a proper ESN. In another case, CC can search the content for the reason either the current version of this media is not satisfied or the content it needs is not yet known for the SP. In this case, a searching procedure will be carried on firstly among ESNs which conserve the information of contents in a distributed way. And then, if the searching result is positive, a list of information of contents will be returned to client to choose. CC can choose a proper version based on its hardware ability. For example, it can choose a high resolution video if it has enough bandwidth resource.

. *E-Cast content discovery protocol* takes effects on both of the two cases. It works similarly to the FIND-VALUE procedure of protocol Kademlia [9]. We present the second case the first. In the second case, the content information entered by CC is hashed to a 160bits value, called SearchValue (SV). A searching procedure starts at the same time in all of the clusters to look for an ESN which has EID closest to SV. And then, each cluster returns the information of its ESN which has the closest file information and the related file information registered on this ESN to SP.

### 4.4  E-Cast Overlay Multicast Routing Protocol

An ESM coexists with one service provider. It is responsible for computing the multicast tree for one content session whose source is on a content provider or on an ESN which has cached the content. Specially, it contacts regularly with ESN cluster leaders to get the fresh information of ESN which has cached "hot" media to updates its local information. In the part of an ESN, it knows its neighbour ESNs and all its local content consumers. Moreover, the ESN reports regularly its information about "hot" media to its cluster leader.

## 5  Performance Evaluation

We simulated the E-Cast topology construction protocol on the PeerSim simulator. Since the importance of this protocol is its two-level cluster structure which takes consider of the underlying network condition. We especially evaluated its efficacy in reducing latency and in balancing link charge. The underlying network topologies were given randomly to insure the reliability of evaluation.

## 5.1 PeerSim Simulator

There are many simulators for evaluating a new protocol, like Narses, 3LS, NS2, Peer-Sim, etc. Each of them has its advantages and disadvantages. PeerSim simulator is simple to simulate a scalable network topology, which can reach to $10^6$ nodes, and has a graph factory to produce varied network topologies. Those characters are suitable to evaluate the efficacy of E-Cast topology construction protocol. PeerSim has been developed with extreme scalability and support for dynamicity in mindOur simulation is to evaluate the efficacy of the two-level cluster topology construction on the scalable network, and besides, we need to compare the longest propagation time from the source to terminals for unicast and two overlay multicast architectures (E-Cast and Narada), so the underlying network condition should be kept the same. For all these reasons, the cycle-based engine was chosen. Benefiting on the graph generator of PeerSim, after some modifications, one underlying network topology can be produced randomly each time and our experiments were carried on these random topologies to get a result more accurate. The figure 3 is a network topology example with 100 terminals and 5 ESNs.

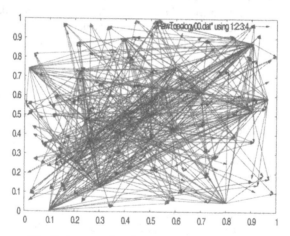

**Fig. 3.** An example of E-cast network topology

In this graph, the point aimed by one or several arrows represents a terminal (content consumer). The point reached by arrows and also from which starts one or several arrows represents an proxy node (a router for the unicast or an ESN for E-Cast and Narada). The points has just arrows setting out from it represents an original media source.

## 5.2 Simulation Model

The experiments were carried on the random network topologies which has one original media source. For each topology, we simulated three transport architectures: (1) unicast,

(2) E-Cast and (3) Narada̅. To insure the reliability of evaluation, we tested 10 times for each architecture and the average of results of 10 times was taken as the final result.

Model assumptions are the followings:

1) The Euclidean distance between two directly connected nodes was considered as the IP packet transfer delay on this link. For example, if terminal node 25 connects directly with proxy node 3, and the Euclidean

2) Distance between proxy 3 and terminal 25 is 12 units of distance, the delay from proxy 3 to terminal 25 is 12 ms. And if node 25 connects with proxy 5 passing by proxy 3, and the distance between proxy 5 and proxy 3 is 30 units of distance, the delay between proxy 5 to terminal 25 is 42 ms.

3) Since packet loss is not evaluated in the E-Cast topology construction protocol, it was assumed that all the terminals can always receive one duplicate of packet by one or a series of proxies even if there is a limit serving amount for one proxy. And there is no congestion in the system.

4) The amount of terminals served by a proxy is limited to avoid all or most of terminals concentrated to one or several proxies. But as mentioned in 2), it doesn't cause an isolated terminal.

Another condition to guarantee that we can compare the results of three architectures is that the algorithm to find the shortest path is always *greedy* algorithm. In unicast, we used it to find the shortest path from the source to each node. In Narada̅, we used it to find the nearest proxy for terminals and nearest proxy neighbour for proxies. In E-Cast, it was used to find the nearest ESN for terminals, the nearest cluster leader for ESN and the shortest path to the source for a cluster leader.

Two parameters were tested:

1) MAX_DELAY: The longest delay from the source to the terminal in the shortest path so that all the terminals receive a duplicate of a packet. This parameter is used to evaluate the effect on reducing the latency of E-Cast.

2) MAX_NUMBER_DUPLICATE: The maximum number of duplicate of one packet passed on one link in order that all the terminals get one. This parameter is to evaluate the capability in balancing network charge of E-Cast.

We evaluated two scenarios:

1) Scenario A: the number of terminals was set on 100, 200, 500, 1000,. The number of proxy was fixed on 50. And for E-Cast, the number of cluster was fixed on 5;

2) Scenario B: the number of proxy began from 5, augmented by 5 for each experiment, until 50. The amount of terminals was fixed on 1000. For E-Cast, the cluster number is fixed to 5;

## 5.3  Results Analysis for Scenario A

In this scenario, the number of proxies was fixed to 50, which means there are 50 routers in unicast, 50 ESN in E-Cast and 50 ESN in Narada̅. The 50 ESNs of E-Cast were grouped into 5 clusters.

The figure 4(a) depicts the MAX_DELAY change with the augment of number of terminals. Since the amount of terminals served by a proxy is limited, the shortest path

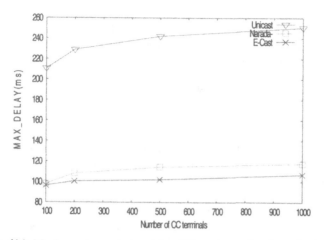

**Fig. 4(a).** Maximum transmission delays VS numbers of end-terminals

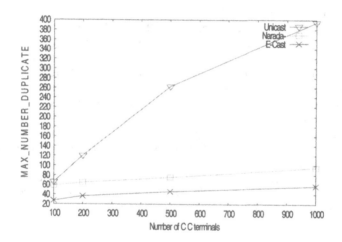

**Fig. 4(b).** Media Packets duplication VS numbers of end-terminals

for the farthest terminal is logically extended with the augment of number of terminals. That's the reason for which the MAX_DELAY in tree architectures are increased. As we know, in unicast, there is always only one source to get media packet: the original source. As a result, one duplicate packet begins always from original source and arrives to one terminal finally. However, in E-Cast and Narada', the ESNs serve also as a media source, the packet can be acquired directly. Consequently, the MAX_DELAY in unicast is much longer than that of E-Cast and Narada'. Between E-Cast and Narada', E-Cast can be still better because the ESNs have been clustered according to their locations in underlying network.

The same character is proved on the effect of MAX_NUMBER_DUPLICAT in the figure 4(b). With the augment of terminals, more and more duplicates of packet were transferred on the shortest path of each terminal. In unicast, the duplicates starts always from the original source, the routers near to the source is heavily charged. They have to transfer the packets for their own serving terminals, and at the same time have to transfer those just passing by them. In E-Cast and Narada‟, the links become also busier but much more softly since ESNs can produce the duplicates. In fact, their augmentation of MAX_NUMBER_DUPLICATE is most caused by the augmentation of local terminals. Between E-Cast and Narada‟, the same reason in 4(a), since the shortest path is improved by cluster the nearby ESNs, the repeating link is consequently reduced.

## 5.4  Results Analysis for Scenario B

In this scenario, the terminal amount is fixed to 1000, and the cluster amount for E-Cast is fixed to 5, we change the number of proxies to evaluate.

The figure 5(a) depicts the different influence on the MAX_DELAY. The augmentation of proxies has great significance for unicast to reduce MAX_DELAY. More routers exist in the system, one terminal can find a closest router to attach with more possibilities. As a result, the curve for unicast decline greatly with the augment of amount of routers. However, since the packet starts always from the original source, the MAX_DELAY is always much greater than those of E-Cast and Narada‟. Like in the Scenario A, the curve of MAX_DELAY of E-Cast and Narada‟ change very softly, in this scenario, they are still not sensible to the change of amount of ESNs. It is because each ESN can be considered as a source, and terminals always look for the nearest source, E-Cast and Narada‟ are very adaptable to the amount of terminal change.

The figure 5(b) depicts the different effects on MAX_NUMBER_DUPLICAT. The tree architectures are all sensitive to the augment of proxy because the more often a link is chosen to be the shortest path or part of the shortest path, it is more charged. As a result, when the number of proxy is augmented, the charge of the busiest is lightened and shared to the others. In E-Cast and Narada‟, ESNs share the charge with the original source, so the MAX_NUMBER_DUPLICATE is already much smaller than that of unicast. Between E-Cast and Narada‟, the cluster leaders of E-Cast can redistribute the charge even better, therefore, E-Cast has the best result. Nevertheless, since terminals connect always with the closest proxy, the rate of improvement is decreased and the advantage of augmenting proxies will be lost in the end.

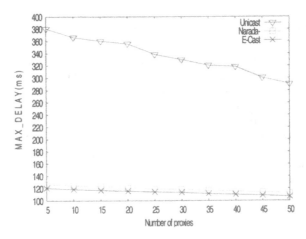

**Fig. 5(a).** Maximum transmission delays VS numbers of ESN proxy nodes

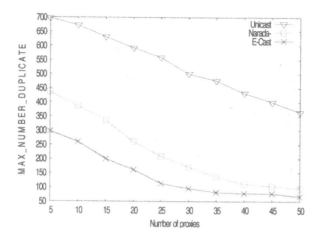

**Fig. 5(b).** Media Packets duplication VS numbers of ESN proxy nodes

# 6   Future Work

The E-Cast system is currently adapted for Video-on-Demand (VoD) service. The multicast transport takes its advantage when ESNs starts to cache media packets. However, in fact, it is simple to be adjusted for live streaming, like IPTV, IP radio etc. The only modification is some of parameters of the *key* in E-Cast content advertisement protocol. We can replace the information of the content by that of a session in the "sValue". This value can be the combination of a short description of a media file and its showing time or schedule. In fact, the disadvantage of some software of IPTV, like PPStream [11], TVCool [12] has shown such a function is very necessary to provide a flexible and satisfactory service. On the two systems, the content is repeated for some days and then is renewed. But a content consumer is always passive to get their media streaming and even cannot know the rate of advance. It merely doesn't matter for the people who pass all their time watching it.  The adaptive E-Cast will be able to let a content consumer to find out all of relative sessions thank to the E-Cast content discovery protocol (called session discovery protocol will more accurate in this case) and choose the most suitable one according to his spare time.

In addition, since ESNs are able to cache the media. This character provides us a possibility to break the single source limit and develop a multi-source model to improve video transport quality and fault tolerant ability on basis of some pre-research works, like [13].

# 7   Conclusion

A novel overlay multicast service management system called E-Cast is designed and evaluated in order to efficiently distribute video streams over multiple and converging wired and wireless network domains. The proposed system automatically locates and clusters newly deployed overlay service proxy nodes named ESNs. The associated overlay topology construction protocol is presented and evaluated. Compared to the well known NARADA system, E-cast is able to considering the underlying network topology to get low latency and balancing the packets transmission charge for the support of scalable and efficient audiovisual services (IPTV, VoD). With VoD services, ESNs are able to cache "hot" media files and share the downloading burden of the original source. The E-Cast content advertisement protocol and discovery protocol based on Kademlia protocol ensures that available media files can be quickly shared and located by end-users. Performance evaluations are carried out using simulation (Peer-Sim) including comparison with unicast transmission and the P2P Narada system. The evaluation results prove that E-Cast has advantage in reducing the latency and balancing the network traffic load.

# References

1. Chu, S.Y., Rao, G., Seshan, S., Zhang, H.: A case for end system multicast. In: ACM SIGMETRICS (2000)
2. Shi, S.: Design of Overlay Networks for Internet Multicast. Ph.D Dissertation, Washington University in St. Louis (August 2002)
3. Banerjee, S., Kommareddy, C., et al.: Construction of an Efficient Overlay Multicast Infrastructure for Real-time Applications. In: IEEE INFOCOM 2003 (2003)
4. Shelley, Q., Zhuang, et al.: Bayeux: An Architecture for Scalable and Fault tolerant Wide area Data Dissemination. In: 11th ACM international workshop on Network and operating systems support for digital audio and video NOSSDAV, New York (2001)
5. Castro, M., Druschel, P., et al.: SCRIBE: A large-scale and decentralized application-level multicast infrastructure. In: IEEE Journal on Selected Areas in Communications (JSAC) (Special issue on Network Support for Multicast Communications) (2002)
6. Zhao, B.Y., Kubiatowicz, et al.: Tapestry: An infrastructure for fault-tolerant wide-area location and routing. Tech. Rep., Univ. of California at Berkeley (2001)
7. Rowstron, A., Druschel, P.: Pastry: Scalable, distributed object location and routing for large-scale peer-to-peer systems. In: Guerraoui, R. (ed.) Middleware 2001. LNCS, vol. 2218, pp. 329–350. Springer, Heidelberg (2001)
8. Kaafar, M.A., Turletti, T., Dabbous, W.: A Locating-First Approach for Scalable Overlay Multicast. In: IEEE IWQoS 2006, New Haven, CT, USA (2006)
9. Maymounkov, P., Mazières, D.: Kademlia: A peer-to-peer information system based on the XOR metric. In: First International Workshop on Peer-to-Peer Systems, Cambridge, MA, USA (2002)
10. PeerSim P2P simulator: http://peersim.sourceforge.net/
11. PPStream, http://www.ppstream.com/
12. TVCool, http://www.cooltreaming.us.tv/
13. Mushtaq, A., Ahmed, T.: Adaptive Packet Video Streaming Over P2P Networks Using Active Measurements. In: Proceedings of the 11th IEEE Symposium on Computers and Communications, Cagliari, Italy (2006)

# Intra-Domain Delay-Based Quality of Service Using Differentiated Routing

Ioannis Papanagiotou and Michael Howarth

Centre for Communication Systems Research,
Department of Electronic Engineering, University of Surrey,
GU2 7XH Guildford, United Kingdom
{I.Papanagiotou,M.Howarth}@surrey.ac.uk
http://www.ee.surrey.ac.uk/CCSR/

**Abstract.** Differentiated routing is an approach to providing service differentiation in networks, a field that is currently receiving significant research attention. In this report we present an algorithm, namely Intra-Domain Differentiated Routing (IDDR), which supports qualitative delay differentiation in IP networks. We review existing differentiated routing approaches and then introduce IDDR and present initial results. We demonstrate that using IDDR we can achieve qualitative delay differentiation for two classes of flows.

## 1 Introduction

The demands placed on computer networks continue to increase, with increased development of multimedia applications and distributed data processing and retrieval systems. These different applications place different requirements on the underlying network. The need for this quality of service (QoS) differentiation has led to the devising of mechanisms which consider flows' requirements before routing them on the network.

The most popular QoS parameters that are relevant for packet-level traffic characteristics are latency, jitter and loss probability, and also bandwidth. Streaming multimedia may require guaranteed bandwidth to ensure that a minimum level of quality is maintained. IP telephony, Voice over IP (VoIP) and video teleconferencing (VTC) require strict limits on jitter and delay. Low delay is essential as it reduces the lag imposed by unforeseen network conditions. Video also requires a low packet drop rate since a single packet loss can give rise to unwanted artefacts on the screen which degrades the video quality. This paper focuses on delay as the QoS metric.

QoS in IP networks has traditionally been provided using differentiated forwarding. Packets from flows that require different QoS are routed along the same paths but are given different forwarding treatment. Packets assigned higher priority (high QoS packets) are forwarded faster than best-effort (BE) packets. Differentiated forwarding has historically been based on one of two frameworks, namely Integrated Services (IntServ) and Differentiated Services (DiffServ). Integrated Services works on a per-flow basis, i.e. it serves each flow differently according to its needs. Differentiated services classify all flows entering a network into one of a predefined number of QoS classes. Differentiated forwarding has not been widely implemented since it has

G. Pavlou, T. Ahmed, and T. Dagiuklas (Eds.): MMNS 2008, LNCS 5274, pp. 127–138, 2008.

generally been perceived by both the research community and network operators to be too complex.

Differentiated routing is an alternative that is currently receiving attention and is the focus of the work described in this paper. Using differentiated routing, packets of different QoS classes follow different paths to their destinations. In the literature there are papers where it is claimed that differentiated routing can be used to improve the performance of a network in terms of delay compared to a network running pure Shortest Path First (SPF) routing algorithms [2, 4, 5, 6].

There are two major concerns regarding differentiated routing in an IP environment. Firstly, by routing flows through alternative longer paths we increase the network load, because any individual flow is using more of the network's resources. Secondly, if each router dynamically chooses the next hop independently for each packet to a given destination, undesirable traffic shifts may occur which might in turn lead to service degradation. This for example might result in out-of-order delivery of TCP packets, causing a drop in goodput; or it might result in significant jitter in UDP packet delivery, reducing the effective QoS. We overcome this issue by routing packets of the same flow through the same path.

It is the key hypothesis of the research described in this paper that differentiated routing provides a promising platform for the delivery of QoS. Our objective is to develop mechanisms for differentiated routing for quality of service while minimising or avoiding the two potential drawbacks described above.

In this paper it is shown that differentiated routing can be used to provide delay differentiation between two classes of flows. Our algorithm, Intra-Domain Differentiated Routing (IDDR), is based on the Shortest Path First with Emergency Exits (SPF-EE) algorithm originally developed by Wang and Crowcroft as a mechanism for avoiding congestion [1]. We here extend the algorithm and refocus it for delay-based QoS. In Section 2 we consider previous approaches to QoS using differentiated routing and generally improvements in network performance achieved using differentiated routing. Section 3 describes the IDDR algorithm. Section 4 describes results from a simulation of IDDR, showing the feasibility of delay differentiation using differentiated routing. Finally, Section 5 provides conclusions and describes future work which would improve IDDR's performance.

## 2 Related Work

This Section reviews a number of algorithms that have been used either for intra-domain service differentiation or for optimised network performance as regards delay and resilience. We initially discuss algorithms that are intended to run on plain IP environments; these are followed by algorithms that make use of Multi-Topology Routing (MTR), and finally those intended for MPLS enabled networks.

### 2.1 IP-Based Routing

Wang and Crowcroft in [2] consider the problem of finding paths that satisfy multiple constraints. Both single mixed metric and multiple metric solutions have been evaluated. A single mixed metric is a function of two or more metrics, such as delay and bandwidth, and can only be used for qualitative QoS at best since it acts only as an indicator in path selection. Multiple metric solutions constitute an NP-complete problem when two or more additive or multiplicative constraints are combined. It is shown that it is computationally feasible to utilize bandwidth with any one other additive or multiplicative constraint i.e. this is not an NP complete problem. QoS algorithms that could be integrated in the widely used Open Shortest Path First (OSPF) [3] protocol are presented in [4]. These algorithms differ in complexity with accuracy being the trade-off, and consider only bandwidth and hop-count. In [5-6] Sahoo presents a Load Sensitive Routing (LSR) algorithm using alternate paths. Although the paper's title refers to QoS, the work does not appear to provide service differentiation among groups of flows; instead, it is shown that LSR outperforms OSPF when it comes to delay and jitter.

## 2.2 Multi-topology Routing

Multi-topology routing (MTR) has several planes, with different link weight configurations for the single network topology; this yields as many routing topologies. MTR is considered to be very effective for network resilience by Menth et al. [7]. In their work they point out that currently resilience in IP networks relies mainly on reconvergence after a node failure via the periodic exchange of link state information. MTR offers improved resilience by providing backup paths in case of node failures. Gjessing [8] presents two existing methods for network resilience in IP networks, both of which make use of backup topologies, namely Resilient Routing Layers (RRL) and Multiple Routing Configurations (MRC) [9-10]. The difference between those approaches is that RRL omits certain links in backup topologies while MRC sets a high link costs to them. MTR is being considered as an approach for differentiated routing based on the notion of Network Planes [11]; these may be interconnected across multiple domains to create Parallel Internets that provide differentiated QoS.

## 2.3 MPLS-Based Algorithms

MPLS was originally developed to provide faster packet forwarding than traditional IP routing [12]. Xiao et al. [13] describe a path computation algorithm using Constraint Based Routing (CBR) which works both online and offline. A QoS routing scheme using MPLS is presented in [14]. The algorithm utilizes both routing and forwarding differentiation. To account for delay and jitter, Weighted Fair Queuing has been used. Routing differentiation is used for network resilience, but unfortunately the authors do not provide comparison with any well established routing protocol. Wang [15] presents another algorithm which performs service differentiation according to bandwidth. The assumption is that all packet-level service requirements such as delay, jitter and packet loss rate can be translated into an equivalent bandwidth requirement. The algorithm describes the importance of critical links: the impact of one Label Switched Path (LSP) request on future LSP requests needs to be considered. In [16] Calle et al. present an algorithm that is based both on failure probabilities and failure impact of particular segments in a network. Even though it has proved to be useful it is based on statistical data regarding network failures and therefore cannot handle unpredictable traffic behaviour.

# 3  Intra-Domain Differentiated Routing (IDDR)

In this Section we present our algorithm, IDDR, which provides service differentiation in terms of delay. The algorithm is based on Shortest Path First with Emergency Exits (SPF-EE) [1]. The latter is intended to improve network resilience, as it modifies plain Shortest Path First (SPF) routing in the event of congestion. SPF-EE is dynamic and highly adaptive to network changes. The algorithm requires routers to keep routing trees of all neighbouring routers, in order to create on-demand alternative paths for flows heading towards congested links. SPF-EE uses these alternative paths - or emergency exits as the authors call them so as to avoid congestion. Although the algorithm was originally intended to address network congestion, we show in this paper that it can be adapted and enhanced to provide delay differentiation to classes of flows. We now explain SPF-EE in brief, since it constitutes the fundamentals of IDDR. We then proceed to describe our modifications to the algorithm which result in IDDR.

## 3.1  Shortest Path First with Emergency Exits (SPF-EE)

SPF-EE takes as its starting point conventional shortest path routing using Dijkstra's algorithm. SPF-EE then extends OSPF: each node makes use of the data available in the Link State Database (LSDB) and derives routing trees for itself and each of its neighbours. Consider node A in Fig. 1 running SPF-EE. Using the derived routing trees, the node A calculates for each neighbour the next hop of the alternative path to each and every destination; by browsing each neighbour's routing tree, except the tree of the node that is the SP next hop, node A then checks whether the destination is on a sub-tree rooted under node A itself or the Shortest Path (SP) next hop. If it is neither then the neighbour is considered to be the next hop Alternative Path (AP). Each node will then produce a routing table similar to the one produced using OSPF, but with one more field to record the alternative paths. Fig. 1 illustrates an example of a flow travelling from node A to node F when link A - B is congested. Node A will browse the routing trees of its neighbours, omitting node B's routing tree since B is the next hop of the SP from A to F. The valid candidates for next hop of an AP are nodes C and D. However, in the routing tree of node D, destination node F is on a subtree rooted under source node A; therefore it is invalid because if the packet were forwarded from A to D, D would then forward the packet back to A, creating a loop. As a result the only valid AP in this case is the one through node C, which can forward a packet on to F.

   If there is no alternative path for a specific destination a Reverse Alternative Path (RAP) is set up, using the following mechanism: a query message is sent to the current node's neighbours, which in turn look in their neighbours' routing trees for an AP. If an AP is found a reply is sent back to the current node, identifying the neighbour which found the AP and the next hop of the AP from the point of view of the neighbour node. If a RAP cannot be found from the immediate neighbours, the latter send query messages to their neighbours and the procedure goes on until a RAP is established or it is decided that the procedure is too costly to continue. The final reply message that the originating node will receive will include the whole path to the exit. Upon a successful RAP establishment, RAP tables in both the current and exit node are updated.

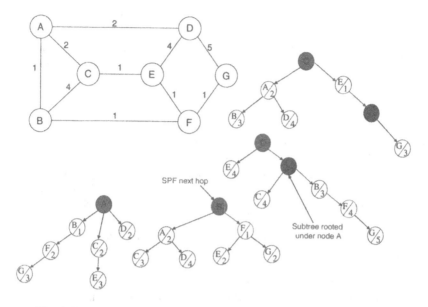

**Fig. 1.** Example topology and routing trees of node A and its neighbours

In SPF-EE, path selection (i.e. the use of either the standard SP or the AP) depends on the length of the outgoing queues of each node. Under normal light loading of the network, packets are forwarding using the standard shortest path. However, if an outgoing queue of a node, e.g. outgoing queue of node A towards node B for destination F (Fig. 1), reaches a certain predefined threshold, then node A redirects the packets to the AP, in this case node C. If the queue to the AP is also above the threshold, then the node looks – in real time – for a new AP and if it does not exist it tries to establish a RAP. If no APs or RAPs can be found for a specific destination then traffic is forwarded to the SP next hop.

In summary, we can see that SPF-EE provides both a shortest path and one or more alternative paths, which in general involves more hops. We hypothesise that this differentiation of paths can be used to provide delay-based differentiated routing; we therefore adapt SPF-EE as described in the following Section.

## 3.2 IDDR: Adapting SPF-EE for QoS

We aim to provide two qualitatively differentiated classes of QoS flows: high QoS, i.e. low delay; and best effort, i.e. higher delay. The main difference between IDDR and SPF-EE lies in the path selection. IDDR allows best effort (BE) traffic to be routed *only* through the alternative paths (APs), while high QoS flows are routed through the shortest paths (SPs). If the SPs are over-utilised the additional high QoS flows are also allowed to use APs. The higher cost (usually longer) paths taken by the BE traffic increase the total delay of the best effort flows, increasing service differentiation. To avoid problems such as out-of-order delivery of TCP packets or UDP jitter, packets of the same flow need to follow an identical path.

A feature of IDDR that results in improved network resilience is the computation of all APs along with the SP for each destination during network convergence (i.e. at the time that link state information is propagated through the network); therefore, the lag imposed during path selection is minimised. A real time computation of a secondary AP, as in SPF-EE, would cause further delay and possibly would result in an increase of dropped flows, since during computation the flows would still be routed through the congested link.

IDDR works as follows. After having received link state information about the network, nodes run Dijkstra's algorithm [17] in order to calculate the shortest paths to all destinations. Each node builds its own routing tree and those of its neighbours. Each leaf of the tree consists of the node's ID and the cost of the path from the root of the tree to the node, as shown in Fig. 1. Each node will then find every available AP, following the procedure explained in Section 3.1. The current node retrieves the cost to the neighbour which constitutes an exit and then it adds it to the cost between the neighbour and the destination; therefore each node can deduce the cost of each AP, if more than one, which are then classified and inserted to their routing table in order of ascending cost.

To limit the traffic volume on links used by high QoS flows we introduce a parameter, the IDDR threshold "$n$", which bounds percentage link utilisation by the value of "$n$". The introduction of this link utilisation gives the network operator some control over the delay of the high QoS flows. The reduced shortest path traffic volume reduces the delay suffered by the high QoS flows. This method using the IDDR threshold, by its nature, also reduces the throughput of the network since it effectively reduces the capacity of its affected links.

The features described above have transformed a congestion avoidance algorithm, SPF-EE to a delay differentiation algorithm, namely IDDR.

## 4  Simulation Design, Results and Analysis

We now describe the simulation of IDDR. The software, used to simulate the operation of IDDR in a QoS-enabled network, is implemented in C++.

To model the delays encountered by the flows we have initially used a simple model from queuing theory, where the arrival time $1/\lambda$ and service time $1/\mu$ are negative exponentially distributed (Poisson process). For each outbound link in each node we model the link delay as a function of link utilisation and link capacity using the following formula:

$$t_q = \frac{\rho}{1-\rho} \qquad (1)$$

where: $\rho = \lambda/\mu$ is the link utilisation and $t_q$ is the link delay.

Whilst this simple model does not take account of the typical heavy tail distribution found in Internet traffic flow [18], it nonetheless provides useful initial insights into the performance of the proposed IDDR algorithm.

### 4.1 Test Topologies

The topologies used to generate our results are: (a) five random topologies created by the BRITE topology generator [19], (b) the test topology by Calle [20] depicted in Fig. 12, and (c) the real topology of the Géant research network [21]. The Géant Topology is of particular interest since it is a real-world network, which implies that its settings incorporates more sophisticated TE, even if that has the objective of optimising the SPF algorithm operation, and not that of IDDR.

The random BRITE topologies each consist of 30 nodes with link connectivity using the Waxman model. Each node is randomly placed in space, has at least 2 links attached and the link capacities take values from 10 to 100 units with those values being uniformly distributed. In Section 4.3 we present the results of one of those BRITE topologies since results on all of them are very similar. Calle's topology consists of 15 nodes, 5 of which are interconnected with high capacity links and form the core of the topology. In particular, in Fig. 2, the bold core links have a capacity of 100 units while the remaining links each have a capacity of 50 units. Finally the Géant topology retains all its characteristics unchanged such as the link weights and capacities.

Our link weight settings for both the BRITE and Calle topologies adopt the standard traffic engineering approach of assigning the link weights for each link to be inversely proportional to the capacity of the link. As mentioned above, for the Géant topology we use its real link capacities and link weights.

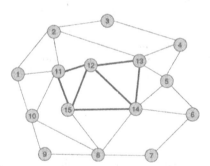

**Fig. 2.** Calle's Topology, from [20]

### 4.2 Metrics

Before we proceed to present simulation results, we introduce the following terms:

- *Total traffic* is the sum of all the data rates (bandwidths) of flows injected into the network;
- *QoS ratio* is the percentage of total traffic that requires preferential treatment, i.e. is "high QoS" or low delay traffic.

The total traffic injected to the BRITE random topologies and Calle topology can vary in the simulations. We have varied the number of flows, and the bandwidth of each flow, as well as the QoS ratio. The total traffic is randomly generated from any node to any other node in the case of random BRITE topology. For the Calle topology we have introduced the notions of edge nodes and core nodes. The former are the routers that form the perimeter of the topology (i.e. nodes 1-10 in Fig. 2) while core nodes are all other routers, i.e. those that are not on the perimeter (nodes 11-15 in Fig. 2). Traffic in Calle topology is randomly generated from any edge node to any other edge node in case of the Calle topology. That way we can gain insights as to how IDDR performs on networks that mainly handle transit traffic. For the Géant topology a real traffic matrix from TOTEM has been used [22].

Our analysis of the results is based on the following metrics:

- *Delay*: the sum over all the links along the path used by any individual flow of the queuing delays experienced on each link, as given by equation (1) above. This enables us to depict the extent of service differentiation IDDR can offer.
- *Throughput*: the actual volume of traffic that is successfully passed by the network; because in some tests the utilisation of some links reaches the limiting capacity, some traffic can not be accommodated on the network.
- *Network Utilisation*: defined by the following formula

$$\eta = \frac{\sum b_i}{\sum c_i} \qquad (2)$$

where $\eta$ is the network utilisation, $b_i$ is the traffic volume on link $i$, and $c_i$ is the capacity of link $i$. Network utilisation is therefore a measure of the fraction of total network resources that are being used. It illustrates the demand of each algorithm on the network resources

- *Network Utilisation per Flow*: the network utilisation divided by the throughput. This is therefore a measure of the network resources that each flow consumes.

## 4.3   Results

We have run the simulations for various scenarios. All results presented here have the QoS ratio set to 50%. We have assumed that with the rapidly evolving multimedia applications, which flood networks with real time traffic, the ratio of the total traffic that will need preferential treatment will approach 50%. The total traffic injected on BRITE and Calle's topologies has been set to 2000 and 900 flows respectively. Each flow has a bandwidth of 1 unit. These numbers were chosen so that when SPF runs on those topologies both network utilizations are around 50%. In Géant Topology we have multiplied the bandwidth of each flow by a factor in order to achieve the desirable network utilization. The above settings apply for the results depicted in Figs. 3-5.

Fig. 3 illustrates the percentage delay difference between high QoS flows and BE flows, given by:

$$\text{Delay difference} = 1 - \frac{\delta_{QoS}}{\delta_{BE}}$$

where $\delta_{QoS}$ is the mean delay of all QoS flows and $\delta_{BE}$ is the mean delay of all BE flows. This shows the percentage reduction in delay encountered by the high QoS flows compared to the delay encountered by the BE flows. It is evident that in all cases even for an IDDR threshold close to 1 (i.e. when links carrying QoS traffic are allowed a high utilisation) a reasonable delay differentiation is found. For the BRITE network the delay differentiation decreases significantly as the IDDR threshold increases. In the Calle topology the delay differentiation does not change substantially with IDDR threshold. The Géant topology delay differentiation drops for higher IDDR threshold values, however from threshold value of 0.4 onwards it outperforms BRITE topology. It is encouraging to note that the Géant topology, a real topology, retains high delay differences even for high values of IDDR threshold.

We next compare the throughput of the networks when running IDDR compared to their throughput with normal SPF routing. In Fig. 4 we see that in case of BRITE and Géant topologies SPF routing outperforms IDDR in throughput, i.e. the SPF throughput is higher than that of IDDR. This is to be expected as the IDDR threshold restricts the utilisation of all links which are used by high QoS flows. In Calle's topology, however, the flexibility offered by APs seems to balance out the restrictions set by the IDDR threshold. The IDDR threshold value of great interest though is around 0.9 (i.e. on any link which carries high QoS flows the link utilisation cannot exceed 0.9). At this value in the Calle topology the IDDR throughput is slightly higher than that of SPF.

In Fig. 5 we consider the network utilisation per flow, i.e. the resources consumed by each flow. It is evident that IDDR consumes more resources than SPF because some flows take paths that have a higher cost than the least cost. IDDR makes use of APs for BE flows and, in case of lack of congested SPs, for high QoS flows as well. This means that all the BE flows will follow paths which have a higher cost than the SPs, and therefore typically tend to comprise more links. Therefore it is not surprising that IDDR has a higher utilisation, since this is the cost-tradeoff for the delay differentiation. In summary, in Fig. 5 we see that the reduced throughput in IDDR in conjunction with the increased network utilization means that IDDR is slightly more expensive resource-wise than plain SPF routing.

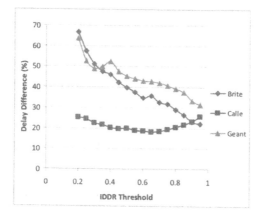

**Fig. 3.** Percentage Delay Difference between High QoS- and BE-Flow

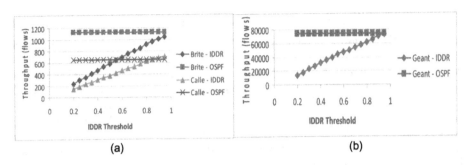

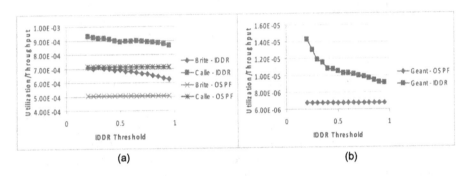

**Fig. 4.** Throughput vs. IDDR Threshold (a) for BRITE and Calle topologies and (b) for Géant topology. (The Géant topology results have been plotted on a different graph since its throughput is much higher than that of the other two topologies).

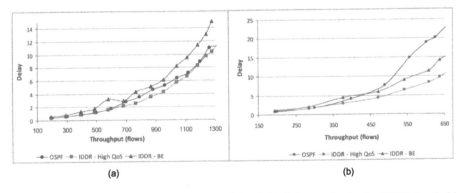

**Fig. 5.** Network Utilisation per flow vs. IDDR threshold (a) for BRITE and Calle topologies and (b) for Géant topology

**Fig. 6.** Delay vs. throughput graph for (a) BRITE and (b) Calle topologies for IDDR threshold set to value 0.9 and total traffic in the range of 200-2100 flows.

Finally, in Fig. 6 we compare IDDR with OSPF for their delay as a function of throughput. In the case of the Calle topology IDDR keeps the delays of high QoS flows significantly lower than SPF flows for a wide range of throughput and from 450 flows onwards delays of BE flows are significantly lower as well. However, in the case of the BRITE topology delay of BE flows is constantly higher than that of the flows in SPF, while high QoS flows are only slightly better than SPF flows in terms of delay. Nevertheless assuming that the best-effort traffic is mainly non delay-sensitive traffic, it is evident that IDDR is a promising solution for service differentiation in a network.

## 5 Conclusion

In this paper we have presented an algorithm for delay differentiation and tested it through simulation using a simple delay model from queuing theory. We have found significant qualitative delay differentiation by using IDDR. The network throughput is reduced only slightly compared to standard SPF routing. We believe that both throughput and delay differentiation could be further improved by performing traffic engineering on the network optimised for IDDR. In addition a future more refined simulation of the algorithm, using a package such as Network Simulator 2 (ns-2), that accounts for more complex queuing models and source packet modelling, would give us more advanced insights into the operation of IDDR.

## Acknowledgement

Ioannis Papanagiotou is supported from the UK Engineering and Physical Sciences Research Council (EPSRC).

## References

1. Wang, Z., Crowcroft, J.: Shortest path first with emergency exits. In: SIGCOMM 1990, vol. 20(4). ACM, New York (1990)
2. Wang, Z., Crowcroft, J.: Quality-of-service routing for supporting multimedia applications. IEEE Journal on Selected Areas in Communication, IEEE Journal 14(7), 1228–1234 (1996)
3. Moy, J.: Corp. Cascade Communication. "OSPF Version 2", IETF, RFC 2178 (July 1997)
4. Guerin, R.A., Orda, A., Williams, D.: 'QoS routing mechanisms and OSPF extensions. In: GLOBECOM 1997, vol. 3, pp. 1903–1908. IEEE, Los Alamitos (1997)
5. Sahoo, A.: An OSPF based load sensitive QoS routing algorithm using alternate paths. In: Computer Communications and Networks Proceedings, pp. 236–241. IEEE, Los Alamitos (2002)
6. Sahoo, A.: A load-sensitive QoS routing algorithm in best-effort environment. In: MILCOM Proceedings, vol. 2, pp. 1206–1210. IEEE, Los Alamitos (2002)
7. Menth, M., Martin, R.: Network resilience through multi-topology routing. In: 5th International Workshop on Design of Reliable Communication Networks Proceedings, 2005 (DRCN 2005), pp. 271–277 (October 2005)
8. Gjessing, S.: Implementation of two Resilience Mechanisms using Multi Topology Routing and Stub Routers. In: International Conference on Internet and Web Applications (ICIW 2006), vol. (1), p. 29. IEEE, Los Alamitos (2006)

9. Hansen, A.F., Kvalbein, A., Cicic, T., Gjessing, S., Lysne, O.: Resilient routing layers for recovery in packet networks. In: International Conference on Dependable Systems and Networks Proceedings, 2005 (DSN 2005), pp. 238–247. IEEE, Los Alamitos (2005)

10. Kvalbein, A., Hansen, A.F., Cicic, T., Gjessing, S., Lysne, O.: Fast IP Network Recovery Using Multiple Routing Configurations. In: INFOCOM 2006, pp. 1–11. IEEE, Los Alamitos (2006)

11. Wang, N., Ho, K.-H., Pavlou, G.: Adaptive Multi-topology IGP Based Traffic Engineering with Near-optimal Network Performance. In: Das, A., Pung, H.K., Lee, F.B.S., Wong, L.W.C. (eds.) NETWORKING 2008. LNCS, vol. 4982. Springer, Heidelberg (2008)

12. MPLS stack software, a mechanism for packet forwarding in networks [Online] (Data Connection 2007), http://www.dataconnection.com/mpls/whatis.htm (Cited: October 24, 2007)

13. Xiao, X., Hannan, A., Bailey, B., Ni, L.M.: Traffic engineering with MPLS in the Internet. IEEE Network 14(2), 28–33 (2000)

14. Li, Z., Zhang, Z., Wang, L.: A novel QoS routing scheme for MPLS traffic engineering. In: International Conference on Communication Technology Proceedings, 2003 (ICCT 2003), vol. 1, pp. 474–477. IEEE, Los Alamitos (2003)

15. Wang, B., Su, X., Chen, C.L.P.: A new bandwidth guaranteed routing algorithm for MPLS traffic engineering. In: International Conference on Communications, 2002 (ICC 2002), vol. 2, pp. 1001–1005. IEEE, Los Alamitos (2002)

16. Calle, E., Marzo, J.L., Urra, A., Vila, P.: Enhancing MPLS QoS routing algorithms by using the network protection degree paradigm. In: GLOBECOM 2003, vol. 6, pp. 3053–3057. IEEE, Los Alamitos (2003)

17. Tanenbaum, A.: Computer Networks. Prentice Hall, Englewood Cliffs (2003)

18. Crovella, M.E., Bestavros, A.: Self-similarity in World Wide Web traffic: evidence and possible causes. Networking. IEEE/ACM 5(6) (December 2007)

19. Boston university Representative Internet Topology gEnerator [Online], http://www.cs.bu.edu/brite (Cited: March 10, 2008)

20. Calle, E., Marzo, J., Urra, A.: Protection performance components in MPLS networks. Computer Communications, Science Direct. 27(12), 1220–1228 (2004)

21. Topology : The Network : GÉANT [Online] (October 2004), http://www.geant.net/server/show/nav.159 (Cited: March 20, 2008)

22. TOTEM (TOolbox for Traffic Engineering Methods) Project [Online] (March 4, 2008), http://totem.run.montefiore.ulg.ac.be/datatools.html (Cited: March 20, 2008)

# Multiconstrained Optimization of Networks with Multicast and Unicast Traffic

Pedro Sousa[1], Miguel Rocha[1], Paulo Cortez[2], and Miguel Rio[3]

[1] Dep. Informatics / CCTC - Univ. Minho - Braga - Portugal
pns@di.uminho.pt mrocha@di.uminho.pt
[2] Dep. Information Systems/ Algoritmi - Univ. Minho - Guimarães - Portugal
pcortez@dsi.uminho.pt
[3] University College London - London - UK
m.rio@ee.ucl.ac.uk

**Abstract.** This paper presents an OSPF routing optimization framework taking into account a set of multiconstrained QoS requirements of the networking domain. The proposed optimization approach, based on Evolutionary Computation, is able to handle network scenarios with both unicast and multicast traffic, providing high quality configurations for single-topology or multi-topology routing approaches. The results clearly show the effectiveness of the devised optimization methods, allowing for the development of management tools automatically providing enhanced configurations to improve the QoS performance of the network.

## 1 Introduction

Nowadays, TCP/IP networks are facing the challenge of providing effective support to a number of advanced services with strict QoS requirements. Services such as Interactive TV, virtual reality, video-conferencing or video surveillance are examples of services that would gain from QoS enabled multicast content delivery. An effective network support to these services requires data delivery with minimal loss along with acceptable end-to-end delays, an even more crucial issue considering the cases of interactive applications requiring strict commitments regarding round-trip time delays. Another relevant point is the fact that the widespread use of multicast has never occurred in the Internet. However, in closed TCP/IP networks, where its scalability problems are not a deterrent, multicast has been used to support some advanced services.

In this context, Traffic Engineering (TE) techniques can be used to improve network performance by achieving near-optimal configurations for routing protocols. TE approaches can be classified into: Multi-Protocol Label Switching (MPLS) [3][2] and pure IP-based intra-domain routing protocols. In the case of MPLS, packets are encapsulated with labels at ingress points, that can be used to route these packets along an explicit label-switched path. However, the use of MPLS presents significant drawbacks when compared with traditional IP routing mechanisms. As regards intra-domain routing protocols, the most commonly

G. Pavlou, T. Ahmed, and T. Dagiuklas (Eds.): MMNS 2008, LNCS 5274, pp. 139–150, 2008.

used today is Open Shortest Path First(OSPF)[12]. Here, the administrator assigns weights to each link in the network, which are then used to compute the best path from each source to each destination using the Dijkstra algorithm [4].

A number of studies have proposed TE procedures which optimize the weights of intra-domain routing protocols to achieve near optimal routing, taking as input the expected traffic demands. This was the approach adopted by the work of Fortz and Thorup (2000) [6] which proposed some local search heuristics to deal with this NP-hard problem. Another approach was the use of Evolutionary Algorithms (EAs) to improve these results [5]. Additional research has been carried out with the objective of pursuing multiconstrained QoS optimization for unicast traffic [11].

In this paper, EAs are employed to provide network administrators with OSPF weights able to optimize network behaviour, taking simultaneously into account unicast and multicast demands of a given domain (for an example see Fig. 1). The conducted study considers two distinct scenarios: (i) optimizing overall network congestion or (ii) optimizing both the overall network congestion and end-to-end delays for multicast traffic.

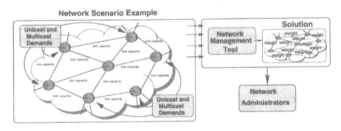

**Fig. 1.** Example of a network scenario

This work is based on the reasoning that in the optimization process both the unicast and multicast demands should be considered simultaneously, in contrast with previous work where optimization is performed in two distinct phases, the first for unicast traffic and the second devoted to multicast optimization [13]. Furthermore, it presents a novel approach that allows the simultaneous optimization of the overall network congestion and multicast end-to-end delays, considering scenarios that use traditional OSPF weights and also the possibility of using a multi-topology approach where two layers of weights are considered.

## 2    Problem Formulation

### 2.1    Unicast Traffic

In this section, a model for minimizing congestion in a network only with unicast traffic demands will de described. This is based on the framework proposed in [6]. The general routing problem [1] that underpins this work represents routers and links by a set of nodes ($N$) and arcs ($A$) in a directed graph $G = (N, A)$.

In this model, $c_a$ represents the capacity of each link $a \in A$. A demand matrix $D$ is available, where each element $d_{st}$ represents the traffic demand between nodes $s$ and $t$. For each arc $a$, the variable $f_a^{(st)}$ represents how much of the traffic demand between $s$ and $t$ travels over arc $a$. The total unicast load $l_a$, the link utilization rate $u_a$ and the congestion measure $\Phi_a$ for arc $a$ are given in Equations 1, 2 and 3, where $p$ is a penalty function that has small values near 0, but as the values approach the unity it becomes more expensive and exponentially penalizes values above 1 [6].

In OSPF, all arcs have an integer weight, used by each node to calculate the shortest paths to all other nodes in the network, using the Dijkstra algorithm [4]. The traffic from a given source to a destination travels along the shortest path. If there are two or more paths with equal length, traffic is evenly divided among the arcs in these paths (load balancing) [9]. Let us assume a given a weight assignment, and the corresponding values of $u_a$. In this case, the total routing cost is expressed by Eq. 4 for the loads and penalties calculated based on the given OSPF weights. In this way, the *OSPF weight setting problem* is equivalent to finding the optimal weight value for each link, in order to minimize $\Phi$. The congestion measure can be normalized ($\Phi^*$) over distinct scenarios to values in the range [1,5000]. It is important to note that in the case when all arcs are exactly full ($l_a = c_a$), the value of $\Phi^*$ is $10\frac{2}{3}$, a value that will be considered a threshold that bounds the acceptable working region of the network.

$$l_a = \sum_{(s,t) \in N \times N} f_a^{st} \quad (1) \qquad u_a = \frac{l_a}{c_a} \quad (2) \qquad \Phi_a = p(u_a) \quad (3) \qquad \Phi = \sum_{a \in A} \Phi_a \quad (4)$$

## 2.2 Multicast Demands

A model that considers minimizing congestion only considering multicast traffic in the network will be described, that is based on the work by Wang and Pavlou (2007) [13]. If there are unicast and multicast demands, this model can be used to perform a two-step optimization process (explained in Section 3.2). The multicast demands are given for a set of $G$ groups, where for each group $g \in G$ the following parameters are defined: a root node $r_g$, a bandwidth demand $M_g$ and a a set of receivers ($V_g$). The multicast optimization problem is typically defined as the computation of a bandwidth constrained Steiner tree, with the objective of minimizing overall bandwidth consumption, using integer programming. The target is to instantiate a number of binary decision variables: $y_a^g$, are equal to 1 if link $a$ is included in the multicast tree for group $g$; and $x_a^{g,k}$ are equal to 1 if link $a$ is included in the multicast tree for group $g$, in the branch from the root node to receiver $k$. The objective is to minimize the overall bandwidth consumption ($L_1$) as expressed by Eq. 5.

$$L_1 = \sum_{g \in G} \sum_{a \in A} M_g y_a^g \tag{5}$$

The deployment of the obtained Steiner trees can be enforced by using an explicit routing overlay, through MPLS on a per-group basis. An alternative with some advantages, previously discussed, is to consider that the routing will be achieved by using an intra-domain protocol such as OSPF. In this case, the tree for a given group will be built from the shortest paths between the root node and each receiver. Therefore, the values assigned to $y_a^g$ variables will be computed as follows: $y_a^g$ is equal to 1 if link $a$ is in the shostest path from the root node $g$ to at least one of the receivers in $V_g$, and is equal to 0 otherwise.

In previous work [13], EAs have been proposed to optimize OSPF weights for multicast traffic. The objective function used in this case is based on the overall network load ($L_1$) but also on the excessive bandwidth allocated to overloaded links ($L_2$), that can is given by:

$$L_2 = \sum_{a \in A} [w_a \sum_{g \in G} (M_g y_a^g) - c_a] \quad (6) \qquad w_a = \begin{cases} 0, if \; \sum_{g \in G} M_g y_a^g \le c_a \\ 1, otherwise \end{cases} \quad (7)$$

The EA's fitness is, therefore, given by:

$$f(L_1, L_2) = \frac{\mu}{\alpha L_1 + \beta L_2} \quad (8)$$

where $\mu$, $\alpha$ and $\beta$ are constants, whose values are set to $10^7$, 1 and 10 respectively.

## 2.3  Unified Congestion Model with Unicast and Multicast Demands

In this work, a unified approach will be proposed that is able to reach OSPF weights that optimize the network congestion measure, simultaneously considering unicast and multicast demands. In this case, the multicast load $ml_a$ for a given link $a$ is given by Eq. 9.

The values of $y_a^g$ will be calculated from the OSPF weights as explained in the previous section. So, the total load on a given arc $a$ is given by $l_a = ml_a + ul_a$ where $ul_a$ is the unicast load in arc $a$ (given by $l_a$ in the previous section). It should noted that $l_a$ here takes the meaning of the total load in the network, while in Section 2.1, $l_a$ is only used for unicast loads since in that case those were the only loads considered. After calculating the overall values of $l_a$ for all links, the process proceeds as described in Section 2.1, in order to reach the normalized congestion measure $\Phi^*$. Another interesting measure of the network performance in this scenario is the excessive bandwidth in overloaded links (BOL). This is a generalization of $L_2$ but now applied to the global loads and not only to the multicast traffic. (Eq. 10).

$$ml_a = \sum_{g \in G} M_g y_a^g \qquad BOL = \sum_{a \in A} z_a(l_a - c_a) \qquad z_a = \begin{cases} 0, if \; l_a \le c_a \\ 1, otherwise \end{cases} \quad (11)$$
$$(9) \qquad\qquad\qquad (10)$$

## 2.4  Modeling Delays in Multicast Traffic

In this section, the previous model is enriched by considering also end-to-end delays associated with multicast traffic. Delay requirements were defined at the group level: a maximum allowed delay $md_g$ is defined for each group $g$, that is applied to every pair (root, receiver) in that group. This means that the maximum allowed delay must be respected for all receivers.

A cost function was developed to evaluate the delay compliance for each scenario. The *delay compliance ratio* for a given receiver $k$ in a group $g$ is defined as in Eq. 12 where $s$ is the root node $r_g$ and $t$ is the receiver $k$ of group $g$. In this expression, $Del_{st}$ stands for the average delay of the traffic between the nodes $s$ and $t$, a value calculated by considering all paths between $s$ and $t$ with minimum cost and averaging the delays in each. The delay in each path is the sum of the propagation delays in its arcs and queuing delays in the nodes along the path. Note that in some network scenarios the latter component might be neglected (e.g. if the propagation delay component has an higher order of magnitude than queuing delays[1]).

A penalty for delay compliance can be calculated using function $p$ ($\gamma_{kg}$ in Eq. 13). This, in turn, allows the definition of a delay minimization cost function, given a set of OSPF weights ($w$) (Eq. 14) where the $\gamma_{kg}(w)$ values represent the delay penalties for each end-to-end path, given the routes determined by the OSPF weight set $w$.

$$dc_{kg} = \frac{Del_{st}}{md_g} \quad (12) \qquad \gamma_{kg} = p(dc_{kg}) \quad (13) \qquad \gamma(w) = \sum_{g \in G} \sum_{k \in V_g} \gamma_{kg}(w) \quad (14)$$

This function can be normalized dividing the values by the sum of all minimum end-to-end delays (for each pair of nodes the minimum end-to-end delay - $minDel_{st}$ - is the delay of the path with minimum possible overall delay):

$$\gamma^*(w) = \frac{\gamma(w)}{\sum_{g \in G} \sum_{k \in V_g} minDel_{st}} \quad (15)$$

where, as before, $s$ is the root node $r_g$ and $t$ is the receiver $k$ of group $g$.

It is possible to define a new optimization problem that is multi-objective, where the aim is to find the set of OSPF weights ($w$) that simultaneously minimizes the functions $\Phi^*(w)$ and $\gamma^*(w)$. The algorithms described in the following sections use a linear weighting scheme where the cost of the solution is given by:

$$f(w) = \alpha \Phi^*(w) + (1 - \alpha)\gamma^*(w), \alpha \in [0, 1] \quad (16)$$

This scheme is effective since both cost functions are normalized in the same range and the parameter $\alpha$ can be tune the trade-off between both components.

## 3 Optimization Algorithms

### 3.1 Evolutionary Algorithms

Evolutionary Algorithms (EAs) [8] are a popular family of optimization methods, inspired in the biological evolution. These methods work by evolving a

---

[1] In this work experiments the network queuing delays at each network node were not considered. However, if required, they might be approximated resorting to queuing theory and taking into account the scheduling mechanisms in use and the capacity and utilization rates of the output links of the network nodes along the path.

population, i.e. a set of individuals, each encoding solutions to a target problem in an artificial chromosome. Each individual is evaluated through a fitness function, that assigns it a numerical value, corresponding to the quality of the encoded solution. EAs are stochastic methods due to their selection process. In fact, individuals selected to create new solutions are taken from the population using probabilities. Highly fit individuals have a higher probability of being selected, but the less fit still have their chance.

In the proposed EA, each individual encodes a solution in a direct way, i.e. as a vector of integer values, where each value corresponds to the weight of an arc in the network (the values range from 1 to $w_{max}$). Therefore, the size of the individual equals the number of links in the network. If multiple topologies are used, i.e. different sets of weights for unicast and multicast, the size of the individual is twice the number of links and the two sets of weights are encoded linearly, i.e. the first $L$ genes encode the weights for unicast traffic, while the latter $L$ links encode the weights for multicast ($L$ is the number of links).

The weight values for individuals in the initial population are randomly generated, taken from a uniform distribution. In order to create new solutions, several reproduction operators were used, more specifically two mutation and one crossover operator: *i) Random Mutation*, replaces a given weight value by a random value, within the allowed range; *ii) Incremental/decremental Mutation*, replaces a given weight value $w$ by $w + 1$ or by $w - 1$ (with equal probabilities); *iii) Uniform crossover*, a standard crossover operator [8]. The operators are all used to create new solutions with equal probabilities. The selection procedure is done by converting the fitness value into a linear ranking in the population, and then applying a roulette wheel scheme. In each generation, 50% of the individuals are selected from the previous generation, and 50% are bred by the application of the genetic operators over selected parents. A population size of 100 individuals was considered.

## 3.2  Optimization Approaches

Three distinct optimization approaches are compared, with the aim to optimize OSPF weights in networks where both unicast and multicast demands are available. All these methods use EAs as the optimization engine. The first method is a **2-step optimization process (2S)**, based on the proposal from Section 2.2 [13], that can be described as: *i)* the OSPF weights are optimized (using EAs) to minimize congestion penalties ($\Phi^*$) only taking into account the unicast demands; *ii)* the bandwidths used for each link in unicast traffic are deduced from the link capacities and *iii)* a second optimization process is conducted, where a different set of weights is calculated from multicast traffic only, by running a new EA with $f(L_1, L_2)$ (Eq. 8) as the fitness function. This method can only be used in the optimization of network congestion and assumes that a protocol that allows multiple sets of weights, each for a distinct type of traffic, is deployed. This is the case, for instance, of the multi-topology protocol MT-OSPF [10].

The remaining alternatives are based on the model proposed in Sections 2.3 and 2.4. Using this model, two different optimization approaches may be followed:

**Single topology (ST)**, i.e. a single set of OSPF weights is used for both types of traffic demands and **Multiple topologies (MT)** , i.e. two sets of OSPF weights are used, one for unicast traffic and the other for multicast demands. These two methods can address both the problem of network congestion, where the fitness function is simply $\Phi^*$, calculated as shown in Section 2.3, as well as to optimize both congestion and multicast end-to-end delays. In the latter case, the cost function is given by the Eq. 16 (in this work $\alpha$ was set to 0.5).

## 4   Experiments and Results

To evaluate the proposed algorithms, a number of experiments were conducted. The experimental platform is presented in Fig. 2. All algorithms and the OSPF routing simulator were implemented using the Java language. A set of 3 network topologies was created using the Brite topology generator [7], varying the number of nodes ($N = 30, 80, 100$) and the average degree of each node was kept ($m = 4$). This resulted in networks ranging from 110 to 390 links. The link bandwidth was generated by a uniform distribution between 1 and 10 Gbits/s. The networks were generated using the Barabasi-Albert model, using a heavy-tail distribution and an incremental grow type (parameters $HS$ and $LS$ were set to 1000 and 100). Next, the unicast demand matrices ($D$) were generated (two distinct matrices for each network). A parameter ($D_p$) was considered, representing the expected mean of congestion in each link (values for $D_p$ were 0.2 and 0.3).

The generation of the multicast traffic demands was based on the following: Firstly, for each network the number of groups $G$ was set equal to the number of nodes. The root node for each group was randomly chosen from the set of nodes (with equal probabilities). For each group, the number of receivers was generated from the range $[2, n/2]$, where $n$ is the number of nodes. The set of receivers $V_g$ was created with the given cardinality, by randomly selecting a set of nodes different from the root. Finally, the demand $M_g$ was generated taking a parameter ($R$) into account. $R$ is defined as the ratio between the total multicast demands and the total unicast demands. Given $R$ and given the unicast demands, a target is calculated for the total multicast demands. The group demands are generated by dividing the target value by the different groups in an uneven way, so that groups with different demands are created resulting in a more plausible scenario. In the experiments, the value of $R$ was set to 0.5.

For the generation of the delays for each group, the strategy was to calculate the average of the minimum possible delay between the root node and all

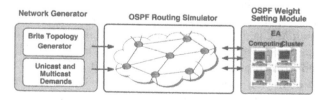

**Fig. 2.** Experimental platform for EA's performance evaluation

**Table 1.** Results for the optimization of the overall congestion

| Nodes | Demands $(D_p)$ | Metric | ST | MT | 2S |
|---|---|---|---|---|---|
| 30 | 0.2 | $\Phi^*$ | 1.38 | 1.31 | 1.83 |
|  |  | BOL | 0 | 0 | 42 |
|  | 0.3 | $\Phi^*$ | 3.32 | 2.83 | 7.78 |
|  |  | BOL | 257 | 128 | 875 |
| 80 | 0.2 | $\Phi^*$ | 1.44 | 1.38 | 1.74 |
|  |  | BOL | 0 | 0 | 7 |
|  | 0.3 | $\Phi^*$ | 2.63 | 2.50 | 3.97 |
|  |  | BOL | 227 | 247 | 821 |
| 100 | 0.2 | $\Phi^*$ | 1.35 | 1.31 | 1.69 |
|  |  | BOL | 0 | 0 | 7 |
|  | 0.3 | $\Phi^*$ | 4.51 | 3.18 | 4.54 |
|  |  | BOL | 2122 | 665 | 1113 |

receivers of the group. A noise value is added that can change this value by $\pm 25\%$. A parameter $(DR_p)$ was considered, representing a multiplier applied to the previous value (values for $DR_p$ in the experiments were 3 and 4). The termination criteria for all optimization approaches consisted in a maximum number of solutions evaluated. This value ranged from 100000 to 300000, increasing linearly with the number of links. For all cases, $w_{max}$ was set to 20 and 20 runs were executed in each instance and the results presented are the means.

Two sets of experiments were conducted in the aforementioned instances, regarding: (i) the optimization of the overall network congestion and (ii) the simultaneous optimization of congestion and multicast end-to-end delays. The results are given and discussed in the next two sub-sections.

## 4.1   Results for Congestion

In this case, there were 6 scenarios (3 networks, 2 values of $D_p$), 3 optimization approaches (2S, ST, MT). Table 1 shows the results for this task. The first column gives the number of nodes in the network; the second shows the demand generation parameter $(D_p)$; the third shows the performance metrics; the remaining columns give the results of each approach.

A different perspective is shown in Figs. 3 and 4 where the congestion measure $(\Phi^*)$ for the three networks is plotted. In each plot, the two scenarios in terms of demands are shown. The values are shown in a logarithmic scale, given the exponential nature of the penalty function. It is clear from these results that the 2S approach leads to sub-optimal results, in terms of overloaded links and network congestion (visible both in the BOL and $\Phi^*$). Both the MT and ST show better results, being able to keep the network in an acceptable behaviour. When comparing ST and MT, the results are quite near, i.e. the gain obtained by using MT is not impressive, although it increases with the value of $D_p$ (the problem is harder). In practical terms, this means that if the network has lots of bandwidth resources and low demands, it is probably not worth to pay the cost of deploying a multi-topology protocol. On the other hand, using this kind of protocol allows the network to support higher demands with the same resources.

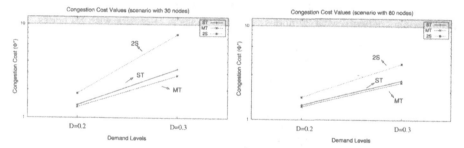

**Fig. 3.** Results for congestion measure - network with a) 30 nodes and b) 80 nodes

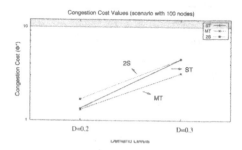

**Fig. 4.** Results for congestion measure - network with 100 nodes

## 4.2 Results for Congestion and Delays

In this case, the number of considered scenarios increases to 12, since two values of $DR_p$ are considered. The optimization approaches in this case are only MT and ST, since the 2S method can not be applied in this case. The results of the experiments are summarized in Tables 2, 3 and 4, for each of the networks. In each table, the first two columns show the parameters $D_p$ and $DR_p$, the third gives the metrics and the last two show the results of both algorithms.

A different perspective is shown in Figs. 5 and 6. In these figures a distinct data representation is used, with the congestion values represented in the *x-axis* and the delays cost values in the *y-axis*. As before, the white area represents the acceptable working region, meaning that the proposed routing configurations are able to support the traffic demands of the domain and simultaneously obey the delay requirements of the considered multicast groups.

Note that in this perspective, acceptable OSPF configurations are expected to be harder to find. As an example, for the the case of the multi-topology approach, the OSPF weights devised to handle the multicast traffic are expected to provide network paths able to support both the traffic demands and the delay requirements of the multicast groups. In the same perspective, scenarios only using a single level of OSPF weights will be faced with the challenge of finding a single level of link weights able to induce both unicast and multicast paths able to satisfy both the overall traffic demands and the multicast delays requirements.

**Table 2.** Results for congestion and delay optimization - network with 30 nodes

| Demands ($D_p$) | Delays ($DR_p$) | Metric | ST | MT |
|---|---|---|---|---|
| 0.2 | 4 | $\Phi^*$ | 1.65 | 1.38 |
| | | BOL | 2 | 0 |
| | | $\gamma^*$ | 1.36 | 1.12 |
| 0.2 | 3 | $\Phi^*$ | 1.74 | 1.38 |
| | | BOL | 2 | 0 |
| | | $\gamma^*$ | 1.66 | 1.41 |
| 0.3 | 4 | $\Phi^*$ | 7.35 | 3.62 |
| | | BOL | 985 | 211 |
| | | $\gamma^*$ | 5.05 | 1.32 |
| 0.3 | 3 | $\Phi^*$ | 24.7 | 3.24 |
| | | BOL | 3039 | 162 |
| | | $\gamma^*$ | 1.91 | 1.54 |

**Table 3.** Results for congestion and delay optimization - network with 80 nodes

| Demands ($D_p$) | Delays ($DR_p$) | Metric | ST | MT |
|---|---|---|---|---|
| 0.2 | 4 | $\Phi^*$ | 2.14 | 1.99 |
| | | BOL | 195 | 151 |
| | | $\gamma^*$ | 2.49 | 1.45 |
| 0.2 | 3 | $\Phi^*$ | 3.15 | 1.54 |
| | | BOL | 449 | 0 |
| | | $\gamma^*$ | 4.85 | 1.75 |
| 0.3 | 4 | $\Phi^*$ | 3.43 | 2.73 |
| | | BOL | 737 | 298 |
| | | $\gamma^*$ | 2.58 | 1.70 |
| 0.3 | 3 | $\Phi^*$ | 5.84 | 2.50 |
| | | BOL | 2139 | 184 |
| | | $\gamma^*$ | 6.66 | 2.29 |

**Table 4.** Results for congestion and delay optimization - network with 100 nodes

| Demands ($D_p$) | Delays ($DR_p$) | Metric | ST | MT |
|---|---|---|---|---|
| 0.2 | 4 | $\Phi^*$ | 1.59 | 1.41 |
| | | BOL | 0 | 0 |
| | | $\gamma^*$ | 2.08 | 1.28 |
| 0.2 | 3 | $\Phi^*$ | 1.85 | 1.44 |
| | | BOL | 15 | 0 |
| | | $\gamma^*$ | 7.36 | 2.10 |
| 0.3 | 4 | $\Phi^*$ | 5.09 | 3.21 |
| | | BOL | 2715 | 809 |
| | | $\gamma^*$ | 3.55 | 1.92 |
| 0.3 | 3 | $\Phi^*$ | 14.1 | 3.93 |
| | | BOL | 7437 | 1356 |
| | | $\gamma^*$ | 17.3 | 3.90 |

Taking into account the results of Figs. 5 and 6 some conclusions might be drawn. As expected, scenarios assuming lower levels of traffic demands and delay requirements (e.g. $D_p = 0.2$ and $DR_p = 4$) present better QoS results in all of the considered scenarios (both for the ST and MT approaches). In the same perspective, for harder assumptions of network demands (e.g. $D_p = 0.3$ and $DR_p = 3$) most of the results show an increase in the congestion and delay

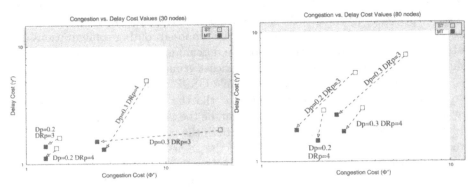

**Fig. 5.** Results for congestion vs delay - network with a) 30 nodes and b) 80 nodes

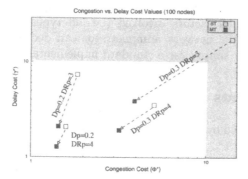

**Fig. 6.** Results for congestion vs delay - network with 100 nodes

costs. In particular, in scenarios with high levels of traffic demands and delays, some of the ST results fall into the gray filled area of the figures, representing a network behavior with some degree of packet loss and/or delay violations.

In addition, the effectiveness of the MT approach can be clearly assessed observing the fact that results obtained from the MT approach are shifted to the lower left corner of the figures (black squares), thus with lower values for the congestion and delay cost functions when comparing to ST. It is also important to note that even providing low quality results when compared with the MT approach, the ST performance is still acceptable for a large part of the studied scenarios. This allows to conclude that under low or medium network demands the optimization framework presented in this work is able to find single topology network configurations assuring a good overall QoS performance in the domain.

Finally, it should be highlighted the quality of the MT results in all the scenarios, independently of the difficulty levels of the demands. This means that even if heavy traffic demands and strict multicast delay requirements are considered, acceptable QoS performances is obtained, corroborating the viability and effectiveness of the proposed optimization framework.

## 5    Conclusions

The optimization of OSPF weights brings important tools for traffic engineering, without demanding modifications on the basic network model. This work presented EAs for routing optimization in networks with unicast and multicast demands. Resorting to a set of network configurations and unicast/ multicast demands, it was shown that the proposed EAs were able to provide OSPF weights that can lead to good network behaviour, in terms of the overall network performance, as well as regarding multicast end-to-end delays.

The proposed approach was favourably compared to a 2-step optimization procedure, proposed in previous work, that leads to sub-optimal results in terms of network congestion and overloaded links. The advantages of using a multi-topology protocol in these scenarios were also studied and it was concluded that these are most advantageous when the network resources are limited.

The main contribution of this work is the capability of optimizing the OSPF weights considering all factors involved (i.e. all types of traffic). Using the proposed methods, the network administrator can decide if a multi-topology protocol is needed or simply use a standard implementation of OSPF.

## Acknowledgments

This work is supported by the Portuguese FCT project PTDC/EIA/64541/2006.

## References

1. Ahuja, R.K., Magnati, T.L., Orlin, J.B.: Network Flows. Prentice Hall, Englewood Cliffs (1993)
2. Awduche, D., Jabbari, B.: Internet traffic engineering using multi-protocol label switching (MPLS). Computer Networks 40, 111–129 (2002)
3. Davie, B., Rekhter, Y.: MPLS: Multiprotocol Label Switching Technology and Applications. Morgan Kaufmann, USA (2000)
4. Dijkstra, E.: A note on two problems in connexion with graphs. Numerische Mathematik 1, 269–271 (1959)
5. Ericsson, M., Resende, M.G.C., Pardalos, P.M.: A Genetic Algorithm for the Weight Setting Problem in OSPF Routing. J. of Combinatorial Optimization 6, 299–333 (2002)
6. Fortz, B., Thorup, M.: Internet Traffic Engineering by Optimizing OSPF Weights. In: Proceedings of IEEE INFOCOM, pp. 519–528 (2000)
7. Medina, A., Lakhina, A., Matta, I., Byers, J.: BRITE: Universal Topology Generation from a User's Perspective. Technical Report 2001-003 (January 2001)
8. Michalewicz, Z.: Genetic Algorithms + Data Structures = Evolution Programs, 3rd edn. Springer, USA (1996)
9. Moy, J.: OSPF, Anatomy of an Internet Routing Protocol. Addison Wesley, Reading (1998)
10. Psenak, P., Mirtorabi, S., Roy, A., Nguyen, L., Pillay-Esnault, P.: Multi-topology (MT) routing in OSPF. IETF RFC 4915 (June 2007)
11. Rocha, M., Sousa, P., Rio, M., Cortez, P.: Qos constrained internet routing with evolutionary algorithms. In: Proc. IEEE Conference Evolutionary Computation, pp. 9270–9277. IEEE Press, Los Alamitos (2006)
12. Thomas, T.M.: OSPF Network Design Solutions. Cisco Press (1998)
13. Wang, N., Pavlou, G.: Traffic Engineered Multicast Content Delivery Without MPLS Overlay. IEEE Transactions on Multimedia 9(3) (April 2007)

# Stabilizing Intelligent Route Control: Randomized Path Monitoring, Randomized Path Switching or History-Aware Path Switching?

Alexandre Fonte[1,2], José Martins[1], Marilia Curado[1], and Edmundo Monteiro[1]

[1] University of Coimbra, CISUC/DEI, Coimbra, Portugal
[2] Polytechnic Institute of Castelo Branco, Castelo Branco, Portugal
{afonte,marilia,edmundo}@dei.uc.pt, jemart@student.dei.uc.pt

**Abstract.** Multihoming Intelligent Route Control (IRC) plays a significant role in improving the performance of Internet accesses. However, in a competitive environment, IRC systems may introduce persistent route oscillations, causing significant performance degradation. In this study, three design alternatives to cope with this issue are investigated: Randomized Path Monitoring, Randomized Path Switching and History-aware Path Switching. The simulation results show that Randomized Path Monitoring is an effective alternative to Randomized Path switching when the sampling frequency is conservative. The results also indicate that the use of a sophisticated IRC algorithm, such as history-aware path switching, does not bring noteworthy benefits in terms of stability.

## 1 Introduction

Multihoming is a well-known technique to improve performance and reliability of Internet accesses. It consists on increasing the Internet connectivity, by leasing multiple broadband lines (e.g., Business DSL) from two or three ISPs (Internet Service Providers). The use of multihoming allows stub ASs (Autonomous Systems) to experience a potential performance improvement of at least 40% [1]. In this context, Intelligent Route Controllers (IRC) are, thus, being increasingly used by multi-homed stub ASs, as they provide a holistic way to solve their traffic challenges by shifting traffic between ISPs [2,3].

Unfortunately, the use of IRC has a major weakness, that is, oscillations can take place due to factors such as its intrinsic selfish nature, self-load effects, and synchronization between the probes [4,5]. Specifically, the last two situations were studied in [4]. As a solution, the authors proposed a set of IRC techniques that might reduce IRC oscillations by adding randomness in the path switching process. In this paper, we answer the following question *adding randomness into the sampling process or using path history to assist IRC decisions are effective alternatives to refrain IRC oscillations?*

The rest of the paper is structured as follows. Section 2 gives a brief overview of the IRC algorithms explored in this study. Next, Section 3 presents the results of the evaluation of these algorithms. Finally, the major conclusions of the work performed are summarized in Section 4.

G. Pavlou, T. Ahmed, and T. Dagiuklas (Eds.): MMNS 2008, LNCS 5274, pp. 151–156, 2008.

## 2    A Brief Overview of IRC Algorithms

Dynamic path switching is the key technique used by most available IRC systems to get better end-to-end performance [2,3,4,6]. With this approach, the IRC selects, in every routing cycle, the next-hop ISP to forward packets that has the smallest value of the chosen performance metric. Obviously, IRCs need to previously probe all the candidate paths by sending, for instance, ICMP and TCP probes at a given frequency $f_i$. In addition, the path selection performed by IRCs must take into account end-to-end performance bounds, so that the perceived application quality does not suffer degradation. For instance, the ITU-Ts G.114 recommendation suggests a one-way delay bound of 150ms to maintain high quality voice.

The work described in this paper seeks to answer the question about which is the best approach to cope with the oscillations associated with IRCs. To achieve this objective, three classes of IRC algorithms are investigated, as follows:

**DLV** (Deterministic Last Value) - DLV is the basic IRC routing algorithm. The IRC selects as the best path, the path that has the smallest value of the metric $M(t_i)$, computed in the last time slot $t_i$. In other words, in DLV, the path shifts are deterministic.
**FSP** (Fixed Switching Probability) - FSP adds randomness to the path switching process. In this case, the IRC picks the best path with a given switching probability $P \in [0, 1]$.
**LpEMA** (Low pass Exponential Moving Average) - LpEMA introduces a certain degree of path history in the IRC route decisions. To compute the actual metric estimate $e_i$, the IRC combines the previous metric estimate $e_{i-1}$ and the actual metric $M(t_i)$ using an adaptive Exponential Moving Average (see Eq.(1)) [7]. Then, the IRC picks the best path, the path that has the smallest metric estimate $e_i$.

$$\begin{cases} e_i = (1 - \alpha_i)e_{i-1} + \alpha_i M(t_i) \\ \alpha_i = \alpha_{max} \frac{1}{1 + \frac{|m_i|}{m_{norm}}} \end{cases} \tag{1}$$

where $\alpha_i$ is an adaptive exponential weight, which is calculated using the classical formula for low pass filter, $m_i$ is the gradient between two metric samples (i.e., $\frac{M(t_i) - M(t_{i-1})}{t_i - t_{i-1}}$), and $m_{norm}$ is the normative gradient calculated over a given time window (e.g., 10 times the interval $t_i - t_{i-1}$).

## 3    Evaluation of IRC Algorithms

This section presents the performance evaluation of the DLV, FSP and LpEMA Intelligent Route Control algorithms. The evaluation was performed on a J-Sim simulation model for IRCs[1]. Two sampling processes were used to compare the three algorithms, namely, a periodic sampling process (Periodic sampling) and a pseudo-Poisson sampling process (p-Poisson sampling), with $N_i$ samples uniformly distributed over a slot of time $t$, afterwards referred as the window $t$.

---

[1] http://www.j-sim.org/

## 3.1   Simulation Setup and IRC Parameterization

The network topology was built using the BRITE[2] topology generator and it contains 100 ASs with a ratio of ASs to inter-domain links of 1:3. During the tests, 300 IRCs sources send homogeneous traffic aggregates to remote prefixes. Each traffic aggregate is composed of a fixed number of multiplexed Pareto flows (i.e., VoIP flows) with Poisson arrivals.

The RTT bound for DLV, FSP and LpEMA is set to 300ms. In this study, the results obtained with DLV are used as a reference for comparison with FSP and LpEMA. The performance of FSP is studied under two different values of the switching probability $P$ (0.1 and 0.5). On the other hand, the LpEMA configuration relies on $\alpha_{max}$, typically ranging from 0.5 to 5. In this study, we pick out a middle value for $\alpha_{max}$ (2.5).

To avoid the self-load effect [4], we combined latency and spare bandwidth into a single metric, i.e., $M = \alpha_1.latency_t + \alpha_2.\frac{1}{abw_t}$, where $latency_t$ is the median of the measured RTTs in a window $t$ of 30s, and $abw_t$ is the estimated spare bandwidth in the peering link during $t$. To facilitate the tuning of $\alpha_i, i = 1, 2$, we adopted the framework in [6]. Finally, DLV, FSP and LpEMA use a route threshold ($R_{th}$) set to 10, as common stability mechanism [6].

## 3.2   Comparasion of IRC Algorithms

Figures 1 to 6 illustrate two empirical Complementary Cumulative Distribution Functions (CCDF) of the number of path shifts performed by the three IRC schemes for two bin sizes, used to count the path shifts along the simulation. If the probability of a number of Path Shifts (PS), in a bin, is greater than or equal to $x$ is high (i.e., P(PS in a bin$\geq x$) is high), it means route oscillations are highly present in every bin. It must be pointed out that a line starting at a value smaller than 1, means that a fraction of the bins do not have path shifts.

Three main conclusions can be drawn from the analysis of these results. First, the comparison between the DLV and FSP shows that IRC oscillations can be reduced by adding a certain degree of randomness in the route control decisions. In fact, these results show similar trends of a previous study [4]. However, when IRCs use the RTT performance metric rather than the loss rate metric, DLV and FSP present a similar number of path shifts for path switching probabilities below 0.5. This behavior might be explained by a weaker aggressiveness of the RTT metric when compared to the loss rate metric used in [4].

Second, the results also show that the oscillations can be reduced by adding a certain degree of randomness in the sampling process. In fact, figures 3 and 4, illustrate that, for lower frequencies of sampling, DLV combined with p-Poisson sampling performs better than when combined with periodic sampling. In particular, when $f = 0.2Hz$, DLV combined with p-Poisson sampling has a smaller probability (20% smaller) to reach the same number of path shifts in a bin. However, when the sampling frequency is higher, both DLVs perform similarly.

---

[2] http://www.cs.bu.edu/brite/

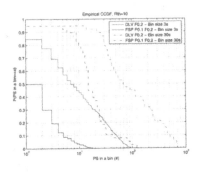

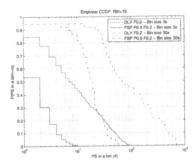

**Fig. 1.** CCDF of PS, DLV vs FSP (P=0.1), Periodic, $f = 0.2Hz$

**Fig. 2.** CCDF of PS, DLV vs FSP (P=0.5), Periodic, $f = 0.2Hz$

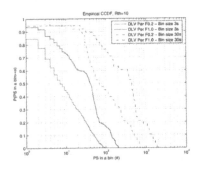

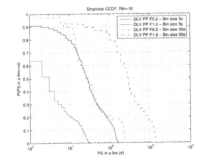

**Fig. 3.** CCDF of PS, DLV, Periodic, $f = 0.2Hz$ and $f = 1Hz$

**Fig. 4.** CCDF of PS, DLV, p-Poisson, $f = 0.2Hz$ and $f = 1Hz$

This arises from similar overlappings of the IRCs measurement windows, which are also significant for p-Poisson when the sampling frequency is high.

Third, the results in figures 5 and 6 indicate the use of a sophisticated IRC algorithm, such as LpEMA, may not bring any benefit in terms of the reduction of oscillations. LpEMA can be viewed as a cascaded DLV and a *low-pass filter* block, and so in theory it should reduce the number of path shifts. However, its ideal tuning depends on the particular stability pattern of the network [7].

Figures 7 to 12 illustrate the CCDF distribution of the traffic latency. The main conclusions of the analysis of these results are described next. First, the results show that there is a correlation between the frequency of sampling and the observed RTTs. More specifically, as the sampling frequency increases, the probability of the traffic to experiment higher RTT also increases. This is even more noticeable when RTT is smaller than 70ms. However, in case of Periodic sampling, there is a clear turn-over point, and a long tail over 70ms, over which higher frequency leads to smaller probabilities to get higher RTTs. This characteristic is common to all IRC algorithms. Second, the results in figures 7 and 8 confirm that when DLV is combined with p-Poisson sampling, the traffic

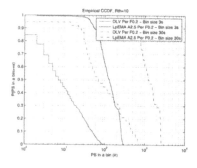

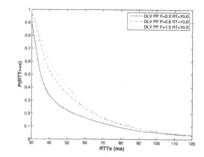

**Fig. 5.** CCDF of PS, DLV vs LpEMA, Periodic, $f = 0.2Hz$

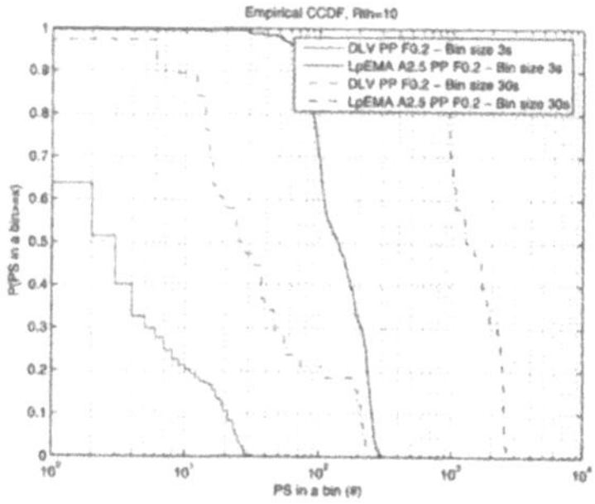

**Fig. 6.** CCDF of PS, DLV vs LpEMA, p-Poisson, $f = 0.2Hz$

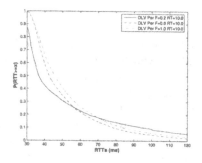

**Fig. 7.** CCDF of RTTs, DLV, Periodic

**Fig. 8.** CCDF of RTTs, DLV, p-Poisson

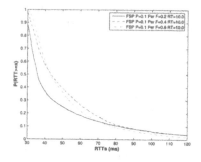

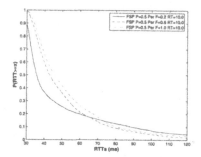

**Fig. 9.** CCDF of RTTs, FSP, $P = 0.1$, Periodic

**Fig. 10.** CCDF of RTTs, FSP, $P = 0.5$, Periodic

experiments a potential performance benefit of 20%, while a smaller number of path shifts is needed. However, when the sampling frequency is high, the improvement is negligible. Third, when changing the FSP probability $P$ (from $P = 0.5$ to $P = 0.1$) to reduce oscillations the effect on the RTT distribution is negligible.

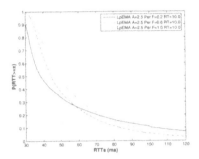   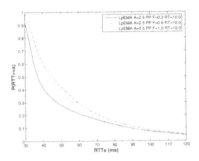

**Fig. 11.** CCDF of RTTs, LpEMA, $\alpha_{max} = 2.5$, Periodic

**Fig. 12.** CCDF of RTTs, LpEMA, $\alpha_{max} = 2.5$, p-Poisson

## 4    Conclusions

In this paper, the evaluation of the three main classes of Intelligent Route Control algorithms was performed in order to find out which is the best alternative to cope with the oscillations associated with this type of schemes. The results showed that the addition of a randomness component to the route control process drastically reduces the number of path shifts needed to meet the traffic challenges. The addition of a randomness component to the path monitoring mechanism is an effective alternative to this solution. However, the decision to adopt a randomized path monitoring solution depends on the time scale used by the IRC system to probe all candidate paths. In particular, short time scales might hurt its effectiveness due to the overlapping of the IRC measurement windows. Finally, the use of sophisticated IRC algorithms, such as history-aware path switching, is questionable, since these mechanisms require additional tuning, according to the particular stability pattern of the network.

## References

1. Akella, A., et al.: A Measurement-Based Analysis of Multihoming. In: The Proc. of ACM SIGCOMM 2003, Karlsruhe, Germany (2003)
2. Cisco Systems, Inc., Optimized Edge Routing
3. Internap Networks Inc., Flow Control Platform
4. Gao, R., et al.: Avoiding Oscillations due to Intelligent Route Control Systems. In: The Proc. of IEEE INFOCOM 2006, Barcelona, Spain (April 2006)
5. Qiu, L., et al.: On Selfish Routing in Internet-Like Environments. In: Proc. of ACM SIGCOMM 2003, Karlsruhe, German (August 2003)
6. Yannuzzi, M., et al.: On the Advantages of Cooperative and Social Smart Route. In: Proc. of ICCCN 2006, Arlington, Virginia, USA (October 2006)
7. Burgstahler, L., Neubauer, M.: New Modications of the Exponential Moving Average Algorithm for Bandwidth Estimation. In: Proc. of the 15th ITC Specialist Seminar (July 2002)

# A Dimensioning and Deployment Tool for on Demand Policy-Based Resource Management System

Kamel Haddadou[1], Samir Ghamri-Doudane[1], Yacine Ghamri-Doudane[2], and Nazim Agoulmine[2]

[1] LIP6, Pierre & Marie Curie University, 104 avenue du Président Kennedy 75015
Paris – France
{Kamel.Haddadou,Samir.Ghamri-Doudane}@lip6.fr
[2] LRSM, ENSIIE & University of Evry joint research group, 18 allée Jean Rostand, 91025
Evry Cedex – France
ghamri@ensiie.fr, Nazim.Agoulmine@iup.univ-evry.fr

**Abstract.** Today the Policy-Based Management (PBM) approach is recognized as an efficient solution to simplify the complex task of managing and controlling networks. To this end, the IETF has introduced a reference framework to build PBM systems. However, this framework only addresses the provisioning of relatively long validity period services based on pre-defined SLAs (Service Level Agreements). Furthermore, very little work addresses the scalability properties of the instantiation of this framework in a real network. In our previous work, we presented an extension of the IETF PBM framework in order to support dynamic provisioning of short term services (end-system signaling) as well as an instantiation scheme that is scalable (distributed provisioning of edge routers). This instantiation scheme is based on the distribution of the provisioning process while keeping centralized only the parts that involve critical resources, namely the Bandwidth Brokerage. In this paper, we propose an extensive analytical study of this extended architecture. The results of this work are intended to be used as a guideline to help network operators to design a scalable PBM system in order to offer to their customers' services with QoS assurance in an on-demand basis.

## 1 Introduction

A major challenge in emerging multi-service, QoS-capable telecommunication networks is the deployment of high-quality multimedia applications. Both of network operators and end users are willing to offer and use multimedia communications with a large range of QoS-guarantees. To achieve this aim, an efficient control and management of network resources are submitted to be the key issues in the telecommunications world. We argue that a combination of QoS signaling and Policy-Based Management (PBM) [1] is required to enable proper multimedia sessions.

PBM aims to facilitate the management activity as it allows network administrators to define high-level objectives of network management schemes based on a set of policies. The latter is a set of pre-defined rules controlling network resources. Rules established by the network administrator, include actions to be triggered when a set of

G. Pavlou, T. Ahmed, and T. Dagiuklas (Eds.): MMNS 2008, LNCS 5274, pp. 157–169, 2008.

conditions is fulfilled. PBM approach allows in its turn the translation of these high-level rules to a set of low-level device-compliant configuration commands [2].

In a previous work [3], we proposed a novel architecture that integrates QoS signaling with dynamic per-session QoS provisioning. Thus, our proposed architecture was twofold. First, we proposed to transfer parts of the network management and control mechanisms to the user's terminal. This latter is rendered responsible, for each of its sessions, to generate QoS requests towards the PBM system and to wait upon the reception of request acceptance by this one. Then we proposed to distribute the resource provisioning process while keeping centralized only the parts that involve critical operations, namely the Bandwidth Brokerage. The performance improvement in terms of scalability of such architecture was demonstrated through practical experiments. In this paper, we propose an extensive analytical study of this extended architecture. The results of our current work are intended to be used as a guideline to help network operators to design and dimension their scalable on-demand policy-based resource allocation system. So, this later will allow them to offer to their customers services with QoS assurance in an on-demand basis.

As far as we know, the only contribution to the specification of an analytical model for PBM systems is the one proposed in [4]. This analytical study aimed at demonstrating that a dynamic PBM architecture could be scalable according to the size of the administrative domain. This work is without doubt very interesting however the hypotheses of the authors are not realistic. Indeed, their analysis did not take into account numerous practical constraints related to the implementation of the PBM architecture, and it also ignores the fact that the critical resources cannot be distributed. This means that when wishing to dimension a PBM system for real networks, the analytical model proposed in [4] cannot be used. Conversely, we design in this paper an analytical model that depends closely on functional constraints and we compare it to real experiments showing its accuracy to model a real system.

The rest of this paper is organized as follows: Section 2 introduces our previously proposed architecture. Section 3 develops the analytical model and analysis of our architecture. The dimensioning formulas for on-demand policy-based resource allocation systems are presented in Section 4. This is followed by the description of the deployment strategy to be used by network operators. Finally, Section 6 concludes the paper and presents some future works.

## 2  Scalable On-Demand Policy-Based Resource Allocation

It appears nowadays that management systems following the PBM architecture are neither responding to operators' scalability issues nor to customers needs. In fact, customers are willing to dynamically request network resources depending on their instantaneous needs and without having to contract a SLA for a long period of time. This tendency is confirmed by the forthcoming 3G IP Multimedia Subsystem (IMS)/Multimedia Domain (MMD) [5] network architecture. Indeed, this architecture is evolving toward including per-session resource management and control using policies. However, from the operator perspective, the integration of dynamic resource allocation to the existing IETF's PBM architecture is not feasible at a large scale.

In order to overcome these limitations, we proposed in a previous work [3] a novel solution for on-demand policy-based resource allocation in IP networks. This solution aims to distribute the decision making operations among several distributed PDPs. Therefore, the PBM architecture has been decomposed into a set of functional components. The idea of this decomposition is to identify which components represent critical sections in the decision-making process. Once this phase achieved, the solution consists on proposing a new instantiation model where non-critical components are distributed according to none functional requirements (such as performance objectives, network size, etc.). Hence, the impact of critical operations on the overall management system performances is minimized. To maintain the consistency of the decision-making process, critical operations are kept centralized. These operations are identified as those operations that need to access to critical resources (shared information, common databases, etc.) in the system.

The critical operations in our framework were identified as those related to the bandwidth brokerage. All other operations related to decision making appeared as replicable. Based on these statements verified in our previous work [3], we propose to keep centralized the Bandwidth Brokerage while distributing all other functional components. Fig. 1 presents in details our framework (Fig. 1(b)) and its instantiation (Fig. 1(c)), and shows its differences with the IETF's PBM framework (Fig. 1(a)).

As our objective was to demonstrate its scalability features, we both realized a complete implementation of our proposed framework. The practical experiments highlighted the scalability property of our approach. These experiments also permitted to identify the effect of each component of the framework on the overall performance of the management system. A detailed description of our proposed architecture and its practical performance evaluation can be found in [3].

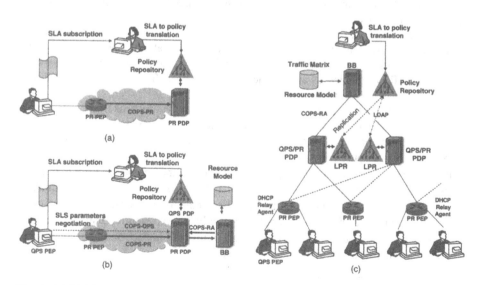

**Fig. 1.** (a) IETF PBM architecture, (b) Proposed on-demand policy-based resource allocation architecture, (c) Scalable inystantiation of the proposed architecture

## 3  Analytical Analysis

In order to understand the behavior of our architecture, we have developed an analytical model. Our main goal in designing this model is to understand the problem analytically and to try to provide network operators with a dimensioning tool to help them to design their system efficiently. First, we will describe the components and characteristics of the analytical model, then we will apply this model to practical experiment results and compare them, in order to validate our model.

### 3.1  Analytical Model

Based on the instantiation schema presented in Figure 1(c), we deduce that all the customer requests follow the same path: (1) PDP processing, (2) Local Policy Repository (LPR) access (LDAP), (3) bandwidth brokerage, and if there is enough resources (positive response from the Bandwidth Broker): (4) configuration of the appropriate edge router, (5) service completion, and (6) resource release (access to the BB and to the adequate edge router). According to this we specify the queue network model shown in Figure 2.

The first queue (P), which represents local processing at a PDP, is composed of C parallel independent servers, each of which corresponds to one connection controlled by a PDP. The aim is to study the scalability of the framework, i.e. to compute the maximum value of C before reaching system instability (i.e. here we are interested in the limits of the system). Each server serves the requests at a certain rate. We have chosen an exponential1 distribution which is fairly representative of the real world. As we are interested in the number of active connections in the system, the number of PDPs has no effect on the model design. Each PDP handles a part of these connections and C represents the total value.

The second queue (L) characterizes the LPR access. This queue is also composed of C parallel independent servers, since an LDAP server is able to handle the requests in parallel. For the same reasons as for the PDP service time modeling, the service time of the LPR is modeled as an exponential distribution. The number of LPRs has no effect on the model design, either.

The third part of the model (B) represents the bandwidth broker. It is a single server queue, as the BB processes the requests sequentially, and it should be noted that there is only one BB in the system. Its service law is approximated by an exponential distribution.

The fourth part (the N parallel queues) symbolizes the set of configurable edge routers in the operator network. We assume that these routers are targeted equitably by customer requests (probability set to 1/N). Each edge router is modeled as a single server queue and its service time is approximated by an exponential distribution. For high values, the edge router number (N) has no significant impact on the performance of our system (this assertion will be argued later).

---

[1] The reason for choosing the exponential distribution as the service time is that all our experiments have shown that the mean and the standard deviation values are close enough for both PDP and LPR. Indeed, the characteristic of this distribution is that its standard deviation is equal to its mean.

The next queue (S) characterizes the effective service time, i.e. the time necessary for a user to complete the desired service. Finally, the last queues (W and F) represent the waiting time between two consecutive requests from the same customer (initiated using the same QPS connection). The Queue F is visited in the case of a blocked call (Failure: insufficient resources to satisfy the client request), while the queue W is visited after a successful call.

After service completion, the system should release the reserved resources, which represents another access to the BB and the corresponding edge router. Consequently, the outflow of the edge router queues is connected to both the service and waiting queues, with the same probability: 1/2. Also, depending on the available resources, the Bandwidth broker may accept or reject the client request. Thus, the outflow of the BB queue is divided into two different paths with a blocking proportion: 'α'. This latter depends on the call blocking probability (p), and is calculated as follows:

First, let us redefine the relevant parameters:

p: The call blocking probability.

α: The blocking proportion at the outflow of the Bandwidth Broker queue in the proposed model.

$T_{<I>}$: The throughput of the queue <I>, with $I \in \{P, L, B, R, S, W, F\}$. Note that, in the steady state and for each queue in the network, the input and output throughputs are the same. $T_R$ corresponds to the aggregated throughput of the N Parallel queues (R).

Then, based on the queue network flows in the steady state, we extract the following equations:

$$T_B = T_L + T_S$$
$$T_R = (1 - \alpha) \times T_B$$
$$T_S = \frac{T_R}{2}$$

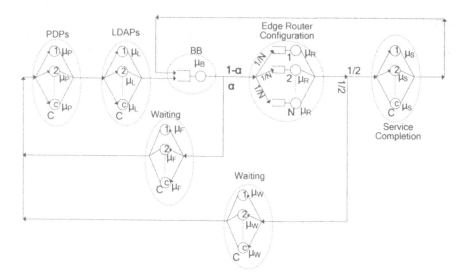

**Fig. 2.** Analytical model of the PBM system

Also, based on the definition of the call blocking probability, it is obvious that:

$$T_S = (1-p) \times T_P \quad \text{with:} \quad T_P = T_L$$

Finally, from the previous equations, the following formula is extracted:

$$\alpha = \frac{p}{2-p} \tag{1}$$

This proposed model is a BCMP model and can be solved as a product form solution [8]. As we are interested in the scalability performance of such a system, we have studied the system in the worst case, by assuming that each customer disconnecting from the system is immediately replaced by a customer entering the system. Thus, the resulting model is a closed queue network, where inputs and outputs are removed.

### 3.2 Test-Bed Results

In order to validate our analytical model, we compare its results to those obtained using practical experiments. To that end, an integrated test-bed containing all our architecture entities has been implemented. The BB, the PEP, the PDP, and the signaling protocol have been implemented using Java 1.5. The policy repository and its replicas (LPRs) are instances of the LDAP repository, in which the management information is modeled using CIM. The management information replication and updates are handled automatically by LDAP [9]. In addition to PBM components, specific Linux-based traffic conditioning software has been used to enforce the QoS decisions (traffic classification and packet marking) in the Linux-based edge routers.

As shown in Figure 3, the obtained practical results demonstrated that the overall-system delay is always below the ITU-T recommended signaling-delay limit [6] and that the system throughput is higher than the 200 req/s as recommended by the ITU-T [7]. For a detailed performance evaluation of our architecture the reader can refer to [3].

From the practical experiments using our test-bed, we have determined the median value of the PDP's mean service time, which is set to 7ms. Similarly, the LPR mean

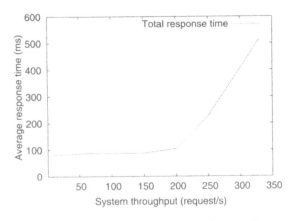

**Fig. 3.** Average response time as a function of system throughput

service time is set to 40ms and the edge router configuration mean time is fixed to 35ms. For the BB, the mean time necessary to process a request is equal to 2,25ms ($\mu_B$). Finally, the obtained value for the call blocking probability (p) is equal to 4.6%. This value is extracted from the practical evaluation during the stable state.

## 3.3 Instantiation and Validation of the Model

In addition to the values obtained from experimental results and depicted above, we chosen the following values to validate our model: the number (N) of edge routers is set to 58 (as assumed in the test-bed). For the BB, the mean time necessary to process a request is equal to 2,25ms ($\mu_B$). The service execution time and the waiting times are assumed to follow an exponential distribution with a mean equal to 2 minutes ($\mu_S$), 5 minutes ($\mu_F$) and 15 minutes ($\mu_B$) respectively. The 'α' parameter is computed using the call blocking probability value (p) and is equal to: 2.35%.

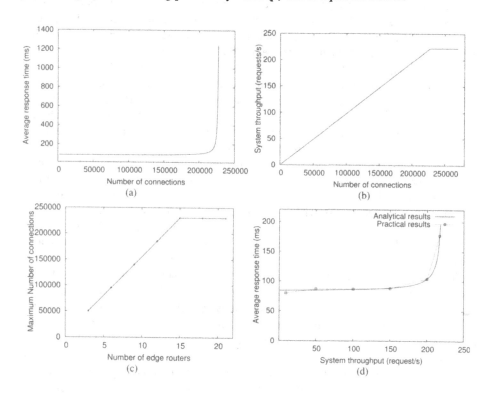

**Fig. 4.** Analytical evaluation:
(a) Average response time to resource allocation requests, and (b) system throughput as a function of the number of connections.
(c) Maximum number of connections shown as a function of the number of edge routers.
(d) Average response time to resource allocation requests as a function of the system throughput: practical vs. analytical results.

Based on the analytical model, which is a BCMP model, it is possible to compute the different scalability and performance parameters of the proposed framework. The parameters which are essential for our study are (1) the average response time, which is the delay time to be served by the PDP, the LPR, the bandwidth broker and, if the call is accepted, the appropriate PR PEP queues respectively, and (2) the effective system throughput calculated as the number of requests correctly served per second ($T_P$). These parameters are calculated for different values of C, the number of customers (connections) in the system. Therefore, this value is increased until the system reaches an unstable state.

The analytical results are represented by the curves in Figure 4(a-b) and we see that the instability point corresponds to a value of C = 230,000 concurrent connections. The average response time remains low enough (less than 150 ms) when the connection pool is under 220,000. Beyond this number, the average time increases very quickly and reaches values of several seconds. At the same time, effective throughput increases linearly until it reaches its maximum value which coincides with the instability point, and then it remains steady. From this, we can conclude that the maximum throughput of our system is about 227 effective requests per second and the value obtained is in concordance with the result obtained in the test-bed.

In the last experiments, we fixed the number N of edge routers, PR PEPs, in the system to 58. In some cases, this value may have a perceptible influence on the scalability performances of the architecture. So, to deal with this assertion, we vary the N value in the range [3 ... 21] and compute the maximum connection number (stability threshold) for each of them. The obtained results are shown in Figure 4(c). When the N value is less than 16, it has a direct impact on the scalability of the system. However, beyond this point, the two parameters become completely independent. This can easily be explained by the fact that the provisioning operations of each edge router are in fact critical sections. Hence, for a low number of edge routers, the time between the arrivals of two consecutive provisioning decisions within the same edge router is very low. For a high number of edge routers, which is the case for most of the 1st and 2nd tier ISPs, the bottleneck of the system is clearly the BB. All the scalability and performance parameters are strongly dependant on this latter.

Furthermore, in order to validate the proposed analytical model and all the corresponding results, we have compared these results with the test-bed results presented in section 3.2. We can see that the results are very similar (Figure 4(d)). This Figure presents the average response time to requests plotted as a function of the effective system throughput (the number of accepted requests per second). In the case of the analytical results, the curve is simply inferred by combining curves (a) and (b) of Figure 4, in which we only consider the stable state of the system (i.e. throughput values below 227 req/s). We see that the performance values obtained in each case are very close. Therefore, we can confirm that the proposed analytical model is representative of the performance of the entire system and can therefore be used as a dimensioning tool to calculate the capacity of the system to handle allocation requests while ensuring the ITU-T maximum response time boundary of 6s and the stability of the system.

## 4 Analytical Results and Dimensioning Formulas

Based on the analytical model presented above, we target here to extract relevant dimensioning formulas, which can act as a simple guideline for the instantiation of the PBM system.. Indeed, the main objective of our study is to provide these relevant dimensioning tools, since we have already identified the behavior of each component as well as the bottleneck of the proposed architecture. More precisely, in the subsequent study, we target the following scalability parameters: (1) $T^{Max}$: the maximum effective throughput of the system and (2) $C^{Max}$: the maximum capacity of the system (i.e. maximum number of active customers before reaching instability). Indeed, these two parameters will be the basis of our system design and dimensioning tool.

First, let us define and organize all the flow equations of our model (the queue network flows):

$$
\begin{cases}
T_L = T_P \\
T_B = T_L + T_S \\
T_R = (1-\alpha) \times T_B \\
T_S = \dfrac{T_R}{2} \\
T_W = \dfrac{T_R}{2} \\
T_F = \alpha \times T_B \\
T_P = T_W + T_F
\end{cases}
\Rightarrow
\begin{cases}
T_L = T_P = \dfrac{1+\alpha}{1-\alpha} \times T_W \\
T_B = \dfrac{2}{1-\alpha} \times T_W \\
T_R = 2 \times T_W \\
T_S = T_W \\
T_F = \dfrac{2\alpha}{1-\alpha} \times T_W
\end{cases}
\tag{2}
$$

Previously, we have shown that the bottleneck of system is the bandwidth broker or the PR PEPs, depending on the number N of edge routers. Consequently, the maximum throughput of the system, which is designated by: ($T^{Max} = T_P^{Max}$), is dependant on these components. Since the BB and the edge routers are modeled as single server queues, we have:

If the BB is the bottleneck: $T_B^{Max} = \dfrac{1}{\mu_B}$

If not: $T_R^{Max} = \dfrac{N}{\mu_R}$

Also: $T_R = (1-\alpha) \times T_B$

Thus, based on these definitions, we can extract the following condition on our system:

$$
\text{If } \left( N > (1-\alpha) \times \frac{\mu_R}{\mu_B} \right) \text{ the BB is the bottleneck of the system.} \tag{3}
$$

Furthermore, based on the flow equations in 2, the maximum throughput of the system is defined by:

$$
T^{Max} = T_P^{Max} =
\begin{cases}
\dfrac{1+\alpha}{2} \times T_B^{Max} & \text{if } N > (1-\alpha) \times \dfrac{\mu_R}{\mu_B} \\[2ex]
\dfrac{1+\alpha}{2 \times (1-\alpha)} \times T_R^{Max} & \text{if not.}
\end{cases}
$$

$$\Rightarrow T^{Max} = \begin{cases} \dfrac{1}{(2-p)\times\mu_B} & \text{if } N > \left(\dfrac{2\times(1-p)}{2-p}\right)\times\dfrac{\mu_R}{\mu_B} \\[3mm] \dfrac{N}{2\times(1-p)\times\mu_R} & \text{if not.} \end{cases} \tag{4}$$

$$\Rightarrow T^{Max} = \text{Min}\left(\dfrac{1}{(2-p)\times\mu_B}, \dfrac{N}{2\times(1-p)\times\mu_R}\right) \tag{5}$$

When applied to our test-bed, these formulas (equations 3 to 5) show the following result: If ($N > 15$), the bottleneck of the system is the BB and, in this case, the maximum effective throughput is $T^{Max} = 227$ req/s.

Also, the number of active connections (customers) in the system can be defined as:

$$C = \sum \overline{N_{<I>}} \quad I \in \{P, L, B, R, S, W, F\}$$

With: $\overline{N_{<I>}}$ : The mean number of customers in the queue <I>.

However, if we assume that most of the customers are in the service and waiting queues during the steady state, the number of customers can be approximated by:

$$C \approx \overline{N_S} + \overline{N_W} + \overline{N_F}$$

With: 
$$\begin{cases} \overline{N_S} = T_S \times \mu_S \\ \overline{N_W} = T_W \times \mu_W \\ \overline{N_F} = T_F \times \mu_F \end{cases} \Rightarrow \begin{cases} \overline{N_S} = \mu_S \times T_W \\ \overline{N_W} = \mu_W \times T_W \\ \overline{N_F} = \dfrac{2\alpha}{1-\alpha} \times \mu_F \times T_W \end{cases}$$

Then: $$C \approx \left(\mu_S + \mu_W + \dfrac{2\alpha}{1-\alpha}\times\mu_F\right)\times T_W$$

Consequently, the maximum capacity of the system is defined as follows:

$$T_W^{Max} = \begin{cases} \dfrac{1-\alpha}{2\times\mu_B} & \text{if } N > (1-\alpha)\times\dfrac{\mu_R}{\mu_B} \\[3mm] \dfrac{N}{2\times\mu_R} & \text{if not.} \end{cases}$$

$$\Rightarrow C^{Max} \approx \begin{cases} \dfrac{(1-\alpha)\times(\mu_S+\mu_W)+2\alpha\times\mu_F}{2\times\mu_B} & \text{if } N > (1-\alpha)\times\dfrac{\mu_R}{\mu_B} \\[3mm] \dfrac{((1-\alpha)\times(\mu_S+\mu_W)+2\alpha\times\mu_F)\times N}{2\times(1-\alpha)\times\mu_R} & \text{if not.} \end{cases}$$

$$\Rightarrow C^{Max} \approx \begin{cases} \dfrac{(1-p)\times(\mu_S+\mu_W)+p\times\mu_F}{(2-p)\times\mu_B} & \text{if } N > \left(\dfrac{2\times(1-p)}{2-p}\right)\times\dfrac{\mu_R}{\mu_B} \\[3mm] \dfrac{((1-p)\times(\mu_S+\mu_W)+p\times\mu_F)\times N}{2\times(1-p)\times\mu_R} & \text{if not.} \end{cases} \tag{6}$$

In order to validate this approximation, we initiated a comparison with the results obtained using the analytical model previously presented. The curve (a), in Figure 5, shows the impact of the mean waiting time on the maximum system capacity, while the curve (b) focuses on the impact of the mean service time of the BB. In all cases, the results, obtained using the approximation formula (equation 6), are very close to the exact values (the analytical model values).

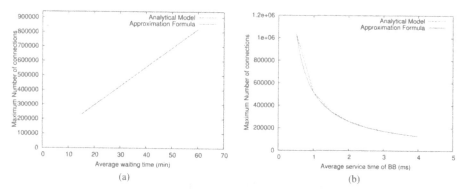

**Fig. 5.** Maximum capacity of the system (number of connections) shown as a function of (a) the average waiting time, (b) the average service time of the bandwidth broker: Analytical Model vs. Approximation Formula

## 5  Deploying a Scalable PBM System

From the proposed analytical model and the previous dimensioning formulas, it is possible for an operator, once he has characterized the behavior of their customers in terms of average service duration $(\mu_s)$ and average waiting time between two consecutive requests for the same customer $(\mu_w, \mu_F)$, to calculate the maximum number of active connections that will be supported by the PBM system. However, in order to instantiate this architecture in a real network, the operator also needs to determine the number of PDPs (respectively LPRs) to deploy physically in the network. The number of PDPs depends on the capacity of each instance to process a certain number of active connections simultaneously. Of course, this delay depends on the frequency of resource allocation requests issued by the QPS PEP and the hardware architecture of the device that is supporting the PDP software. We have conducted a number of experiments to highlight the evolution of the processing performance of the Management Center (PDP+LPR) on a particular platform according to the number of active customers (i.e. The number of customers currently connected to the PDP).

The test-bed includes an instantiation of the PDP and the LPR on two different computers running on a Linux-based OS. Each of them has the following characteristics: RAM=512Mo, CPU=P4-2489Mhz, Cache Memory=512Kb. Each PDP is connected to 58 edge routers. Each connected customer generates a resource allocation request every minute (this is deliberately high but in the reality it should be lower).

The results of these experiments are illustrated in Figure 6, which shows how the processing performance of the Management Centre evolves with the increase in the number of active customers. From this figure we see that the PDP is able to manage efficiently up to 7,000 active customers without any real loss of performance. With this load, the system doesn't use the memory swap and the RAM usage increases linearly with the number of connected customers. In addition, the mean CPU usage ratio of the PDP is around 12%. When the customer pool is below the 7000 limit, the Management Centre service time is always below 100ms with a mean of about 45ms (this is approximately the same value used in the analytical study: $(\mu_p + \mu_L)$.

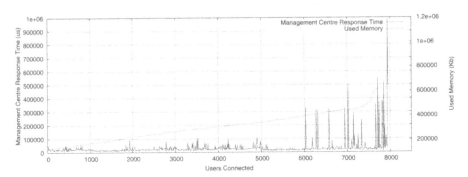

**Fig. 6.** PDP performance vs. PDP load

Above this number of active customers, the experiments show long service times. This is principally due to the high usage of the physical memory and the need for the system to start swapping. At this point, the system is in an unstable situation and the Management Centre service delay increases significantly with the number of active customers. According to these results we can consider that, for this hardware architecture, the maximum number of active customers a particular PDP with this particular hardware can support efficiently is 7,000.

From these results and the analytical study, we can provide a very simple guideline for the instantiation of the PBM system. Depending on customers' behavior (average service duration and average waiting time between two consecutive requests), the analytical model gives the maximum capacity of the PBM system (i.e. maximum number of active customers). Let $C^{Max}$ denote this maximum capacity. This capacity can be expressed in terms of the number of necessary PDP devices. According to the experiments, the number of PDPs needed should be equal to $C^{Max}/7,000$ (if using the same hardware architecture as in the experiments). If, for example, an operator expects to have a maximum of 220,000 active customers and if he is willing to provide a Voice over IP service and let's say that in this case the average duration of a phone session is $\mu_s = 2\,\text{min}$ and the average time between two consecutive calls for each customer is $\mu_w = 15\,\text{min}$, then the number of PDPs to instantiate will be $220,000/7000 \approx 32$ PDPs. This means that if the operator deploys one BB and 32 PDP, and provides the customers with the QPS PEP software, he will provide a scalable and stable on-demand policy-based resource allocation system until it reaches 220,000 active connections. This number does not represent the number of customers, which can be much greater, since not all the customers are active at the same time. No doubt, numerical performance can be enhanced using more advanced hardware.

## 6  Conclusion and Future Work

In this work, we have presented an analytical model for an on-demand policy-based resource allocation and provisioning system for stateless IP networks. Our objective behind this work is to use this analytical model to derive dimensioning formulas to be used to design such systems. As it stands, the performance of the system depends on the performance of the BB as well as the underlying PDP instantiations. Using these results, we also proposed a simple approach to calculate the number of PDPs to deploy in the system and ensure the targeted scalability feature. Both the derived dimensioning formulas and the deployment rules can be used by network operators as a design tool for their on-demand policy-based resource allocation and provisioning system.

As for future work, one point that can be considered is the design of a distributed scheme for the dynamic assignment of PDP to the customers (QPS PEP). This dynamic assignment should necessarily deal with the balancing of load among PDPs and the limitation of the load within each PDP to a desirable value (i.e. to a maximum of 7000 connections per PDP for our plate-form implementation).

# References

1. Verma, D.: Policy-Based Networking–Architecture and Algorithms. New Riders Publishing (2000)
2. Aib, Boutaba, R.: On Leveraging Policy-Based Management for Maximizing Business Profit. IEEE Transactions on Network and Service Management 4(3), 25–39 (2007)
3. Haddadou, K., Ghamri Doudane, S., Ghamri Doudane, Y., Agoulmine, N.: Designing Scalable On-Demand Policy-Based Resource Allocation in IP Networks. IEEE Communications Magazine 44(3), 142–149 (2006)
4. Pujolle, G., Korner, U., Perros, H.: Resource allocation in the new fixed and mobile internet generation. ACM International Journal of Network Management (2003)
5. 3GPP TSG SA WG2. IP multimedia subsystem (IMS). Stage 2 (release 8). Technical Report SP-36 v8.1.0, 3GPP (2007)
6. ITU-T Recommendation No. E.721: Network grade of service parameters and target values for circuit-switched services in the evolving ISDN (1999)
7. ITU-T Recommendation No. E.500: Traffic intensity measurement principles (1998)
8. Bolch, G., et al.: Queuing Networks and Markov Chains. In: Modelling and Performance Evaluation with Computer Science Applications. Wiley- InterScience, Chichester (1998)
9. Hodges, J., Morgan, R.: Lightweight Directory Access Protocol (v3): Technical Specification. RFC 3377 (2002)

# Author Index

# Lecture Notes in Computer Science

Sublibrary 5: Computer Communication Networks and Telecommunications